FURTHER CHAT

The Second Year on the Internet

by
K. Allen

published by Flying Finish Press

ISBN 978-0-6151-8655-9

**Identification
has been removed
to
protect
the
Not-So-Innocent**

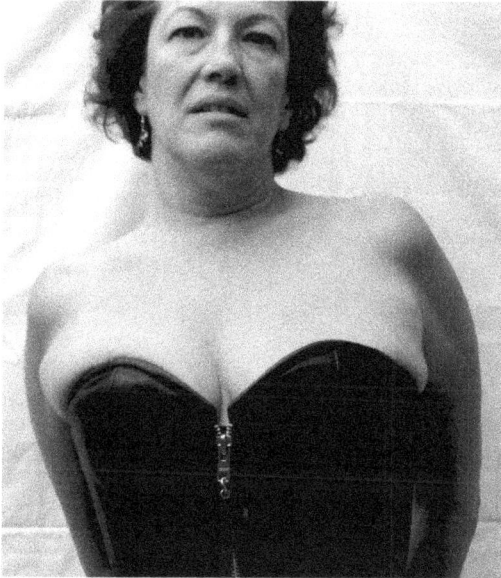

You may know me by my **Имя интернета** or you may not. Either way you know you're in for a wild ride.

photographs by C. Cochran

MAY
2006

May 2
Get in Touch With Your Inner Cat
Hey there, care to roll around in the long grass? Big strong
males who can withstand my passions like you shouldn't be
afraid. I may even turn a delightful shade of pink and
purrrrrrrrrrrrrrrr.

May 6
Cat toys should be white males who do not have to answer
for any marks upon their bodies and are aged 35 to 55 years
with a sense of humor. I prefer males of about 6ft in height.
Some extra padding is fine but they must have fur upon
their bodies; at least some fur. Having their own place with
a comfy bed is also preferred.

May 11th
It is all Very Well and Good to talk all macho in your
replies/comments on my blog - but do you email me? You
do not. Which is a shame, really, as I do so enjoy playing
with my cat toys. Especially those large furry ones who
chuckle gently as they enfold me in their arms; those who
smile and think I am being cute when I grrrrowl at them;
and those who ruffle my fur whilst grinning at me and
dancing just out of reach. Pesky, adorable, exasperating,
and delightful males!!! Try emailing this time!

May 15
Poison, but you Have to have a Taste: Can you truly
acquiese to being used for my pleasure alone without
regard for your own? Can you lie there, naked in the half
light, passively awaiting your fate? Perhaps even trembling
with desire beneath the caress of my claws and fangs as I
meander all over your body with agonizing slowness? Will
you beg for your orgasm? shall we see how much
'stimulation' you can take?

May 20

If You Aren't Good................................ I will shred your pillows and hide under your bed. The only way to coax me out is to put down a saucer of single malt scotch, step back and to say sweet things. Either that or I will bite your ankles every time you come near! Once out from under the bed, I plan on indulging in nuzzle-nipping you as we roll around on the bed. This time you had better be UP for it!!

May 30

22nd of June at noon. Please see a Selection Committee member to get on the list.

RULES
1. you will NOT talk
2. you WILL fuck every person of the other gender
3. BYOC
4. BYOB
5. Ante' up $40 for the hotel room

Cat toys are cheerfully invited.
Women are welcome if they are SERIOUS.
Couples welcome if they play with everyone else of the other gender FIRST.

Went on vacation down to Alabama to witness the birth of my first grandchild.

JUNE
2006

June 3

Rain. Why am I NOT surprised? But gasoline is cheaper here so it isn't ALL bad. I want some serious sun!!! Brought one of my few non-skimpy bathing suits with me. But it is one of those 'tan through' suits - spf level 10 at the most.

Today is the day we meet HIS side of the family - the approved members thereof. Naturally you would not want to introduce me to your drug addled mommy. GRRRRR SNARL SNARL Just imagine what fun THAT would be. Fortunately Daddy was released from custody last night so I get to meet him. JEEZ! How 'southern' can one get?!?!? Hope my fur doesn't get ruffled!!!

June 4

This morning at 0056 Central time, weighing in at 7 lbs 1 oz with an Apgar score of 9.9, and at 22 inches long, the newest Kitten was born!!! So tomorrow we'll be hanging around the pool, all 4 of us, drinking champers!!!!

June 5

Sport-Dating: Nothing against it and in fact, I think more women should indulge themselves with a bit of sport but it isn't my style somehow. I much prefer a more, more relaxed approach. Something more along the lines of a group of very, very close friends who happen to share the same interests. *VEG* I also happen to be a teddybear fancier - always have been. There's just something so very attractive about them. La Gran Domme - Yes, yes, now that I have attained this rank there's no need to consign me to knitting and a rocking chair on the front porch. THAT's NOT GOING TO HAPPEN!!

Now, clearly, if a male is younger than 40, he need not apply! But all of you mature dogs had better watch your backs!! Esp since I have been 'un-fed' for a week now!! But my teddybear didn't fit into my suitcase. Back soon!!

June 8
"She who must be obeyed" has returned and will be vetting males as soon as things settle down a trifle. The banks, the IRS, etc - they all require dealing with, not to mention my truck's acting up again! They were supposed to have fixed it!! Drat them!! So back it goes into the shop - GRRRRR. If it's not one thing......it's some guy somewhere! LOL No, not really. You all know I just love men! Some men. Okay, okay a few of you men! Stop being a pest!

Jun 9
Some People are Confused: about how a kitten can not only be evil but evil twice over. Seems they have forgotten the Monty Python rabbit. The one whose defeat required the use of The Holy Hand Grenade. "Skip a bit, Brother." You remember. Yes, that's the one. So now you understand why an evil, evil kitten adores wicked teddybears. Its that gleam in the eye and that oh so elegant waving of the tail. You KNOW you cannot resist. I shall get you into my bed, or yours, it is only a matter of time.
Spontaneous Acts of Kindness-Are to be greatly appreciated by all those receiving them for they indicate that someone gives a damn about you. Why are we here if not for such indications? We wish, even if in just a small way, for someone to care about us. We also wish for the opportunity to show someone else that we can care for someone other than ourselves. Yes this is about sex. Sex is the most personal of sharing with and caring for others. The real hunger is for affection and shared joy. And, yes, even I feel it.

Jun 10
Sexual Frustration - is a very dangerous game if played with me. There is a definite value in making sure that I remain fully satisfied for when I am not, my promise to NOT bite and to NOT claw is null and void.

Some men like to exert a measure of control and dominance by having you wait for them or by having you ask permission to orgasm and so on. Not a good idea. Not with me. Such demands will be laughed at and further requests of this nature will result in your somewhat painful re-education.
My sexuality is my own.

Jun 11
Teddybear, Teddybear Turn around! Mmmmmmmmeow! Looks nice, baby! Come and let me nuzzle in your fur. My, what big muscles you have! You all 'big and bad boys' buying any of this hmmm? Chuckling but it might happen.

June 12
Chat Room Protocols:
This has to be said because so many do not know or, like children, refuse to behave themselves.

1. Do NOT ever use someone's real name or disclose any real information about them in the open chatroom.

2. Do NOT reveal anyone's past handles even if you know what they are in the open chatroom.

You may think it's cute or fun to 'take the mickey out of someone' but you might have just revealed that person to their stalker. Women have security issues for damn good reasons.

3. Then there are good manners - use them. This means being civil and good natured and NOT using all capital letters since the use thereof signifies YELLING, and few people enjoy being yelled at.

Remember that you can be banned from chat and from the site as well if you are simply too obnoxious. At the very least, you will be IGNORED and thus erased from the screen as if you never had existed.

June 13
"That boy is lower than a snake full of buckshot!"
or how about "that boy's one head short". So now we have a small contest - with the winner getting something I haven't decided what yet. Come up with your wittiest negative description and enter it in the comment box below!!

June 14
These are the current parties now on the books.

this Thursday a happy hour M&G at TGIF in Springfield, VA

there's a gb scheduled (kinda) for this Friday - see HP, and another for this weekend - see DM.

vetting of men will be done this Friday after 9pm at the secret place and also at The Shade Tree in Centreville, VA - these are the regular M&Gs so just come along.

Then there's a huge M&G on the 24th but for info on that you will have to check elsewhere, I have yet to receive the info on that one.

I am always interested in bringing people out to polo on Saturdays 7 to 11pm. Drop me an email.

We also have two parties we'd like to do:

1. Scotch Tasting
2. Naked Twister

Both would require the use of a private home which we have yet to find. You understand the difficulties I am sure.

One Particular Person Would do well to mind his own business. What we do has nothing to do with you. We are NOT harming, forcing, or doing anything even remotely similar to anyone. I have found your diatribe against me. I have rebutted each and every point. And I have saved it. Thank you for the increased ammunition. I also have the emails sent to others by your friends, the other persons involved's blog entries on this topic and they all bear out my version of the facts. You would do well to remain silent. Anything further from you will be sent on to the CEO of this site along with the archive I have saved.

Jun 15
POLO! HURRAY!! Time to celebrate because both Great Meadows and Chetwood are having polo this season!
Two nights out in the country instead of one!

Now to gather up my 'polo buddies' and scamper off for another fun and invigorating *W* evening *EG*!

We bet a penny on our team and whoever's team loses gets to buy the ice cream. More I cannot say but you know we all enjoy it very, very much.

15

Jun 17

New Brakes!! YEEHAW!! I shall no longer have to grind to a halt! They are installing new ones even as we speak - you have to love handy resident males!! Saw what they took off and it was NOT pretty - metal to metal, darlings. Not good.

But now I shall be able to careen around corners on two wheels in perfect safety!!

Jun 18

Naked and in the Pool! Few things more refreshing than a midnight swim in the pool with minimal lighting and some lovely friends.
We went to polo, which they all agreed was waay kewl and lots of fun. They we all went back to her place, very nice, and hung out by the pool out back.
Then, alas!, it was time to scamper home!
We all will do this again!

Happy Father's Day! - to all men so privileged. May your kids turn out just like you. *EG*

Cute and adorable!

had you worried there for a minute, huh?

Jun 19
Reprinted by Special Request
Male Slut Selection Tips Nov 3, 2005

Other than appealing to you to the point where you are wondering how his hands and lips would feel on your skin, you have to carefully consider several other criteria when selecting a male slut or when selecting a male to turn into a slut.

1. can he get his mind around the concept of any woman, at any time he's required, anyway she wants him? can he be passed around amongst the ladies like a six-pack? would he enjoy it?

2. does he have the cojones to submit without being obsequious or fawning? you want a man not a dog after all.

3. is he presentable? if all you wanted was a penis, you could go buy one. can he converse and how are his manners?

4. is he willing to learn and open to new ideas and experiences?

5. does he genuinely like women? you know what I mean by that and yes, we can tell if he does.

Now all we have to consider is his amount of available free time, transport and wherewithal since you do not want to end up having to support him. Self sufficient but willing men with the necessary free time is what you want. If he volunteers, that's even better!!

I HATE TO DO THIS
something DREADFUL has come up and unfortunately I have to cancel this Thursday's Seminar. Sorry, my lovelies, but it is going to be HELL this week and perhaps next week as well. Time will tell. Perhaps in July after the 4th? But who can tell - I am distracted.

Jun 20
Some people need an update. Wrap your mind around the concept that a chatroom is just chat. Yes, I have men whose company I enjoy. This does not mean that I cannot relax in the chatroom exchanging banter with others - even after great sex. Men might want to curl up and nap afterwards, but most women get a surge of energy that will prevent them from sleeping. So I chat. Deal with it but NOT by calling me a liar. Stupid, stupid man!

Ah! So Sweet! There are men who can wear a collar and leash with a great deal of panache. I have seen this. He was wearing only a 'bad boy' grin and sitting on my sofa at the time.

Jun 21
Sunbathing topless! Let the girls out and take them outside to play in the sun! If you are a teddybear, you may apply the lotion.

Well, it is a nice thought but I have some work to do before I can do that - dreaming only makes it more difficult to focus.

Published a small primer today at lulu called beguile. You can only comment if you like it.
LOL Remember I am tender and delicate for the next two weeks.

OK That's It!! I am hiding beneath a certain teddybear's bed and I am NOT coming out until all of you men get naked, dowse yourselves with single malt scotch, and let me have my way with you!!!

Jun 24

Wheeeeeeeeee!! A lovely pair of mischievous and witty persons, the kind who dance naked in thunderstorms, looking to find out what makes you laugh, sparkle, and come to life in our arms. WOW! What a party!

Seeking similar high energy and joyous hwp couples, as many as will fit on the bed, to join us for varied heterosexual activities during the week: days and early evenings. Sleep? That's what meetings are for!

Blasting the music whilst I romp down the highway - WOW!! What fun! Until the nice policeman pulls me over. Rammstein's DuHast at Mach 3 is just about right. I do not know why you are hanging onto that 'Jesus Handle' like that! Relax! I haven't killed anyone all week!

fast cars, fast horses & fast men!!!

Jun 26

His sexual subjugation should be joyous and life affirming. This somewhat less than silken dalliance should be fun for both with each one pleasing the other. This result cannot be achieved without mutual regard and respect. There also has to be a mutual sexual attraction. If the blood is not roaring within, then nothing good can come of playing in this fashion. In many ways, the actual acts are the same and only the perspective changes. Fellatio becomes feeding off the male, for example, when done from a female superior position. The male takes on the passive role during sex unless called upon to please his lady. While there are no set rules, play should be mutually satisfying with both having orgasms.

Jun 27

Now gathering nursery rhymes and songs for the Wriggling Demon Spawn - she's soooo cute! - anyone know the words to "Louie, Louie"?

Romance? You mean that wine and dine with theatre tickets, picnics and flowers kind of thing?
OR
Do you mean the home every night, work all day, remembering soccer games and recitals and your mother-in-law's birthday, being a good spouse and wise parent - bearing up as a decent person amid other decent persons kind of thing.
OR
were you referring to something more like cocktails and polo games on the weekends and hanging out by the pool kind of purrrrry thing?

Jun28

What's That? Up There in the Sky? Yes the sun is shining once again!!! This means that I get to go out and play today! Anyone have any ideas?

"I'm in the mood for trouble. Simply because I am hungry!"

Jun30
and I quote:
"EEK ~ PAT THE BUNNY??? Somehow I thought you were born with the OED to your bosom!"

Well, one has to begin somewhere! Fortunately I soon replaced that OED with men. That binding chafed.

Hugs back, gf!!

JULY
2006

Jul 1, Purrrrrrrrrrr

Something very nice about hanging out with your favorite teddybear. Polo would not be the same without him. Met some good people. Unfortunately this particular set was comprised of tired women and male bimbos. Nice but no sparks. Then it was off to the 'secret spot' for some real fun! Danced a lot. Kissed a few men. Had a great time then and afterwards.

True or Not?

"Women need to realize that their bodies are temples -- or at least men like to think so -- and that they shouldn't be shared with any Tom, Dick or Harry. Once a woman realizes this, three things will happen:

1. She'll appreciate herself a lot more, and in turn the man will gain more respect for her and realize that he has a valuable treasure.

2. The man who had to work hard and commit in order to bed a woman will appreciate her more. After all, time was invested in her.

3. The sex will be brought to a whole new passionate level when she finally makes love to the man who fought for her -- by being patient.

Today too many people -- including myself -- place too much importance on sex. This explains why so many marriages don't work. People base their whole relationship on sex and don't realize that when the passion disappears, and the honeymoon phase dies down, there is nothing left but each other's flaws."

This article was in response to a woman asking why men have issues with a promiscuous woman. She said "I was honest, told him the truth when he asked how many men I had slept with, and then I never heard from him again." I disagree with the author's response.

This is especially so when you consider that men perpetually complain about not getting enough sex!

We are all people here; just trying to get along as best we can. Treating each other kindly and with respect, unless they demand otherwise, will go a long way to improving all of our lives.

Jul 3
Boat Party
 Sunning, swimming, speeding, and sex, sex, SEX! Absolutely love a day on the water with some very special friends!
Thank you!!

Party, party, party
 Polo every Friday and some Saturday evenings - see me.
Regular meet n greets for locals=
July 15th a Major meet n greet no specific invitation needed - just show up.
Next private gb somewhere around the third Thursday of August. Get vetted soon. (Cat toys excepted.)

Jul 4, 2006
Happy 4th
 Just in case you are in any doubt, I LOVE FIREWORKS esp THE BIG BANGS!!!

GO, RED GLARE, GO!!

Jul 5,
Oddments
Tap your heels together three times while chanting "there's no place like Sears. There's no place like Sears."

Make a right hand turn from the left hand lane with a kid in the back yelling "No Eng- lace!" out of the window.

Stand there with two kids clinging to your pant legs, two movers with a moving van full of your furniture, and a sheaf of diagrams in your hands while your darling drives off to work waving bye bye.

"Your daughter's not making those animal noises anymore." said by her teacher in a parent teacher conference.

"Mom, there's a van in the living room!"

Hell, and you guys think being single and without kids is fun? HAH!

Jul 6
Can't Blog Getting ready to go to a sex party!! WHEEEEEEEEEEE!!

Jul 8
No. You cannot have a blog today either!

evil laughter

Jul 9

Weekends!! In summation:

Friday, polo, the secret spot then back for a very very nice romp.

Saturday, frantic morning settling up the final bit of disaster, you will recall previous posts on this topic, and then a nice afternoon basking and doing a spot of work, then 'in w Jim' Sunday, yardwork getting all dirty and covered in mud whilst wearing my 'Daisy Duke's. If I had the pix of me in my Daisy Duke's I would have posted it. But since the pockets hang well below the hemline you get the idea I am sure.

Schedule for this week:

Monday: Mike's circa 6pm to 9pm be there or be square - come out and meet the infamous me.

Tuesday: sorry seeing someone *EG*

Wednesday: M&G in Fredericksburg

Thursday: sorry I am seeing someone

Friday: OMG tis packed with fun things to do!

POLO this time CATERED, UNCLE SAM'S, then the secret spot! Will there even be time for sex?

Saturday: up to the M&G in Frederick MD

BUSY BUSY BUSY

Jul 10

Karma Police I was surprised last weekend by not getting the reaction I expected. Amazingly enough he seemed pleased by public recognition! Obviously 'he with whom the adventure began is a man of more parts than I had previously thought.

So, he's reviewing the manuscript while I am reviewing the proof copy of my previous book - ette. I have this thing with being too concise. I tend to assume y'all are keeping up and on the same wavelength so I touch on subjects in passing.

I read the same way. If you have seen Monty Python & The Holy Grail, you have seen that part where Brother Maynard says "Skip a bit, brother." that's how I read. There's no need to dwell on a point - touch and go. We shall see how many red marks my two works collect.

Jul 10,
 Seems I Cannot Help Myself !! Another Klepto-Blog!
1. What, if any, significance does your handle have
2. What is your favorite color?
3. What size bed do you sleep in?
4. The majority of the time, do you sleep alone or with someone?
5. Do you shower at night before bed or in the morning?
6. What all parts of your body do you shave?
7. What is one thing about you that people find the most interesting?
8. Do you have any children? How many? Boys, girls, or some of each?
9. Do you have any grandchildren?
10. Are your parents still living?
11. What is your birth order? Oldest? Youngest? Somewhere in the middle?
12. What is the most tragic thing that has ever happened to you?
13. What is the BEST thing that has ever happened to you?
14. Do you like public displays of affection or are you too shy or "macho" for that?
15. What is your favorite food? Drink?
16. Do we know each other, other than online?
17. If not, would you like to?
18. Would you ever go on a date with me, knowing that we would NOT have sex?

19. What are you most interested in and hoping to accomplish by being a member here?
20. Do you have a hobby? If so, what is it?
21. If you could own any vehicle you wanted, what vehicle would it be?
22. What is your favorite indoor activity?
23. What is your favorite outdoor activity?
24. What Country, State, City were you born? Do you still live there?
25. What year did you graduate high school?
26. What were you voted as "most likely to be" your Senior yr in High School? Did it hold true?
27. Did you go to college? Did you graduate? What's your degree in, if you have one?
28. If we went out on a date, where would you take me?
29. Would you pay? Would I pay? Or would we go dutch?
30. Do you have any goals or dreams? Would you care to tell what they are?
31. Will you post this on your blog so I can fill it out for you? If you don't have a blog, will you start one, so I can fill it out for you?

Jul 11
Would You Buy This Book? The ad shows the upper right hand quadrant of a well-endowed ladies' bra and shoulder with a small booklet slid under her shoulder strap so you could clearly see the title and author??
btw he edited my book so much that you'd think he had bled all over it. Liked the content hated the presentation, type face etc, etc, etc.
Well back to the corrections and revisions *sigh*.

Jul 12,

Caution to the Winds! Passionately overwhelming him with kisses while unbuttoning his shirt outside his front door!

If I threw myself into your arms, would you know what to do once you had caught me?

There's nothing better than a cute, congenial, furry, cigar-smoking teddybear in a bathrobe sitting nearby wearing a 'bad boy' grin!

Three Definitions of Chemistry

 He walked into the sports bar, horrible place, and joined the group, sitting down next to me. Everyone was talking and yet I could only think of how would his hands and lips feel on my skin. It didn't matter that he was not a young, hard-bodied, glamour male. I didn't care. It was all I could do to remain calm and not rip his clothes off and fuck him right then and there. I had to content myself with my leg against his but that was because we were so tightly packed together. Very crowded. Ah, but the goodnight kiss was so good - had to do it thrice!

He was soddenly drunk and hanging on the door so he didn't fall down. Didn't matter at all! He was tall with dirty blond hair and buff from being used by his dad as a backhoe. He was chatting with the girl he was dating at the time but he managed to notice my roommate and I sitting there. Another guy wandered in and decided that I was the girl he wanted. I growled at him and flashed my fangs. He backed off saying oh my!

But the drunk hunk loved it! I am not like other girls. Room 9 The Ladies' Choice!

He was sitting at the bar. Nothing special about him particularly. Didn't matter. Oh how I wanted him! The thing was he was willing to accept and enjoy whatever I chose to offer him. We kissed and hugged several times - every time I went up for a drink. Circumstances meant nothing came of it but I will remember him to my grave.

August Group Therapy August 17th at noon
ALL CAT TOYS NEEDED
YIM me!!

Jul 14
Further Klepting
1. What is funny about yourself that makes you smile when you think about it?
2. How can you tell when people are really listening to you?
3. What is something you truly appreciate or enjoy doing that most others probably do not care for?
4. What is something that you got rid of that you wish you had back?
5. What in this morning's paper made you happy?
6. You get angry with yourself when _____?
7. What was the worst thing that ever happened to you in an elevator?
8. What wakes you up in the middle of the night?
9. What is the most interesting question anyone ever asked you?
10. What is a symbol that inspires you?

Today
the sun is shining, the maids are delayed, and I have groceries to get before dashing off to tonight's frivolous activities. FRIVOL, FRIVOL So here I am blogging.

Tomorrow
will be doing housework and yardwork then going off for more FRIVOLITY

Sunday
no frivolity WAH! but sometimes tis good to relax!

Monday
the truck goes into the shop - and they had better FIX it
THIS time! Then it is off to be introduced to a certain cat
and then meet up with a couple for drinks at Mike's for
Possible FRIVOLITY.

Jul 15
No Party Tonight is off due to circumstances beyond
anyone's control.
And the pool party scheduled for the 22nd is also off for
now due to circumstances beyond the owner's control.
VA Beach likely to be the 29th of July.

Jul 16,
On Being Polyandrous It isn't all about the sex and my
sense of adventure. I do truly care about the men in my
circle. Friends with benefits is the best possible
arrangement short of being truly polyamorous in a
commingled household. Imagine being surrounded by
friends, lovers, and other assorted persons who are with
you because they want to be and not just because they must
be. The mutual enrichment of our lives is well worth the
time, I assure you. Love as you live - unstintingly!

Redux
 Women ask men impossible to answer questions because
the question we actually asked is not the question we really
want answered. You only have to lie if you answer the
question we actually asked rather than the one we really
want answered. You would not have to to lie if you ignored
the question we actually asked and answered the question
we really wanted answered. This is especially true if the
question we actually asked requires the man to give an

opinion in his answer which is never permitted. (If a man gives a woman his opinion on any topic he should immediately apologize and humbly beg her forgiveness unless said opinion deals directly with automobiles or power tools.) Be advised that women ask these questions as a test. We are determining your ability to read subtext, deciding whether to continue the relationship or not, and seeing how clever you really are as shown by the quality of your answer. You will remember that women are naturally more sibylline than men and that we enjoy playing that delightful game "Confuse-A-Male". This has been a test. This has only been a test. If this had been an actual emergency requiring an opinion we would have asked a woman.

Jul 18,
Some Guys! "Why must males be at least 40 years of age? Afraid that a younger man may be too much for you?"
Obviously this is an in-experienced male. Because any sensible male knows that a woman doesn't hit her sexual peak until in her 40's and that a self aware and sexually aggressive woman easily out-guns any six men you'd care to name.
Did he REALLY think that his skinny little self would stand the strain of being with me?

Jul 19
To Continue Just to refresh your memory of the topic at hand: "Why must males be at least 40 years of age? Afraid that a younger man may be too much for you?"
This is not the first time, I have had some young guy in his 20's asking me this question. I have tried being nice about it. "Sorry, hun but you just do not do it for me." I have been upfront and not led anyone on. "Sorry but I am not in education." Yet they almost all go from 'please fuck to me' to 'you hag' upon being told no.

31

It seems as if they just discovered they have this wonderful penis that works and they expect everyone to fall to her knees before him! Come on now, guys! Think about this. Imagine you getting hit on by everything even remotely female, including those who have been 'manufactured' 24/7/365. which ones would you pick?

Yeah, yeah in your dreams, eh? You would pick the ones that really took your breath away now wouldn't you? Of course you would. Well, kiddos that is precisely what I am doing. If you do not stir my blood, then you're NOT getting any from me.

I have always been inordinately fond of the 40 and 50 something teddybears. Exploring him and his track record is an adventure I do NOT want to miss! It is the whole man and not JUST his penis that interests me. For one on one sex you have to meet my criteria - period!

Now, any more questions???

Jul 20,

Zooooom! My MGB is small and nimble but not all that fast - only has 4 cyl.s - so there I am in the far right lane cruising in amidst the rigs. What, me nervous??? Hey, this is a woman in a short skirt in a sports car - what trucker's going to mess with that? I am almost an expert on undercarriages too so it is all good here!

Bedridden? Riding men in bed - what a DELIGHTFUL thought! Any of you guys care to lie down? Now? Here? I have a little free time. Nudge, nudge, wink, wink. I promise to return you in good condition - really I will. Honest! Why doesn't anyone ever believe me?

Jul 21

My 4th book done and published late last night. Finally! Today's agenda, the Money Show in DC, grocery getting, get the Expedition out of the shop, a sex party at noon in Old Town Alex, swing by get my date and then off to polo then on to Mamma Mia's after swinging back home so I can change from jeans to a slinky red dress and stilettos. I have to cook up polo food for dinner in there somewhere. Anyone care to lend me a few hands? Gotta run! Ciao, babies!!!

Jul 23,

In Trouble Again! Ah well! Hey Ho for a quiet life in the country! Sorry darlings, but that will never happen because it is more 'may the Devil take the hindmost' with me - too much peace and quiet and I get antsy so I am off to 'misbehave' today with some of my favorite people
C Y'ALL

Jul 24

Being Trenchant

1. If you'd rather talk to Jim than have sex with me, you might as well put a bullet through your brain because you are done. "It's dead, Jim." But it was an important personal matter! Yeah, well, this is a party. You do know about parties, yes?

2. No condoms = no sex and I don't give a damn about your previous 35 years of just getting shots to fix you right on up, hun. How many times does it take getting run over before you learn NOT to play in the street?

3. Yes most women have a nice slow pace and want to be caressed and cajoled into having sex with men they want to know something about. That's MOST WOMEN, mind you - not THIS WOMAN. Once my engines have been spun up

and the blood's roaring - just lie down right here and shut up.

Yes, you all may comment and I may bite back but then - you know I love you all dearly - this week.

So other than throwing his ass over the balcony railing - what else was I do to?

Sex Survey:
1. HAVE YOU GOTTEN LAID IN 2006?
2. EVER HAD SEX IN A PUBLIC PLACE?
3. EVER LAUGH DURING SEX? IF SO WHY?
4. EVER CRY DURING SEX? IF SO WHY?
5. DO YOU LIKE TO CUDDLE AFTER SEX?
6. EVER REGRET SEX WITH SOMEONE?
7. EVER FAKED AN ORGASM?
8. DIRTY TALK, OR SHUT THE FUCK UP?
9. EVER HAVE UNPROTECTED SEX?
10. EVER MASTERBATE WITH YOUR PARTNER?
11. EVER HAVE A ONE NIGHT STAND?
12. EVER HAVE A THREESOME?
13. EVER WATCH PORN DURING SEX?
14. EVER THOUGHT OF SOMEONE ELSE DURING SEX?
15. HAS THE CONDOM EVER BROKE?
16. WHAT IS YOUR MOST EMBARRASSING SEXUAL EXPERIENCE?
17. HOW OLD WERE YOU WHEN YOU LOST YOUR VIRGINITY?
18. WHO WOULD YOU LIKE TO HAVE SEX WITH RIGHT NOW?
19. DO YOU THINK THAT "number 18" IS POSSIBLE?
20. ARE YOU HORNY NOW?

Jul 25
How to Introduce Him to Your Kinky Side
1. Sit on his lap facing him, kiss him while deftly sliding a collar around his neck.

2. Leave a collar out on the coffee table.

3. Use your vibe as 'the second man.'

4. Run your hand up the back of his neck into his hair. Tilt his head back and kiss the base of his throat - gently but lingeringly.

5. When hanging out naked in the house wear stilettos.

Care to add a few to this list, ladies?

Jul 26
Wheeeeee! Sorry but I am having waay too much fun with this party planning! I have the two books being reviewed only he hasn't yet. I will know when he has. So there are three items with, like me, a sting in the tail! Anticipation!
Also from ask men - "It's still important to tease women and bust on them." Perhaps bust on them means something different to men than it does to women but bust on me and there's someone else I'd rather be with thank you very much. I equate 'bust' on her with 'yeah, smack her in the chops a few times'. I hope they meant verbally. But even so.
They also recommend, in order to get more free time away from her, that you take her paintballing or hunting. Yeah that'll work. Until I zap your ass and out shoot you. Not possible with Slut 2 of course but I can hold my own when it comes to firearms both real and paint. BBQ Bunny anyone?

"Damn it is cold out here! Okay the next bull's-eye and we'll go in." Guess who then shot the bull? *I raise my hand* This was while shooting against three more experienced men btw. We were bench shooting 30.06 at the range. Cannot remember the yardage but the target was barely visible through the scope. The bull had to be right...there! Well, I was FREEZING out there!

So you can see - I am having far too much with this! Perhaps I should do something about that? Talk to me, people! Naked sunbathing in the backyard? LOL

Jul 27
This is Not Drama! This is enthusiasm and vitality. I am enjoying myself tremendously. Sorry, no PMS - am the same person 24/7/365 - morning, noon, or night. The same energy, delight, and passion I display here, I bring to bed.
But you won't get me showing up unexpectedly at your door or calling you incessantly on your phone or doing any of those other silly nonsensical games. No, no, no. That's sooo not me.
Are we clear about this point?
Can we now talk more about asset allocation? How about a nice dynasty trust arrangement?

Dynasty Trusts-
This is the ultimate in estate planning and asset preservation. A dynasty trust properly funded and maintained can support your family and increase the family wealth over a hundred years, possibly more.
Setting up a trust, any trust, requires an attorney specializing in estate planning. A dynasty trust is one, however, that requires the services of your entire professional team: your financial advisor, your CPA and the attorney. Unlike most trusts, a dynasty trust must have at least one corporate fiduciary acting as a trustee. Dynasty

trusts must be written with great care since they need to be flexible enough to meet any future contingencies. This is just a brief glimpse into a rarefied world but it may be useful.

To be specific, you write up and fund you dynasty trust using life insurance. You set the total of the beneficiaries' allowances to no more than 4% of annual earnings. The remaining growth goes back into the trust to grow its assets further, to pay the insurance premiums, and to pay the taxes due. You limit the beneficiaries to those who are 'heirs of the blood'. As each beneficiary comes into the trust, actuaries determine how much that beneficiary will use, indexed for inflation, over the course of their lifetime and the fiduciary then insures that person for that amount. This way, the trust is constantly replenished. The minimum required to begin a dynasty trust is five million dollars. All assets other than your personal residence may be put into a dynasty trust. Your personal residence is handled by another trust entirely. You may permit beneficiaries to make contributions into the trust.

The interesting thing is, that while everyone benefits no one actually owns anything.
(How neat is that?)

Can this be done on a smaller scale? Of course it can be! To calculate it out, take your maximum lifetime exemption for estate and gift tax. That is how much you can put into a trust without incurring any liabilities. Currently, you can do this for one million dollars. You then follow the steps as outlined above. The only difference is that corporate fiduciaries will be hard to come by as they usually do have minimums of at least five million. Perhaps you can find one locally that will take you on. Be advised that there will be fees involved. The amount of these fees will increase with the complexity of your affairs. Consulting your financial advisor is the first step.

In a MAN/WOMAN, my likes are...
Favorite Eye Color: two
Favorite Hair Color: some esp body hair
Short or Long Hair: either way
Height: taller
Weight: teddybear but not sloppy

There are my answers! What are yours?

Jul 28,
Old Friends It may have escaped your attention, but Slut 1 has not been heard of for quite awhile now. It got to be too much drama for him, not me but others you understand, so he dropped out of sight. He worked 6 days a week and stayed with the lady who didn't seem to like him very much.
Well he stopped by yesterday. He seemed stressed out and very tired. He needed a "Kitten Fix". I hadn't seen him for about what, 6 months to a year almost? Baby needs to relax more and take his time having some fun. I hope he did get some time playing yesterday - betcha his game's off.
No not that 'game', he did very nicely thank you *W*
So how many old friends have surprised you lately?

I am High Maintenance!
I require sex at least once every day for about 3 hours at a time! So get it up and keep it up, fellas!
Sorry - had to just SAY it.

Jul 29

Common Plaints Often heard in the chat.

1. "Does anyone ever hook up in here?"
Yes we actually do hook up in here but you won't if you whine, whimper demand, or throw a tantrum. So chill out and try actually chatting with people, dude!

2. "Are you for real?"
Yes we know about bots - but think, they promise you everything for nothing. Women do not - they demand at least some effort on your part to show you are interested and not just blowing hot air up their skirts. That is nice of course but we did have more in mind.

3. "Can we go someplace and chat privately? It is so hard to follow in here."
If you ignore people, the chat clears out very nicely! Ignoring imbeciles and unpleasant persons clears the screen and slows down the chat room nicely. So no we don't have any problem- you do! Fix it.

Anyone care to add other favorites?

Jul 30

Looking through Old Photos to see which can be scanned onto digital media for further use in various projects. My, my, my what we used to get up to! Have all sorts of pix of all sorts of people, places and times. Some aren't half bad! I do have a great many of them however so this is going to take quite a while! I even have a few pix of myself when I was a small wee little kitten! Other than pictures all I have left from my childhood is a pair of leather bound books - one a cookbook and one the complete works of Shakespeare.
What do you have from your childhood? Anything left?

Jul 30 cont.
My Kinky Horoscope "Aquarius (Jan. 20- Feb. 1 --

My favorite sluts are Aquarius. Why? Because if you don't expect anything in return, you won't be disappointed. Sounds easy, huh? They will get under your skin though, so beware. It's easy to be hurt by an Aquarius because they don't want you to know what they are thinking. If they are silent but you are in the room with them...chances are they are in heavy thought. But don't worry, chances are they are thinking about you...and fifteen other things. Water bearers look at sex like it is a form of recess. They can turn you on by simply walking in the room. They are the Rain Man of the Zodiac. They give too much of themselves to others that don't give a shit...then get shy to those that care about them. Go figure.

They like kinky. They are easy going. To them, it's a learning experience. Male Aquarians like to tease and live life in a fantasy world. Female Aquarians can't masturbate enough...Males never get the chance to masturbate because everybody wants a piece of them. They like their ankles nibbled. They love back massages. Their ultimate adventure is the "But we might get caught" game.

They will fuck wherever they run the risk of being seen or found by another lover. Don't expect faithfulness from these creatures...it's just not in their DNA. They are open minded to the point that anything shiny will derail their train of thought. Fucking while standing or leaning is a plus here. Fuck with their mind and they will follow you anywhere. They enjoy being fucked in groups of three. Think being Jack Nicholson in bed with the three Witches of Eastwick? This is an Aquarian dream. They need you to make the first move. Not to be dominated. But to bring them back to earth now and again for a little physical funtime. They get lost in the clouds a lot. Don't derail from your personal pleasure course, however, otherwise you will be just talking to them all night. which can be stimulating just as well too. Beware! They are the flirts and teases from HELL! Never take one on a trip to a Home Depot when you are both horny. This can lead to nasty things."

No, not quite accurate enough! Sorry but you missed the point! Should have stuck with 'sex as recess' thing. Now to check out my lovers' horoscopes *EG*!!

Jul 31,
The List
Pool Party August 5th - see Bugsy-7
Boat Party August 5th - see K and J
Backyard BBQ August 12th - see The Princess111
Group Therapy August 17th - see me

this is in addition to the usual Friday evening
Anyone have any additional parties they'd like to post?

Other Astrological Views
"One of the Aquarian's deepest needs is for a satisfying, complementary relationship, which gives them freedom and tolerance along with mental and physical stimulation. With the right person they will be a passionate, uninhibited and understanding lover intent on maintaining their bond for life. Receptivity will calm Aquarians' rebellious tendencies. Unlike many, Aquarians rarely feel any pangs of jealousy.

Their sex-drive is not unduly strong, but their need to explore and be stimulated sometimes gives others the impression their desires are unconquerable. They can be very playful and attentive lovers and will put a great deal of energy into satisfying their partners. Aquarians are open to all forms of experimentation (in the pursuit of new knowledge, of course) and the field of sexuality and

relationships is no exception. Even though deep down they seek security, their love of originality and exploring unusual new fields of endeavor gives them an attraction for partners with interesting, unconventional minds and bodies."
and
"As befits an Air sign, Aquarians tend to approach sex via the mind. If they can share and discuss their thoughts with their lover, matters in bed will be greatly enhanced. Their natural curiosity will also lead them to experiment with creative play between the sheets, so watch out! Pushing the envelope is a natural response for these folks, and they'll continually test the waters for ever greater pleasures. A delicious mystery lurks beneath the surface of these oft-controlled souls, and the lover who can call their bluff is in for a wild ride. The issue of mind vs. body, and which is more important, is also with the Water Bearer. A lover who can convince them of the pleasure principle will set this sexual being free."

What's this 'set me free' and 'not unduly strong sex drive' stuff??? Interestingly, another site said I would be 'slow to arouse'. ROTBLMAO

42

AUGUST
2006

Aug 5

There comes a Point when a lady simply declines to play any further. I'll be sure to let you know when I have reached that point. But for now, to quote a movie,..

"Not yet. Not yet."

Anyone there yet?

Aug 6,

Beautifully wise & Dangerously kind MOST of the time.....but there are those times when a man had better just lie down and enjoy it because the lady's hungry and she's not going to accept any fuss or excuse. You don't want me to break a claw! The question is..............

how much and how long of a fight are you going to put up?

Aug 7

Fair is Fair! Read the Verbiage!

"That only a union between same sex individuals may be a marriage valid in or recognized by this Commonwealth and its political subdivisions.

This Commonwealth and its political subdivisions shall not create or recognize a legal status for relationships of one man and one woman that intends to approximate the design, qualities, significance, or effects of marriage. Nor shall this Commonwealth or its political subdivisions create or recognize another union, partnership, or other legal status to which is assigned the rights, benefits, obligations, qualities, or effects of marriage."

§ 20-45.2. Marriage between persons of opposite sex.

A marriage between persons of opposite sex is prohibited. Any marriage entered into by persons of opposite sex in another state or jurisdiction shall be void in all respects in

Virginia and any contractual rights created by such marriage shall be void and unenforceable.

(1975, c. 644; 1997, cc. 354, 365.)

§ 20-45.3. Civil unions between persons of opposite sex.

A civil union, partnership contract or other arrangement between persons of opposite sex purporting to bestow the privileges or obligations of marriage is prohibited. Any such civil union, partnership contract or other arrangement entered into by persons of opposite sex in another state or jurisdiction shall be void in all respects in Virginia and any contractual rights created thereby shall be void and unenforceable.

(2004, c. 983.)

Y'ALL UNDERSTAND YET?

Aug 8,
Pick Your Philosopher!   You are known by the company you keep *W* so who's your company, baby?
Plato
Marx
Locke
Wittgenstein
Hegel
Descartes
Hobbes
Rousseau
Hume
Other

Hmmmm

All those desirous of my continuing to wear skimpy summer dresses to the secret spot....... vote now!
Yeah, baby!! or NO!!!

Aug 9
Today
1. nap
2. read
3. go to post office
4. do the dry cleaning run
5. go to M&G near Fredericksburg for fun
6. go home
Yes, fast living here! LOL. Miss you, darling!

Why Certain Men do NOT Get Laid
1. they are LOUD!
2. they have no discretion
3. they are too damn nice - not wicked enough
4. they are too macho - they play silly games
5. they argue with me
So, ladies, what are YOUR turn-offs?

Aug 10,
Updated Party List
Sat 12th at 6pm Cookout see The Princess111
Thurs 17th at noon GTS see me
Mon 21st GTS private party
and then the camp out 26th/27th see previous party post for information
as always the Secret Spot will be on Friday after 9pm
Polo continues!
Anyone have any other parties on their books?

Just Read Your Profile
OMG! Too much information!!! Look if I had wanted to read an encyclopedia, I would get a set not look at your profile. Hun you're cute but trim it back a bit!

Part I is about what kind of guy you are not what you like. What are you? Teddybear? Drill Sergeant? Partially insane person dying of testosterone poisoning? Your limit is three full and complete sentences - all grammatically correct and no misspellings.

Part II is The lady you are seeking. What is the one characteristic you MUST have in this lady or those ladies? Kindness? Sense of humor? Brains? Once again you are limited to three sentences as above.

Do NOT ever repeat anything in your profile that is in your stats. Never answer "Prefer not to say"
And DON'T tell us EVERYTHING - we like to 'explore'.

Meet at bars attached to restaurants. Then if you hit it off, you can ease on over for appetizers or dessert or maybe even an entire meal if you two hit it off without any distractions from the conversation. Walk her to her car, wrap her in those nice arms of yours firmly, give her a 'bad boy' grin and a decent lingering kiss lasting at LEAST 20 seconds. Then let her take it from there.
Should work., dontcha think?

Aug 11
The Friday rush has begun!
Soon I'll be 'busy' *EG*
May the devil take the hindmost!!!!!!!!!!!!!

Aug 12
Woman Issue #32
You're at some venue, having a good time, when so-and-so walks in. What do you do? You leave the party, bar, whatever - fleeing the scene! "I just don't want to deal with it!" You'd rather stop having fun just in case Mr. Annoying PITA decides he may want to throw a fit or make a dramatic scene than let him make a fool out of himself and, by inference, of you.
TSK TSK TSK
My favorite way of dealing with these guys is to watch them, in silence, while they throw whatever tantrum they have chosen like I was watching some very boring Congressional hearing on some very arcane bit of tax law. YAWN.
You then ask if he really did enjoy publicly embarrassing himself like that. You then remind him that "hell buddy, I'm not married to you. Take it to someone who cares." Then watch him turn red and disappear. Nothing to do with you. If he cannot behave like a gentleman then he doesn't deserve being treated like one.
And he certainly shouldn't curtail your fun.
Hasn't how you handle 'it' always been more important than what 'it' actually is?

For Men Who do NOT Chat
Alternatives include:
1. using those score signs that they used to hold up in the Olympics
2. semaphore lamps or flags
3. sign language
4. Morse code and Braille
or my personal favorite
5. a sharp whack upside his head with a rolled up newspaper if he's not doing cunnilingus correctly.

Oooo, baby! Anyone have other suggestions?

Aug 13
l'attrait érotique cannot be achieved whilst wearing daisy dukes but is possible if wearing the red dress or my more infamous black dress but I have been informed that naked beneath a sheet in the half light 'afterwards' is my most seductive 'look'.
yeah or nay?
any other suggestions?

Aug 13
The Cookout and why we don't like 'Youngsters' We said the hell with it and went to Tabu for a bit. If we had stayed they would have done either of two things waited until we had left "or like the hotel party down south, they play 'around' you while ignoring you" both of which SUCK. The combination of poor manners, lack of imagination, boring and boorish conversation, and inept sex is not offset by youth and 'hardbody' beauty.
So - no one under the age of 30 years will be invited to my parties unless they are SERIOUS players with EXCELLENT manners. And even the 30 year olds had better 'watch it'! LOL

Aug 14
Mmmmmm 20-50 oh baby!   Things that attract the attention of a worshipper of the Great Goddess Gasoline include:
1. dab engine ol behind your ear.
2. a bit of unleaded on an ankle.
3. lithium grease?
4. tell him your belt is slipping.
5. your cylinders need boring.
Yeah, baby - but that engine lift gets uncomfy!!

Okay I'll see your Challenge and Raise ya......!
Rising Sign is in 16 Degrees Gemini
Extremely active by nature, you like to get around, meet people and do different things. Very restless, you just can't seem to stay put. You need to be involved in several projects at once in order to keep your mind stimulated. You like to read books and to write letters and to talk -- constantly. Seemingly ageless, you will always appear to be much younger than you really are. Very adaptable and inquisitive, you are always open to new ideas and experiences. A "jack-of-all-trades", you are lively and versatile. Because of the high nervous tension that you always seem to have, athletic activity would be a good way for you to burn off energy. But be careful of a tendency to experience things only superficially -- try to dig in and absorb things at a deeper level.

Sun is in 25 Degrees Aquarius.
You get bored with the status quo and are generally open to new things and ideas. An individualist and a free spirit, your friends are quite important to you as long as they do not try to tie you down by making too many emotional demands on you. Your thoughts are offbeat and you're a bit eccentric, but not always very changeable. As a matter of fact, you can be quite stubborn at times. Very fair-minded when dealing with large groups or broad issues, you are not always emotionally sensitive to the needs of individuals. Extremely objective, with good powers of observation, you would be qualified to study technical and complicated subjects, like science, computers or maybe even astrology.

Moon is in 25 Degrees Leo.
You always want to be proud of yourself and will never do anything that will make yourself look bad. You need the respect and admiration of others and enjoy attracting attention to yourself. Everything you do tends to be self-

emphasized and self-exaggerated. Very stubborn, willful and independent yourself, be sure to allow others who are close to you the similar right to "be themselves." Your need for love, affection and reassurance, and your tendency toward vanity, allow you to have your head easily turned by flattery. The more insecure you are, the more you tend to be a showoff. You love games and sports as a matter of fact, you would usually rather play than work. Be careful of a tendency to be snobbish and uppity -- it does not become you.

Mercury is in 02 Degrees Aquarius.
You tend to be very opinionated -- you have strongly felt notions about things and are quite vocal about expressing and defending them. Yet you are also an original thinker -- you enjoy shocking others with your offbeat, original thoughts. You appreciate and need mental and intellectual stimulation. Your judgment is usually fair and impartial -- you can be a good critic because you can remain objective and unemotional about most things.

Venus is in 11 Degrees Aquarius.
You are a friendly and outgoing individual, but close relationships are difficult for you to maintain due to your fear that they will cause you to lose your freedom. You attract friends and associates who are exciting, different and sometimes a bit odd. You are popular with others and enjoy working within a group toward group goals.

Mars is in 10 Degrees Taurus.
Careful, slow and thorough about all that you do, at times you are also willful and stubborn when others try to alter your course. You are definitely not a quitter -- you will work long and hard to get what you want. Your possessions are very important to you. One of your continuing problems is that you tend to regard the significant people in your life

much the same way as you do your possessions -- you become overly attached and much too jealous. You repress your anger when you get upset and that is not healthy. Try to learn to show your anger immediately in order to avoid painful explosions later.

Jupiter is in 00 Degrees Libra.
You are generally good at balancing opinions and judging issues, but you tend to be indecisive when it comes to making up your own mind. You are objective and quite concerned with fair play and justice. But, when it comes to yourself, you are so aware that whatever you do might upset the apple cart that you often choose to compromise rather than do anything that might make you lonely or vulnerable. Relationships are very important to you -- you learn about yourself and grow through observing yourself interacting with others. Your aesthetic tastes are refined, but expansive and expensive.

Saturn is in 13 Degrees Sagittarius.
Basically quite conservative, you respect traditional authority figures and are very thankful and supportive of the laws and institutions which govern your life. You learn and accept new ideas only after having very thoroughly examined them. Ideals and abstract concepts are important to you only if they can be used in some practical fashion. You are so practical and so orderly that you have natural skills in planning, administrating and organizing.

Uranus is in 04 Degrees Leo.
You, and your peers as well, demand complete and total freedom of self- expression. You want to make your mark in the world according to your own lights and will brook no interference from traditional authority figures, especially if they attempt to mold or shape you in any way. You are honest and forthright, but a bit offbeat and eccentric. The

lack of self-discipline may hinder you from reaching your goals as quickly as you would like.

Neptune is in 02 Degrees Scorpio.
You, and your entire generation, are extremely interested in anything deep and mysterious. You will explore and idealize the benefits that can accrue from the study of the occult, healing and psychology. You are willing to experiment with substances like drugs in order to push your understanding of your inner being to the extreme.

Pluto is in 29 Degrees Leo.
For your entire generation, this is a time when the relationship of the individual to society as a whole is being thoroughly re-examined. Major attempts will be made to find a balance between the need to be self-sufficient and the need to honor debts of social commitment.

N. Node is in 24 Degrees Scorpio.
You have a special aptitude for working by yourself, or with a like-minded group of dedicated individuals. Once you've committed yourself to a person or group or project, your loyalty and devotion are total until the group's goals have been realized. Not at all gregarious by nature, you're uncomfortable around strangers, greatly preferring to be in known and familiar situations. Others may regard you as shy or eccentric, but those who know you well are aware of the intense loyalty that you have to your friends.

Some of this nonsense is true. The rest is just fluff excused by them as due to my 'extremely complex personality' HAH!

Why Him?
No, it isn't anything about what he looks like etc, etc, etc
though he is cute;- it is the vibe that came off of him.
Perhaps it is pheromones? It happens so very rarely but
somehow the man just SPEAKS to me and I am powerless
to resist! I MUST HAVE HIM NOW!!!
So, darling just lay down right here.

XXX
Arranging her skirts, she straddled my lap facing me on my
sofa. She was so beautiful. Her eyes laughed and sparkled.
Her lips curved delightfully and when she kissed me so
lightly all of the desire I had for her flared up. Delicately
kissing my lips over and over making me quiver. When she
lifted her face away I became aware of the collar around
my neck. I said nothing as she began undoing my shirt
buttons and running her hands through my chest hair,
caressing me. I stopped her hands at my belt buckle. It was
too soon for me. Yes, I wanted her. But between wanting
and having there lay issues. A messy past, an uncertain
future, and a woman I barely knew snuggling into my arms
as I wore her collar around my neck. There was that ring on
her left hand. Where did that put me? Yes I wanted her,
who wouldn't?, but I am not a young guy heedless of
consequences. No, not tonight. But you know I was kicking
myself as I went upstairs to bed after watching her drive
off.

What I wanted was not what she could give. What I
wanted, she already had. Where did that leave me? Yes,
she's a domme' but I haven't seen a whip yet. She seems
kind and patient. I like her as a person and I care about her
as a friend. But what am I getting myself into? She wants
me? A beautiful woman wants me? And here I am
somewhat bewildered since I am not a young tall
hardbodied hunk who's hung like a horse. I am not bad but

she could have any man she really wanted. I am not rich either. She must just like me for some

reason. What do I know about women? I tried to resist but then she was sitting next to me on my sofa. she had my shirt off and she ran her fingertips slowly and lightly up my spine and blew gently on the nape of my neck and lightly licked my ear.

Okay, okay, I give in! Take me upstairs to my bed! She did. I did. We did. Still no whips. She doesn't need them. Force of personality, drop dead sexy beauty, razor intelligence, and a skill at seduction that you have to experience to believe makes coercion unnecessary. Yeah, I am her slut. My former reluctance makes me smile.

Aug 15
Metaphysics
I have been reading The Harvard Lectures, which I highly recommend, so when a fake profile using my real name and information was made, and the creature came into the chatroom calling me a jealous bitch, I had to wonder - how exactly does one go about being jealous of one's self? How does that work?
Any ideas?

Showing Big Sharp Pointy Teeth
Their profile says, right up there under what kind of swinger they are, "Sex with your partner only". Okay. This means either the two men get together while the women watch and get all steamy and then each goes back to their spouses OR The two women get together while the men watch get all steamy and then back to their spouses again OR her hubby gets me and the others get to watch, okay maybe my man gets a bj and then back to your own spouses. Which begs the question - why don't you just go and watch porn? Seems hardly worth the effort to find,

meet, and have chemistry enough (but not too much?) with another couple if you're only going to play that far but no further.

Seems to be some power play involved as well. The "I can fuck yours but you can't fuck mine" thing. Sorry, but I like my man far too much to go along with that bs.

Then there's the "precious female syndrome" as in my female is far too precious (shy, timid, scared, whatever) to share but she wants me to have my fun. And I am 'expendable'. Sounds like you two have a personal problem. You should talk to someone.

If you're offended, think about what you said in your profile re: the immediately preceding two paragraphs, which is only you two have any importance and we don't count at all.

Seduction 1
The hunger never goes away. I can feel it coming off of your skin as I walk over to where you'e sitting on the barstool. Standing there between your knees I lift your chin with my fingers and lightly kiss you, lingeringly. You do not move. You do not speak. You accept the kiss - the subtle touch of our lips. Will you come to me?

Aug 16
Masculine Persistence
Short answer is: No. Persistence usually ends up with them being blocked if not merely ignored and deleted without reading.

The long answer is: He can ask and ask and ask but hell will freeze over before I acknowledge his existence because he is most unsuitable and does not and never could meet my needs, desires, passions, or requirements because he's either too young, too stupid, too inept, too needy, too damn far away, too damn ugly, too controlling, or just too much of a huge pain in the ass to deal with (pauses for breath) or just too damn annoying for any woman to deal with, let alone a demanding woman like me, for any length of time which he will ever realize or understand because he's too stuck on himself and what he wants to consider the wishes of anyone else.

Enough said? *EG*

Seduction 2
Gently, slowly, lightly tracing graceful arabesques with the tips of my nails and fingertips over the contours of your body as we lay side by side naked upon your bed in the halflit quietude after passion. My lips lightly trailing the movements of my hands, exploring you, tasting you enjoying the feel of your skin and fur, enjoying your scent. Will you come to me?

Aug 17,
Truth or Dare
Here's your chance! Free of charge and no law prohibits this. Your privacy of info is your problem. You aren't on here to be private anyway.

Here's the thing. You get ONE just ONE question. You know how the game is played - so go for it!!

this offer valid until I say otherwise ty

And That's how you throw a PARTY!!!
3 women and 12 naked, naked men - 4 of them Cat Toys. Even had the chance to enjoy a friend I hadn't seen in 6 months - Mmmmmmmmeow!!
Next time don't use my undies to open your beer, dammit!
WOW!! WHAT A GREAT TIME!!!

don't you wish you had been there?

Aug 19
Since I Last Posted I have been busy. In addition to fomenting rebellion amongst the young, who don't want to get into a pissing contest - must be a guy thing - with me, having a wild party, and arranging for other wild parties, I have been reading The Archduke and The Assassin by Lavender Cassels. Very interesting and an example of how a once great country can vanish in an instant. Excellent read for those into history.
Do you people read at all?

58

Aug 19
Some Requests will NOT be honored. I do NOT kiss and tell especially not details. So if you want to know what happened at any particular place or time or party - you will just have to come next time!

Group Dynamics
That is the field of study's actual title yet someone (as far as the "group dynamics" is it really fair to group everyone together?) apparently doesn't think so.

Yes, in certain ways you can group people together since that is what cultures and societies tend to do. All of that "birds of a feather" thing. And people settling down in areas in which they feel comfortable amidst people just like themselves. People also tend to 'hang' with those similar to themselves, hence the 'exclusion' whether meant or not. Very few people can cross societal and cultural lines or leave the familiar for the strange. Myself included.
The point was the responses received.
Stats:
1. got it =1
2. came very close =2
3. leapt into error with both feet =2
Admittedly, the sample was far fewer than I had hoped to get.
Note to those in category 3 above: Just to answer your underlying assumption - I was not the only person who noticed, nor was I the only person who commented upon this phenomenon although I was the only one who noted it publicly. Mainly because I can take the heat and don't mind drawing fire.

All of your comments cheerfully welcomed whether for good or ill!! Please leave some!!

Aug 20
RM-isms
The Resident Males are of the following opinions - yes, they are permitted to have some.
1. men use humor because if she's laughing, she's not going to be seeking your blood just then.
2. men use humor to keep themselves from doing something drastic when the kids do something particularly bone-headed.
3. Some days it is best just to hide in the garage working on the cars or go and mow the lawn.
How very, very true!

The Cozy Red Interview!!!
Interview: Polyandrous Woman Tells Most
We are NOT alone!!!

Aug 21
Fur all Ruffled
Someone, who should damn well know better, has impugned my character by misrepresenting my motives. This time - he WILL PAY!

Aug 22
The Party Process
We, my partner in crime and I, have been holding these for about a year now and we have worked out most of the glitches in our system.

We have a core group of GREAT guys - the Cat Toys. Now we also have the makings of a very nice group of interested ladies! These people are the ones around whom we build a MARVELOUS sex party.
They come or not as their schedules permit.

New people are vetted which means the come out and meet either my partner or I or both of us at some public bar and we chat. *EG* Expect to be questioned most closely.

Then your name goes onto our list. This list is circulated among the Selection Committee members who may vote out or in any man they wish. They then give me their results or the final tabulation. I send invitations out to all men voted in.

You must RSVP !! Once you have said 'yes' then you must either show up or call ahead of time. Anyone who 'no shows' will be blacklisted - forever!

Women are treated differently, of course. We give you TWO chances!!

Everyone clear on this?

So Today
I went and got my hair done. Then I did what I always want to do afterwards - drove over to HIS house and enjoy him!!
Lovely day today!!
And my hair looks great!

Aug 23
Line 'em Up!
Biz is slow, must be August, so I am going to sunbathe (nude) some more after the customary slathering on of unguents.
Do my back?

Aug 24
Nice Meet & Greet Chat, chat, chat and some men showing some interest - we shall see. I may have to strangle one of the men however. The man bit me! GRRRRRRRRRRR No marks or he would have met with his demise right then and there. DOWN, BOY, DOWN!
You would not have done that would you?

Doing Research
for this one 'project' I'm involved with so I scoped out the Younger Women/Older Guys thread.
Now discounting the 'appearance factors', since anyone of any age can be fat or skinny or whatever, there seems to be a few reasons which can be described as 'ego factors', such as you can train her or show off 'what a stud you are' to your buddies, BUT the main reason seems to be procreativity. OKAY. A worthy reason.

Now with further advances in medical science, do you think this will change? I don't. I think that the other factors will move up as limited procreativity becomes less limited although some women my age will sigh and think "damn! more kids!" feeling under some pressure to 'perform' I suppose. It does remain true that it is best to have kids when she's in her 20's though.

I just hope these younger women will share! *EG* I'd make a great 'secondary'! Even my own kids think I'm a BLAST! My daughter did refuse to take me to the supermarket to pick up old men , but she still likes me anyway! My son just shakes his head ruefully and makes that noise Lurch used to make. LOL My primary just stands there and thinks I'm cute and asks me if I'm going to be home for dinner.

But I digress....you didn't mind, did you?

62

Training Your Girlfriend

"When you first start dating a new girlfriend, you want to be on your best behavior. Sure, you want to make a good impression, but what you're really doing is catering to her to get sex.

The problem is, the power base shifts to her right from the outset and she knows it. She's in charge of access to the zipper and she counts on you bending over backward to gain entry. So she's got you.

But there's more to it than that.

You might not be aware of it, but what she's really up to is training you to be what she calls a "gentleman" -- acting nice and accommodating, paying for her meals and chauffeuring her around like a servant. And that's not all. She's also busy laying her traps to lock you into this pattern for the course of the relationship.

Before you know it, she'll have you on her leash, following her around like a puppy dog, eagerly awaiting her next command and lapping up the few sexual kibbles she tosses at you to keep you at "heel."

Sounds despicable, doesn't it? Yet girlfriends do it to men all the time. Why? Because we let them. We allow them to treat us like obedient pets, with sex as our reward for the "correct" behavior.

But what if you don't want to wind up as your girlfriend's puppy dog? Is there any way out of this canine catastrophe? The answer is "yes."

The trick is to beat her to the punch -- act fast and treat her like one first. A girlfriend can make a best friend and ideal companion, but like any bitch (female dog, that is), she needs to be taught how to act around the house. So you have to set the ground rules early by enrolling her in your own private obedience school.

common obedience problems:

Aggression
She's out of control and constantly acts up. Brainwashed by a steady diet of Oprah and "feminist" propaganda, she's now "empowered," meaning that her thoughts run somewhere along these lines: "Men have been holding me back, I want mine now, and I don't care what pair of testicles I have to step on to get it." Since a girlfriend's brain is unable to distinguish emotion from logic, this kind of fantasy thinking will prompt her to act in self-destructive patterns and will cause you undue stress around the house.

Whining
She doesn't like to be left alone. She pouts when you hook up for the weekly poker game with your buddies. She harps at you to buy her something, and when she gets it, she doesn't want it anymore (or demands something even more expensive). She nags that you watch too much ESPN. She's always whimpering that she's too fat, too old or not pretty enough. She craves constant attention.

Barking
Yap, yap, yap. She talks incessantly. But the problem is that she goes on and on and on about nothing . You're on the phone, trying to close a business deal, and there she is in the background, yipping about her new pair of shoes.

Disobedience
Like a dog, she is hard to train. No matter what you want, she always insists on getting her own way, then throws a tantrum or cuts off sex if you oppose her. She's always

escaping from the yard to go shopping. And she won't respect your commands ("roll over," "lie down," "play dead").

Begging
She always "begs" with her hands on her hips -- never on all fours. All you hear from her is, "I want this," "Give me that" (on your credit card, of course) and "My girlfriend's boyfriend bought her a car -- why are you so cheap?". Not to mention that she expects to be regularly taken out for expensive dinners.

House destruction
You just can't leave her alone in your place. You go out for a few hours to play golf, and when you come back, your autographed Bears poster and leather couch have been replaced by flower prints and a shrimp-colored loveseat. And there are friggin' valances on the windows.

Not fetching
An improperly trained girlfriend doesn't know that she should always bring you a beer without having to be asked.

Chasing
Girlfriends are naturally attracted to bright, shiny objects (like jewelry) and fast-moving luxury cars. An untrained girlfriend will abandon you and run after any male who happens by with a few baubles and a Porsche.

Not being housetrained
Girlfriends are notorious for not knowing how to put the toilet seat back up.

training your girlfriend:

You can see how much upset an untrained girlfriend can bring into your life. So how can you counteract these bad behaviors?

Act early and often
Girlfriends have to be taught obedience from day one, or they will soon think that their bad behavior will be tolerated. Once improper patterns have been imprinted on the female brain, they can be extremely difficult to alter -- you can't teach an old girlfriend new tricks. The idea is to set the ground rules at the beginning of the relationship so that she can understand what's expected of her. This means your regular night out with the guys, sharing dating expenses and sex on your terms.

Don't be afraid to say "no"
As many would believe, girlfriends aren't usually as bright as men, so they typically have to be told more than once. And spank her if she continues to misbehave. If she likes it, spank her a lot.

Use operant conditioning
Freely encourage her good behaviors (being in heat, excessive licking, humping, and especially obeying the command, "Down, girl!") with praise and rewards while ignoring the bad. The idea is not to punish her for doing something wrong (unless she's into that sort of thing), but to withhold attention from the behaviors you don't like. This way, she will slowly catch on and eliminate the unwanted patterns from her repertoire. As she starts to become dependent upon your approval or disapproval, she will act more agreeably and respectfully towards you.

practice makes perfect:

All in all, obedience training is one of the best things you can do for your girlfriend and yourself, because a well-trained girlfriend makes for a happy relationship. It can enrich your dating life by eliminating unwanted behaviors and can make your time together much more enjoyable. The ultimate result is that you'll wind up with a girlfriend who will treat you well and work hard to please you... the perfect pet to have around the house."

AND HE DAMN WELL BETTER BE KIDDING!!!!

Aug 25
Recent E-Males
"mmmm, possibly?...I'll take that as wild interest."
LOL Very funny because Yes, guys do that! And it is CUTE!

and

"I know you want to be the master and in control of the situation at all times. But I believe your misunderstood as to what "you" really want. I also think no ones looked deep enough into you to know you."   (his spelling)

Unfortunately guys do this as well! *smacking this guy upside the head* THINK BEFORE YOU WRITE, DAMMIT! Read my blog BEFORE e-mailing me. It will save you from getting so many heavy blows to your head. (Blunt objects optional.)

This one is based upon the belief that one, women do NOT know what they want as well as some guy they never even met does, and two, that all controlling women are just RIDDLED with insecurities that can only be expressed in the 'right' situation i. e. as a submissive to him.

NEITHER of those applies to me. After messing with men for more than 38 years - yeah, I do know what I like and my insecurities have been faced.
OKAY guys! Show me YOUR bad e-feMales!

The Art of the Sustained Joke
Knitting a hang glider out of barbed wire.
Knit one, purl two. Knit one, purl two.
Knit one, purl two. *sip of scotch* Knit one, purl two.
End of the row. Have to turn now.
Ouch! Ouch! Fuck, that hurts! OUCH!
Knit one, purl two. Knit one, purl two.
more scotch

or

Kitten sitting there naked except for gold-rimmed half glasses on a fancy neck chain and an embroidered cardigan, like your grandmother used to wear, draped over shoulders (and stilettos) writing up reports on men vetted in a very large book..."Phineas = # 624"

or

Kitten entering the room wearing only long dangling earrings, thigh-high stockings and stilettos - carrying a brown leather backpack. From the backpack, she takes out a teak steamer lounge chair, with its umbrella attachment and its padding, a table, an ashtray, binoculars, and a never-ending supply of bottles of Laphroaig which she drinks by opening the bottle and inserting the straw. She then lounges there, in all of this glory, watching the chatroom scroll on by using the binoculars to scope out the men.

or

the entire concept of Aunt Agatha Answers All.
which you, no doubt, all remember quite well.

EG

Aug 26,
"Quietude"
flying down the cathedral of the night
exulting, at one with all
at one with you

May I Have Your Attention, Please?
You may have gotten the impression from my blog that the
only thing keeping certain males, who know who they are,
alive and well (i.e. unstrangled) is their skill in bed. While
there may be an element of 'appeasement' or 'feeding the
savage beast' involved in my relationships - I am really not
all that high maintenance. I can often be contented with a
simple saucer of very good single-malt scotch.
Thank you for listening.

More Research
This was posted:

"That's a little cruel, I think, but there's a grain of truth
there....older women know that their physical beauty is
fading fast, and that their chances of attracting a life partner
diminish with every passing year. Add that to the common
(but hardly universal!!!) attitude that they somehow "need"
a man to "take care" of them (financially, emotionally...and
yes, sexually), and you get the "clingy" response. If they
find one they like, they tend to latch on because they're not
at all sure they'll find another one.

This makes it sound like I think all older women are
desperate, man hungry manipulators, and that's not at all

69

the case. At my age, most of the women I meet might fit the definition of "older" and most of them are truly beautiful people. Sexually speaking, Ben Franklin was right, too....there is definitely something to be said for a woman who is flattered by the attention of a good man, no longer inhibited by the naiveté of youth, and determined to prove that there's life in an aging body."

Which I find extremely interesting coming from an 'older man' esp that part about 'proving that there's life in an aging body'.
Ironic dontcha think?

Zoom, Zoom!!
Motorcycling out and about today on the winding 'no line down the middle' back roads of Virginia today! Saw more 'don't blink' towns than one normally sees in this part of the country.
Virginia is beautiful!! Couldn't get real deep in the country, however, as "Baby" isn't allowed onto unpaved roads. Got my ankle caressed as we went along too! Mmmmmmmmeow!
Did you have any fun this weekend? *W*

Vetting Checklist - Physical
All males should be checked for the following physical attributes during the vetting process.
1. stands straight indicating a strong lower back
2. walks with a free and easy stride
3. fully articulating hips, knees, and shoulders
4. flexibility especially through his waist
5. manual dexterity
and
6. enough rhythm to do a slow foxtrot
(extra points if he can rumba)
The strength testing will come later.
How's your rumba these days, Darling?

My Sex Song
"Love You to Death" by Type O Negative
because:
dark, sensual, switching power play, slow, and deep with latent ferocity
What's yours and why?

Aug 28
Stolen From Another!
You are being exiled to a "deserted island" or another planet... You can bring an MP3 player, but with only 10 songs on it.. What tunes would you bring?

Cat Toy Call
Will all Cat Toys please let me know who's in for the party on the 23rd.

Aug 2
Why...
You should beware the entire shredding of pillows and hiding beneath the bed incident - the only way I'll come out is if enticed by naked men bathed in single malt scotch all ready to be licked clean.
EG and don't think I'm kidding.

Aug 29
Another book done!
just keeping you informed.
That's 8 books done.

Aug 30
My Feline Persona
Has been developed over the last few years and is based upon direct observation of various actual feli domestica. Their natural love of sex combined with an inherent dignity and arrogance is consistent with my own personality so it was a natural fit. But there was a problem. While I want to be totally bewitching and beguiling and rock a man's senses into a whirlwind of delight - I am doomed to just being 'cute'. Even worse, I have been informed that I am 'adorable'. ARRRGH! Very disappointing for a girl!
Why won't you men cooperate??

Aug 31
Heavy Metal Poetry

"Pyretta Blaze"

Beautiful yet dangerous
Thermogenic luminous
Like a moth drawn to a flame
I'm the same
All cremated equally

As a spark still I knew
I'll be lured be consumed
She a pyre incarnate incinerate
An inferno turned to flesh

Say the words I long to hear
Pinch bite kiss suck lick and sear
In a pyromantic way
I'm her slave
Living for her to ignite

-by Type O Negative

SEPTEMBER
2006

Sep 1

You Do Have to Get Out and actually meet people!! Had a WONDERFUL time tonight meeting some people - old and new - for a confab and then hung about a bit downtown with my sweety. Fabulous time!

Sometimes all it takes is just a sparkle in his eye! Feeling MUCH better now, thank you!

Recent Postings have been changed to protect all of you innocents from the reality of ME. I assure you that all pix now excluded were of me and nothing salacious was intended. Even today I enjoy a good game of hopscotch! Try it while wearing high heels! Yeeehaw!

as we explored last night - all bad habits should be practiced to excess! don't you agree?

September Party Part 2

Date/Time change due to circumstances well beyond my control - oo you just KNOW how I hate THAT! - Party is now Thursday the 21st beginning at noon and lasting until we all want to go home. This is a private venue and free of charge get together for the FOUR ladies of our delightful acquaintance and the EIGHT Cat Toys who know who they are.

This is a 'day in the country' kind of thing so call in sick with leprosy or something major.

Naked Twister and Scotch Tasting provided by ME and anyone else who cares to bring a little something with them.

CONTACT ME ASAP as the max occupancy is 12 persons!!

To All Those Facing Grievous Times
This too is but to try you!

May I tell you a story? Thank you.
Three years ago I went for a checkup and was given a preliminary diagnosis of heart disease, breast cancer, and diabetes. Further tests would be done in 30 days. Further tests showed that I had NONE of these and I am in fact healthy in spite of the odds.
The point is that for those 30 days of waiting for the next tests and the 30 days waiting for the second set of test results - I was ANGRY.
"You couldn't just give me one, you had to be 'generous' and give me all three?!?!"
(Language cleaned up to protect tender and delicate male sensibilities.)
Nothing more 'refreshing' during trying times than driving out to the middle of nowhere, having a stiff drink or six and telling The Lord exactly what you think of your current lot in life.
Grab your courage with both hands and go forward with a cheerful heart!

Sep 2
Recent Photos Placed herein are not mine and not of me but are graphic reminders to all of you of what can be achieved with a camera and a photographer.
Down with the black bar across the eyes!

Interviewed by C_R
Thank you, C_R and that's a GREAT picture you have!!
How do you think I did on my interview?

Sep 4
Got Bored Cleaning my desk and my office so...I compiled another book. This one on classical music. Besides, I'd rather do almost anything than do 'housework'.
See what happens when there aren't any suitable males around?

The Value of an Education
IS:
1. the person you become
2. the things you learn
3. you have proof of your tenacity
all of which are most enriching!
Of course you got the joke?

Sep 5
TSK, TSK, TSK Look, guys; can we talk? You all have not been getting the message:
1. I don't play games. I may periodically give way to excessive cuteness but it fools no one is not meant to fool anyone.
2. I do not give nor do I receive pain, abuse, or humiliation. So save the 'slap-happy, spanky-spank games' for your others.
3. I am not a Goddess. I am a Demoness. There is a difference.
Now that that has been settled, I am off - back to cleaning my office! *deep sigh of despair*

Sep 6
Errors
I really should check my email before leaving to meet guys but hey, I am busy and I am at work.
So there I am, at the meeting place, looking STUPID as I keep watching the door, wondering if that is him, or is it him, or OMG! I HOPE it ISN'T him!
So I leave after half an hour, return to the office, running an errand in between and there's no call either to my cell or to my office.
Said $^$&%& and checked my email and there it was "Since you didn't answer my questions in the last email I have decided not to come."
Hell, just read my blog - not like I don't have plenty of info on here!
Guy; you had a woman interested in you. What more did you really need to know?

Wicked Woman Day Spa Update
Trials of our new program have been successful!! We therefore will now offer this new package of services to our clients.
Program 2: consists of the following:
1. a delightful romp with one of our demonesses
2. a brief rest break
3. a full massage back and front specially designed for male bodies
4. fellatio
5. a salt scrub in the shower with extra warm water rinsing depending upon degree of furriness.
6. a glass of single-malt scotch with an ice cube while wearing a warm spa robe.

Every male wishing to avail himself of our services is asked to specify whether he wants Program 1 or Program 2 when making his appointment. Thank you.

Sep 7,
Swinging
When a couple committed to each other mutually have sexual relationships with other persons for positive, life-enhancing, reasons.

Several misconceptions concerning this topic linger in the minds of non-swingers.
1. Women are coerced or pressured into it.
2. Sex is sacred and swinging debases sex into simply a way to enjoy pleasure.

In the swing world, Women Rule. How ever they come to swing, once there, women find it liberating, confidence-building, and empowering. They can finally give up being 'nice girls'. They can stop worrying that they aren't 'cute' or 'pretty' enough. They can stop competing with other women and share instead. Women also find that men are not fiends and that often the best lovers are those they never expected. Women can opt in or opt out of any activity as they will and no questions are asked. They no longer have to justify their desires or their sexuality.

There is nothing wrong with pleasure, that is to say positive stimuli. The 'sacredness of sex' in all of this, lies within the relationship between the pair and not within the activity. Mistaking this key point leads non-swingers into error. Sharing joy and delight; enjoying your partner's having fun; learning about each other from watching their interactions with others – these are all good things. You grow both as individuals and as a couple. There is no fraud and no betrayal and you never need to feel as if there were. Everything is known. You have no secrets from each other. Imagine that you two shared with others; how wonderful would that be?

Sep 8
OMG! Letter in The W. Post today extolling the virtues of faith based reproductive medicine.

Several points:
1. The military does not exist to laud your reproductive powers as you seem to feel it should. "where pregnancy is treated like a disease" Yes it is because it has a similar negative effect upon the military's ability to do its job. You could also say the military treats disease like pregnancies. Tis equally true.

2. The lady was rejoicing in an atmosphere where she can "bask in the respect due her reproduction." Apparently she feels 'special' because her body parts work. How very nice. Congratulations on being able to do what almost every other life form on the planet can do.

This is not to say that having a faith and practicing it is not good. This is not to say that that having children is not good.
I am saying that thinking you are a 'princess because you can' or 'thinking others should think you are a princess because you can', or thinking that your only value lies with your having a working womb is WRONG.
You may feel free to agree/disagree as you will.
All comments cheerfully debated *EG*!

Sep 10
The Frantic Life of The Pampered House Cat
Pets, brushings, 2 meals daily, a bed, your private bath, free annual check-ups and free medical and dental care, lots of toys to play with and all you have to do in return is sit on a few laps, purrrrr a bit, lounge around, and look elegant. Not a Problem!!
May be in our next life?

Male Partner Selection
For those who do not yet have a partner, here are some tips to use when you set out to find one.
Other than appealing to you to the point where you are wondering how his hands and lips would feel on your skin, you have to carefully consider several other criteria when selecting a male slut or when selecting a male to turn into a slut.
1. Can he get his mind around the concept of any woman, at any time he is required, anyway she wants him? Can he be passed around amongst the ladies like a six-pack? Would he enjoy it?
2. Does he have the cojones to submit without being obsequious or fawning? You want a man not a dog after all.
3. Is he presentable? If all you wanted was a penis, you could go buy one. Can he converse and how are his manners?
4. Is he willing to learn and open to new ideas and experiences?
5. Does he genuinely like women? You know what I mean by that - and yes, we can tell if he does.
Now all we have to consider is his amount of available free time, transport, and wherewithal (since you do not want to end up having to support him). Self-sufficient but willing men with the necessary free time are what you want. If he volunteers, that's even better!

BTW I am having a rough time of it lately. I really need to be invited out for a massage by a comely and skilled male teddybear!

Serenity
Most of us simply want to go on in our own merry way, injuring no one, and enjoying life. And why not? Certainly there is enough frustration and anger in the world without our adding our little bits of high melodrama.
Embrace serenity at every opportunity! I have to remember this when driving way out on Interstate 66 and the check engine light comes on - again - for the THIRD TIME THIS SUMMER!
Sssshh. Serenity - remember serenity.
Yes. Serenity. I really do have to work on that.

This Week
Wed - off to Annapolis
Fri- polo, then the secret spot
Sat - the Thornton Hill Hound Point-to-Point
also trying to finish 3 books and I might even be able to work some SEX in this week as well!

Live as you Love
"If I told you that I adore you, would have you have me do so stintingly? Or would you have me declare it as I feel it, with all my heart and soul?"
Life, even the most banal life, can become a grand adventure if we would have it so, if we savored each moment, if we enjoyed it most completely.

Men Only Please!

1. Would you take charge, want me to take charge, or a little of both?
2. Would you rather make love to me, fuck me, or a little of both?
3. Would you ever whisper freaky stuff in my ear? If so ... when would you be likely to be a whisper freak?
4. Would you ever talk dirty to me? What's your idea of dirty anyway?
5. Would you kiss me with a little tongue or a lot of tongue?
6. Would you make love to me with your mouth until I begged you for more and then not stop, or would you rather not please me orally?
7. Would it scare you if I squirted all over your face? Your hands? Your cock?
8. Would you want to penetrate me with your cock? Your tongue? Your hands? Anything else?
9. Do you love me shaved or think I need to grow hair? Would you wanna shave me? Shower me? Bathe me?
10. Would you take off all your clothes for me? Anywhere I wanted you to? Would you like it if I took off all of my clothes for you?
11. Would you lick and bite me all over? Would you tease me? How would you tease me?
12. Would you like foreplay for hours, or are you a get straight to the point kind of lover?
13. Would you take your time if I asked you to do so, or would you explode if you had to use control on yourself?
14. What kind of play gives you the most pleasure?
15. What's your favorite time of day to play?
16. Would you want to go fast or slow?
17. Are you loud or quiet?
18. Would you let me pleasure you for hours with my hands and my mouth if I wanted to? Anywhere I wanted to?

19. Would you want to see me dressed in a particular fashion? Privately? Publicly?

20. Do you think that you could carry me to the land of orgasms? Multiple orgasms?

21. Would you fall asleep when we were done?

22. Would you be upset if I woke you up in the middle of the night, fucked or sucked your brains out, and then let you go back to sleep?

(September 11 postings were removed from this narrative due to their highly personal nature which would make identification all too easy.)

Sep 12
Bad Dating Tips for Men
Keep the power

"Ever been on a date and you could just sense that she had all the POWER? As if she had something that you desperately wanted and she KNEW IT? Most guys give away their power when they're with a woman. But do you think women are ATTRACTED to men who do this? No. The solution is to let her know that YOU are the one doing the "selecting," NOT HER. Show that you're picky about who you spend your time with and tease her about how she's screwing up her chances with you. Communicate that she's going to have to be on her best behavior to "qualify" for your time, and you'll be surprised just how far she'll go to get on your calendar."

Put yourself on a pedestal

"How would you act if you KNEW beyond the shadow of a doubt that a woman was TOTALLY into you but you weren't THAT interested in her, and that you decided RELUCTANTLY to give her a chance to hang out with you? What if you were a bit arrogant, but still in the mood to have fun with it and tease her to see how much she really wanted you? Practice coming from this mental space and you'll find that it'll eliminate your nervousness -- INSTANTLY -- and it will give you the edge you need to project a confident, attractive vibe to ANY woman."

Be TOO comfortable

"When a man is intimidated by a woman, she ALWAYS knows. How? Because he'll behave in ways that subtly tell her he's not comfortable with himself, with her and with the situation. The solution is to go to the OPPOSITE EXTREME and create the feeling that you're TOO comfortable. Mimic something she's doing in a funny way -- for example, if she has a really rigid posture, sit up extra straight and say, "I really think you should work on your posture." People are only playful like this when they're feeling comfortable, so this behavior will send the message that you're not intimidated by her in the slightest.

You can also pick up something small like a napkin and swat her with it, especially after you've made fun of her and she's pretending the comment bothered her. Most men don't have the guts to be this bold, so when you DO, she'll see you as a cut above other guys."

Bring out her animal responses

"In the animal kingdom, different animals have signals that tell their mate of choice they're interested. When the male uses one of these signals, the female actually becomes PARALYZED and freezes in a sexually aroused position. Women respond in a similar way to several specific behaviors from men. So if you want to turn her on in a BIG way, smell her neck and shoulders… pull her hair gently by running your hand up the back of her neck and her hair, then make a fist and pull lightly... breath in her ear and whisper a compliment to her or bite her neck gently. Warning: Use these moves with caution -- you may create a WILD animal that will stop at nothing to get what she wants from you."

Try any of these with me, guys - and you will be alone within 5 seconds. Remember, any such disrespect and I will have NO problem forgetting your name.

Pictures
I guess the picture that accompanied my 9/11 story where the soldier in Iraq was petting a small feline friend and was too much for mature adults to see.

Sep 13
had you forgotten?
Last night the silken slow sliding down your body finding that which made you quiver and catch your breath in delight slow very slowly twining around your shoulders your waist your loins feeling you against my cheek your skin and fur on my skin until I too quiver and burn with a predatory desire kissing caressing licking hearing your pleasure the black leather cuffs on your wrists the strap around the bedpost restraining your arms kissing up and along nuzzling enjoying you Purrrrrrrrrr bless and be blessed.

Sep 14
not very happy
SO ANGRY I WANTED TO
put my fist through plate glass window somewhere
or
run over a puppy deliberately
or
spit
But do I actually do any of these? No. What I really did do was drive out, adhering to the speed limit, and fill up the trucks' gas tanks and then nicely drove back home again. Did this twice since there are two trucks and it was my turn. Sedate behavior masking rage.
Feeling 'dramatic' does not mean you have to act 'dramatic'.

Sep 15
sorry to disappoint but you cannot rule the world for
I ALREADY DO!
and they didn't hide the gummy bears well enough!

Come and Be Vetted
Tonight's Agenda
Polo circa 6pm
(pull over at the power sub station and change clothes in the truck)
The Shade Tree 9pm to 9:30pm approx.
Remember to look for the tall lady in the RED dress.
Mamma's thereafter until I get bored.

Sep 16
Thornton Hill Hounds Point-to-Point Races
Spent a lovely time this afternoon, the girls and I, out at Thornton Hill enjoying the races. Hurdles, timber and flat races were held. Mutawage almost won but was beaten in the last strides by Haggard. One horse, who shall be nameless, ditched her rider and wandered off to talk to the hounds who were penned nearby. Other horses were so far back that they just said 'hell with this' and walked their way to the finish ignoring their riders entirely. The girls had a great time, walking about, petting horses, taking pictures and nibbling sandwiches. One huntswoman had a splendid clean-cut, 18-hand, bay under her - I sooo wanted that horse!!! Perfect conformation and had a fluid, easy movement!
It was down south of Sperryville and yet, got the girls back and to work early - in spite of the policeman.

Sep 17
Publicity Thoughts on various topics concerning PDA
1. he pinched my nipple, clothes on, in front of the waitress for two reasons - to shock her, and to see my reaction - childish power play sort of display.
2. seated leaning cheek against him and having his hand caressing my back - not really very public as was at Mamma's at the time, clothes on - no problems with this
3. pulled over at the side of the road engaging in intercourse, partially unclothed - no witnesses=no problem; witnesses=problems so not really public either since 'the public' was absent although a truck went by just after and we had to go back and retrieve his wallet from the side of the road - ooopsie!
4. naked and engaging in group sex - not a problem - we're all friends here could be said to be 'not public' either but that would be semantics don't you think?

5. hanging out naked at a naked open air venue - also not public strictly speaking but no problem there either - if you don't like - don't look
The answer seems to be "It depends".

Teddybears, teddybears - Come out and Play!
Late Monday or 8-ish Tuesday?
Not Wednesday
Of course, Thursday and
perhaps - if I'm lucky,
Friday!!!!
any teddybears available?

Excuses, Excuses!!
"5 Reasons To Dump Your Date

1- She's not a giver
She's not considerate or helpful. She doesn't help you carry the grocery bags upstairs. She doesn't bring a bottle of wine along to contribute to the picnic dinner. She's all "Me, me, me." One of the dead giveaways: she's overly concerned with material things. Joyful giving of herself, her time and her energy is just not part of her language. There's no good reason to have a second date with one of these gals.

2- She has no integrity
She doesn't keep her word. You can't count on her. She's consistently, chronically tardy. She "fibs" a lot and makes things up to satisfy her own little agenda, thinking that you won't get it or at least will let things slide. She even makes up whoppers when she doesn't need to. Yup, she's got some serious character problems. So it's best to weed this woman out of your garden of lovelies as quickly as you can. And I don't care if she looks like an Elle magazine cover girl. Lose her.

3- She's inflexible
You want to take her to the beach, and she doesn't want to go because the wind might mess up her new hairdo. Doing anything that takes her out of her comfort zone is threatening to her. She can't handle any kind of spontaneity. She won't change her agenda to fit in with yours. As far as she's concerned, you're the one who's supposed to rearrange your plans to fit her needs.

4- She's a complainer & a nag
You can't seem to do anything right in her eyes. "Why do you always...? Why can't you ever...?" are two of her favorite questions to ask. She has no concept of the value of building up a man's ego. She couldn't do it if you paid her 50 grand just to fake it. Deep down she's not a happy person, and she wants to bring you down to her unhappy level. Ironically, many of these nagger-type girls think that they are being helpful and constructive when they do their number and have no clue that they are actually pushing men away. Who cares about how she got to be the way she is? Let her work it out with her therapist. It's not your job to try to fix her.

5- She's not fun to be with
The package looks perfect. She's a knockout, and she knows how to dress to impress. She doesn't really seem to have any particular troublesome character traits either. But when you're out with her, you just don't seem to really have fun. You find yourself working too hard to keep the conversation going. She just doesn't "get" your jokes. This is another losing situation that can be quickly perceived, evaluated and terminated.

Remember guys; it's okay to leave first, honest!"

OK, my take: all legit reasons for not seeing her again, esp #5. But do not ditch her and leave her sitting there picking up the check. HOWEVER: before you embark upon another lady, review your history and see if you didn't contribute to any of this. ALSO: be aware that this works BOTH ways!
"May I have an 'amen'?"

Sep 18
Jealousy is Good?
"But like I mentioned before, there are varying degrees of jealousy:

Cute jealousy
Jealousy does not necessarily merit its negative connotation, after all, it's normal for men to be suspicious of their women (and vice versa). Having reservations about her going to a strip bar with friends or not enjoying the sight of her drooling over some guy in a magazine are innocent examples of how some jealousy can be harmless, and a perfectly normal reaction.

Healthy jealousy
Likewise, a man who voices his concern over having his girlfriend go out with a bunch of guys or seeing another man flirting with her is also part of a healthy relationship. Oftentimes, a man is just looking out for his girlfriend's well-being and women usually respect that. They may even be insulted if you don't say anything.

Obsessive jealousy
The problem arises when aggression and/or violence accompanies the jealousy. Once you've reached this stage, you obsessively begin questioning her loyalty to you, and that sends you into a rage, maybe even using physical force."

I totally disagree with the above. There is no excuse for jealousy - EVER. Being suspicious of your lover is NOT normal behavior. Jealousy is NOT a sign of a healthy relationship. TRUST is a sign of a healthy relationship so trust him or her until given reason not to. I am not jealous myself and I will not permit a jealous lover into my life. What do you think?

Hello, Reality?
"8 Reasons For Staying Single

1- You can take the time to find the right woman
By staying contentedly single you can afford to wait for your true soul mate -- if one even exists -- to pop into the picture. You can take the time to casually wade through the barracuda-infested waters of the dating pool and set your hook for the prize catch.

2- You can focus on your career
By staying single you can enjoy the opportunity of building your career to your own satisfaction without draining off the tons of energy a permanent relationship entails. You remain free to put in long hours, work on the weekends or do whatever else you have to do to be successful. This is especially true if you're working in any kind of time-demanding field, such as medicine, law or entrepreneur-ship.

3- You can do what you want, when you want
When you're single, the world is your oyster. You can pick up and go anywhere you want, do anything you want, any time you want. No one is in the background nagging at you to do chores, go shopping, or "grow up." You're absolutely free to hang out with your buddies, party till dawn and find plenty of time for your personal interests and hobbies. Best

of all, you have the luxury of being all by yourself, if you feel like it.

4- You can enjoy a sexual smorgasbord
By staying single, you're not stuck with the same sex partner for the rest of your life. The dating universe is yours to conquer. You can happily sample all the different fare at the sexual buffet, and keep your taste buds primed for the next dish being served. What's more, you never have to wrestle with sexual boredom or lack of variety (and you'll be the envy of all your married friends).

5- You can build wealth
Staying single means not being forced into buying a 10,000-megawatt diamond ring (so your fiancée can impress her friends with the huge price tag she has set on getting her into bed) or any of the other bloodsucking financial drains that marriage entails, for that matter. And you won't be stuck having to regularly shell out for the flowers, more jewelry and the other gifts that a wife demands (it's like paying maintenance fees on a condo). By staying single, you're not legally or financially obligated to anyone but yourself. But once you John Hancock the dotted line on that marriage contract, she has you forever by the balls. You can take this money (that somehow spontaneously becomes "hers" once you get married) and invest it in important things like sex-drenched singles' cruises, buying cool cars or building equity in a house.

6- You can enjoy serenity
Being single means peace and quiet. When you don't live with a woman, you're not subjected to her never-ending mood swings and emotional storms, or her blaming you for everything that she screws up in her life. And, of course, no fights. As long as you keep her as a casual girlfriend and

not a wife, if she gets too uppity you can simply walk away, free and clear.

7- You can keep your toys
When you're single, you can hang on to all your fun toys -- that classic Mustang, the speedboat, the Harley -- all of which seem to magically disappear overnight once you get married. Your wife won't want you to have these things because they take the focus off her and she feels it's her money that she could be better spending on clothes and shoes.

8- You don't have to compromise
Being single means you don't have to constantly find a "middle ground" -- meaning, do what she wants to do (whether you like it or not). This includes being forced to see chick flicks or suffer antique fairs and dinner with her friends. And you'd better toe the line buddy, or you'll have hell to pay and no more sex for you.

While marriage may provide certain benefits, when you choose to stay single, you're keeping the door open for many more options and opportunities in your life. Your male independence is something you should never surrender lightly, even if you think you've met the girl of your dreams."

Okay, can we talk reality here? Your married friends really do not envy you - if they did, they'd ditch the wife and kids and join you in your lifestyle. Do you see that happening? No you don't. What you do see are friends quietly dropping away from you as they get on with their lives. "Yeah, I'll call ya, buddy." I'm not even going to touch on the lack of respect shown by the "never-ending mood swings" remark! Dude, you have entirely missed the point! Agree or Disagree?

Hard to Believe!
Read to believe!

from a certain couple and I quote:

"OH MY GOD. A 51 year old woman wants to know why no one showed up at her gang bang? The tits are almost touching her belly button while laying down. I'll bet with monopause in full force you need a ton of lub. LOL LOL LOL I could laugh out loud all day and still am."

unquote.
the misspellings are his/hers, not mine.

I mentioned that no one showed up for the vetting last Friday evening. Not to a party, just a vetting to get on the guest list for parties.

Mind you this woman here is 28 and her man is 41 and they say in their profile that 'age isn't an issue'. Like hell it isn't! They also complain about 'the fakes' on the Internet
sputtering laughter!
You just can't make this stuff up!

Sep 20
Ditzy? Frankly - you men are REALLY spazzy!

"Why do women play hard to get?
It's human nature to value people that you've invested resources on."

then add in this gem,

"Why else would we endure hours of trivial female chatter and pick up the check at the end of it? There is no other reason than the hope that we will somehow convince her to go to bed with us."

toss in this item:

"If you're in an exciting relationship, don't let it last too long."

And you get a guy who will say this:

"You say: Honey, I'm going to watch the game over at Tim's place.
She says: What for?
Your reply: Because I enjoy watching the game with my buddies. See you later."

and NOT expect to get this in reply:

She says: You won't see me later.

(unless they're married where, as soon as he's left, she's on the phone jacking up his life insurance coverage - j/k)

I have a great deal of sympathy for men and what they are up against. But guys, there's no need to self-inflict this way! We are all people here, just trying to get through life as nicely as we can.

Vetting
What I will ask, why I ask that, and what I am looking for when vetting men.

The process begins as soon as I see you and no you do not have to be Brad Pitt, et al. I'm looking at how you stand and how you move more than how you look. Fur is a definite plus.

Does he identify and approach me with confidence?
We all know why we are meeting and if he can't "get it up" here chances are he will not be able to "get it up" there.

The conversation is important for not only what he says/how he says it - but also for how much of the "heavy lifting" he leaves to me. Equal talk time is perfect.

1. How long have you been online dating/ how many met? Experience level questions. Also trying to gauge interest level. Standard sort of basic qualifying questions you'd get when applying for any position.

2. What do you particularly like - sexually?
Forget what you think I want to hear and just go for it. I will not be shocked, amazed, or injured by whatever you tell me. *EG* I promise. Besides, I may know someone who is looking for just that.

3. What do you do?
Nevermind any stereotypes. Just how much chaos can you take? Analytical or no? What you do for a living tells me how your mind generally works.

4. What are your interests/hobbies?
All work and no play - so just relax and tell me you're really into stamp collecting.

5. The standard marital status, kids, mode of living questions. Meaning how much time you have available and is daytime or evening good for you?
If you're married I might ask if she might like to play too but will not pry any further. That's your problem, buddy.

6. Do you have any questions?
If you do ASK! I understand this is your first time with us. Having questions is only to be expected.

So. do you have any questions?

Sep 21
A Teddybear Came Out and Played!!
MMMMMMMMMMMmmmmmmmm   Mmmmmmmmeow!
Lovely, lovely teddybear who makes me feel sooo purrrrrrry!
First there was Monday and then there was Wednesday! I hope there will be another this Friday!
a woman can never have too many teddybears!

You Ladies Missed Out Big-time!
Those of you ladies who shamed your mothers by standing me up today, missed out on one HELL of a GREAT time! As you all know, once you have accepted an invitation, the ONLY things that excuse you are disease and/or your death. I realize that things come up and that your figure is not perfect but you had a cell number to call dammit! So why didn't you?

Party!
It was supposed to be an orgy out in the country with 6 women and 6 men all having a great time - instead it was 4 men and myself out in the country having a GREAT time! Mmmmmmmmmmmmmeow! Thank you guys for coming and cumming! That was FUN!

Sep 23
It is Time!
We all make choices in our lives and there comes a point when you have to decide to run with the big dogs or stay on the porch with the losers.
'Nuff said?

Sep 23
Halfway to S!
Recently my friend _S wrote her 400th post. I am nearing my 200th hence the title. But those who know from whence I came will know that I may very well be nearing my 400th as well. It is difficult to say now.
What I can say is that it has been so much FUN!!

Sep 24
200th Post !!!!
I am polyandrous with firm deeply felt ties to several men but we don't all live together. Yes I really am as portrayed only more intellectual and usually nicer and that awful word - cute! I am slightly younger than stated in my profile. No I have not yet fucked the 5th Fleet but I am only one woman so it will take time. Own my own professional practice and work almost all the time I'm not more pleasurably engaged. I both work and smoke like a full-bore locomotive. Have two kids and a darling husband who thinks I'm just adorable but that might be because he's way bigger than I am. Either that or its the two H-D motorcycles

I bought him. I hate housework, am a great cook, and he didn't marry me for my driving skills. LOL
Now you know!

Sep 25
Change 1
UPDATE: PARTY WILL BE WEDNESDAY THE 11th AT NOON instead. Adjust your schedules accordingly, please, gentlemen! This is so my lovely Partner in Crime can come out and enjoy all of you men too! I know you have missed her! So we now have 4 women.
Stand by for more 'news as it happens'.

boyfriend vs. boy toy
"She wants a boyfriend if she:

Says that you and her best friend/brother/cousin have a lot in common and would get along.
Discusses her plans or goals for the future and shows an interest in yours.
Doesn't hesitate to introduce you when she runs into someone she knows.
Asks for your help with something she is unable to do on her own.

She wants a lover if she:

Regularly mentions social events she will be attending but never asks you to join her.
Turns down your invitations to social events.
Dismisses your attempts to share any personal information.
Tells you that her schedule can be unpredictable and offers to call you when she's free.

She wants a boyfriend if she:

Tells you specifically why her last relationship failed and what she's learned from it.
Mentions the relationship status of her close friends.
Asks about your previous girlfriends and dating history.
Remarks on how different you are from her past boyfriends.

She wants a lover if she:

Avoids discussing previous men in her life or only makes negative comments about them.
Is less than enthusiastic when discussing a friend's relationship or upcoming wedding.
Tells you that you remind her of her ex.
Lets you know that she is casually dating a variety of men.

She wants a boyfriend if she:

Suggests watching a romantic comedy or scary movie.
Invites you to events that represent how she likes to spend her time or things that are important to her.
Suggests a double date or a social gathering where you will be interacting with her friends, family or coworkers.
Wants to hold your hand or be otherwise intimate with you in public.

She wants a lover if she:

Shows no interest in scheduling daytime dates.
Plans activities that revolve around the consumption of alcohol or are at places that make conversation impossible.
Gravitates toward dating activities that allow for revealing clothing or physical interaction.
Suggests dinner and a movie at her place, then mentions that she can't cook."

Relatively sane advice for men, this time - they haven't always been very smart. The trouble with this comes when she does both boyfriend and boy-toy things with you. In such a situation, a man has to be 'flexible' - that is to say looks good and performs well both in a suit and in the sheets! Can you do that, baby?

Vetting Dates/Times/Venues
FRIDAY at Centreville at 9pm
OR
MONDAY in Occoquan at 6pm
Be there, at either, or be left off the list!

Sep 26
Create Positive Vibes
"As many professionals say, chemistry is the result of "positive vibrations" between two people. Obviously, there is some debate as to what exactly creates these vibrations, but most agree that attraction is amplified when we feel comfortable around someone. Negative vibrations arise from disagreements, overactive egos, competitiveness, and so on. Positive vibrations come about from being fun and exciting, conversing easily and effortlessly, and listening with an interest and a smile. Just sit across from her and act more comfortable than if you were at home in your plush recliner."
Finally, some decent advice for men. LOL

Sep 27
Now Available A revised edition of Introduction to Classical Music as well as a new companion cd of the music on the Recommended Listening List.
I do have a cd ready as a gift to the one who owns the only original copy of the book!
NB: no copyrights were harmed during the recording of this cd.

So Cute!
1st Email =
"No, I'm not mentally impaired. I apparently hit the wrong key as I am still new to this site. I thought I was sending a reply to your E-mail and before I knew it your E-mail went back as my reply. I thought maybe that is what I was supposed to do so I didn't try again. I figured you get a ton of E-mails and didn't need another from me.
MY BAD"

2nd Email =
"I forgot to add you might learn how to spell."

3rd Email =
"Maybe I could be your keyboard slave and type for you! Then I could be rewarded for my efforts!"

A slave typist!! What more could a woman with claws ask for?

There is something about pinning his naked body down onto the bed beneath mine that just gets me all aroused!!!!

Sep 28
Busy, busy
There simply aren't enough hours in the day ....
...devoted to long lingering wild SEX!!!
Lets do something about this!

OCTOBER

2006

10/01/2006

"SUPPORT HEALTHY HOOTERS!!!

You've just been flashed in honor of Breast Cancer Awareness Month!"

Two steps forward. One step back. Ah well. I can endure I suppose. Thinking of it as atonement for my manifold sins.

10/02/2006

"That only a union between same sex individuals may be a marriage valid in or recognized by this Commonwealth and its political subdivisions. This Commonwealth and its political subdivisions shall not create or recognize a legal status for relationships of one man and one woman that intends to approximate the design, qualities, significance, or effects of marriage. Nor shall this Commonwealth or its political subdivisions create or recognize another union, partnership, or other legal status to which is assigned the rights, benefits, obligations, qualities, or effects of marriage."

§ 20-45.2. Marriage between persons of opposite sex.

A marriage between persons of opposite sex is prohibited. Any marriage entered into by persons of opposite sex in another state or jurisdiction shall be void in all respects in Virginia and any contractual rights created by such marriage shall be void and unenforceable. (1975, c. 644; 1997, cc. 354, 365.)

§ 20-45.3. Civil unions between persons of opposite sex.

A civil union, partnership contract or other arrangement between persons of opposite sex purporting to bestow the privileges or obligations of marriage is prohibited. Any such civil union, partnership contract or other arrangement entered into by persons of opposite sex in another state or jurisdiction shall be void in all respects in Virginia and any contractual rights created thereby shall be void and unenforceable. (2004, c. 983.)

IT IS DIFFERENT WHEN IT IS YOUR HEAD ON THE BLOCK

My reasons for opposing all such legislation:

1. The Declaration of Independence and The Constitution of The United States do NOT say "except for you."

2. No one has the right to impose their beliefs onto another.

3. what you or I or the next person does between consenting adults is NO ONE ELSE'S BUSINESS

4. You are wasting time and money. THIS is NOT what I 'hired' you to do. GET BACK TO WORK.

(Unfortunately, the measure passed.)

Situation continuing. If I end up divorced over this....well, someone's going to have to come up with bed space for me until the house is sold and I get my apartment or whatever. I get custody of the scotch!

My men are so damn spoiled! All they have to do is work, putter around the house, spend their allowances, and 'put out' every chance they're asked - which happens every 5 minutes! YET they currently are being HUGE pains in the ass! GRRRRRRRRRRRRR. DO NOT make me get out the whip!!

10/03/2006

Some men can be the most exasperating pains in the ass! No, not my beloved Cat - though he too has his moments. It is this other guy! Yegods, man! Let it go! You know - I may need a drink here if this continues much longer. At least he hasn't kicked me out of bed yet.

"a youth who can't hit a cathedral at 30 yards with a Gatling gun, in three-quarters of an hour," and "be good and you'll be lonesome." -don't you just adore Mark Twain?

Polo season has closed so now it is the start of the hunting season. I will have to see if there are any hill-topping opportunities for neophytes on lead reins. LOL All such info cheerfully accepted. Ciao, babies!!!

Pick-up Lines: I usually just wander over after maintaining eye contact, stand very close, put my fingertips on his chin near his mouth and whisper "Hello." just before I kiss him. Does that count as a pick-up line? *EG* would it work on you, baby?

10/04/2006
My readership is falling off tremendously!! Apparently people prefer fluffy sweetness and light. SOB! That is SOOO NOT me! But R said something nice about me recently = "as inconspicuous as a tarantula on a slice of angel food cake." Thank you, R!! But if this lack of readership continues, I may have to drink more.

What She Considers 'Cheating':
1. confiding in other women
2. dancing closely
3. flirting provocatively
4. anything to do with a sex pro
5. engaging in cyber/phone sex
6. engaging in any actual sex with someone else

Mind you, the lady who ran this survey of 100 women asked 100 women under the age of 35 who, apparently, do NOT swing or participate in other alternative activities. I would be willing to bet that if the lady had asked 100 hard-bitten, old, long time married battle-axes (like me!) that she would have gotten far different responses. My response: NOT keeping me fully informed at all times.

10/05/2006

"There are many things a woman looks at in order to get an impression of a man's personality before she decides to get involved with him. She might analyze his clothes, his demeanor and the way he treats other people, but the things she finds desirable or undesirable may not always be obvious to him.

One of the tools women use to take mental inventory of men is to assess whether or not they're worth keeping based on who they're attracted to. Women are intensely interested in knowing what types of girls their man finds attractive -- hence; the landmine, yet so innocently posed question, "Which of my friends do you find hot?"

The roots of this preoccupation are twofold:
1) Your girl compares herself to every woman she sees

(especially those you find attractive) because she wants to see how she stacks up.
2) She sees the girls you're into as a reflection of the kind of guy you are."

Now, if she's doing this it means she's 'competing' with other women for men albeit more subtly than the usual. STOP THAT! There's sufficient men to go around and you can learn to share, dammit. Unless you are insecure? Hmmm?

Apparently SOME people are thin-skinned and "sensitive" or "delicate" creatures. Interestingly, they are out of the house unescorted by suitable medical personnel. Unfortunately, I had NO WARNING of this and so have lost some blogs BEFORE I could save them elsewhere. Thank you very much.

Be that as it may *waves a paw*.

Someone said something NICE about me the other day. He quoted Raymond Chandler when he described me "as inconspicuous as a tarantula on a slice of angel food cake." Such a sweetheart! Yes, yes the BAD EVIL WOMAN is back! LOL BTW if she's so case-hardened that she needs 12 hours and 12 inches to get off - you are doing something WRONG there, buddy boy! *EG* Ciao, babies!!!

10/06/2006

Oh, really? from another blog: "We are getting very tired of getting together with couples where the male half reveils that he had such a tiny member that it's almost funny to look at or many times he can't stay hard long enough for HER to get some enjoyment. No offense to these males but enjoyment is what we're on here for. Where are all the

110

couples who have males 7 inches and larger?" The misspellings are their own and this couple is late 40's early 50's.

I am not sure if they realize what they revealed in this post, but it seems she's so 'case-hardened' that it takes approximately 12 hours and about 12 inches for her to get off. So you young 'bang my cervix' types just remember you will age and regard the post above as a grim warning! The more 'rough' you get now, the more you will increasingly need to reach orgasm. This has been a public service announcement. We now return you to your regularly scheduled frivolity.

I shall neither confirm nor deny my involvement with any particular male. You all know who I am NOT enjoying. Situation beginning to break; but should be an underlying irritant for some time to come. BTW I was right in my earlier posts. Divorce was considered.

Nov's and Dec's parties will have to be held earlier in those months. How do Nov 17th and Dec 7th, or thereabouts, fit your schedules?

No party for us tonight! This often happens and is one of the reasons I hold my own parties. Not many like sexually aggressive straight women. Yes, I know what you all SAY but when the rumps hit the sheets, frequently it is another story. I've had guys disappear on me in the interval between the bar and the hotel! Driving along and then POOF he's gone! WTF? Amazing. All of these men complaining about not getting enough. JEEZ!

10/07/2006

Once again turned down because I, Nip, am NOT at all bisexual. How so VERY boring. She actually said that if I didn't share my pussy with her, she wasn't going to share the cocks with me! And here we were just saying to a newly swinging couple how lifestylers AREN'T judgmental. Like I have time for this?!?! More of the 'fuck like us or else' - well onto the next couple/couples.

Look, there are plenty of bona fide bi-femmes online - why are you bothering me? Now if you want two aggressive, multi-orgasmic women to gang up on you, making it unlikely that you will survive the encounter intact - that is one thing. We can do that! But 'femme on femme' is out.

If it is an MFM - Ah yes! I'm am UP for that! Like my teddybear said when I asked for more: "Silly, Kitten! That's what gangbangs are for!"

I have saved my blogs now -ALL of them! Watch for my upcoming book! I hear blog-books are very popular in Japan. All designations, I need hardly say, have been deleted to protect the not-so-innocent. Thus far the book is HILARIOUS! Cat gets the first signed copy.

Nasty wet weather *shaking moisture from paws* has kept me inside doing housework. Ah me! My son, employed as a PM CHIMS, is going to be a 'booth bunny' at some trade thing Monday so he's getting himself all trimmed and fluffed. Tis very amusing. Now which tie will he wear with his black suit? Think he'll dab a bit of gasoline behind his ear so they DON'T think he's a geek? Ciao, babies!!!

10/08/2006

Being Exclusive? Is being sexually exclusive with another equal true love and devotion in your mind? Or does it indicate an unhealthy dependence upon the other for your own self-worth? Does sharing him/her with others mean you do or you don't care about that other person? What role does trust play in your relationships? All of us want to matter to another - that is a given. But beyond that, where do you go?

10/09/2006

"What do you say when a younger girl asks how old you are? Always stay in control of conversations, and learn how to bust on women in a way that cranks up the attraction. If a woman asks how old you are, instead of answering, just ask her how much she weighs. And if she shares how much she weighs, guess what? It's always just a pound or two above your limit for a woman's weight! Of course, you do this in a playful, teasing way."

Oh yeah, like THIS will work well! NOT! Guys, do not 'bust on women' - we are not like your guy buddies. We do not 'shake hands and go out for a beer afterwards'. Playful and teasing is permitted only AFTER we have bedded you; never before.

10/10/2006

Cougars: "Often, older women are newly divorced, and looking to sow their wild oats. Getting involved with a man who isn't looking for a serious relationship and wants to have fun is the perfect solution. Younger men have the stamina and carefree attitude to satisfy their need for a wild

113

ride. So, if you're looking to learn a thing or two between the sheets, look no further than an older woman. After all, she's no longer sexually inhibited, knows what she wants, and probably has a few tricks up her sleeve.

More often than not, an older woman has faced her insecurities and fears head on, and has dealt with them to the best of her abilities. She likely has enough life experience to know what matters and what doesn't. Consequently, she's above the petty nonsense that drives you crazy about women your own age. An older woman has figured out what makes her look fat, and what looks good on her, and knows enough about male-female relationships to not bother you with feminine trivialities that usually serve to turn men off anyway. Older women have the self-confidence that could only come from experience and the knowledge that they can handle whatever life throws their way. That is not to say that they never have a bad day, but merely that it's probably due to something more than the fact that they have a pimple and a party to go to that night.

In the end, it's up to you to weigh the pros and cons of such a relationship and decide if it is right for you right now. Let's see, the promise of mind-blowing sex with an experienced, confident woman, without the expectation of a long-term commitment... I know, it's a tough call."

Be advised, however, that she's not going to put up with any masculine BS from you. Remember who you're dealing with and who your competition is. You're playing in the 'majors' now, guy, so you had better be prepared to leave the little league kid stuff behind you.

We are currently developing a complete and overwhelming spa package for certain males. We require volunteers for product development testing. Males must be between the ages of 35 and 55; comely; able to provide the necessary facilities nearby us; DDF; smokers and drinkers preferred. Those meeting the requirements who wish to volunteer are asked to email me here using WW in the subject line.

A respite from care is at hand! Come on. All together now! DEEP SIGH of RELIEF. Aaaaaah! That's it; reeeelax. Are we all nice and happy now? Good. Pay the bills.

Teddybears, teddybears;
lovely, lovely teddybears..............
..............Ciao, babies!

10/12/2006

You didn't get a blog entry today because I was busy - having a sex party!!!!!!!!!!!!!!!!!!!!!!!!

For your amusement, here are a few 'bits and pieces' from my various adventures.

1. asking one man to bite my nipples only to be told 'but that would hurt' whereupon the other men I was with sadly shook their heads and obliged me instead

2. riding him then rolling over while still engaged and almost running out of bed on the side

3. rolling over in bed to face him and snuggle only misjudging the distance and punching him in the eye

4. franticly searching for his garments which he flung off in the mad rush to get with me - in my office - and we couldn't find his shirt!

Oooops! LOL
Ciao, babies!!

10/11/2006

No, you cannot have a blog today.
I am at a SEX PARTY!
WHEEEEEEEEEEEEEEEEEEEEEEEEEEEEEEEEEEEEEEE!
Ciao, babies!!!

10/12/2006

I belong to this group of veeerrryyy friendly people who get together each month for 'stress management seminars' and 'business focus groups'. Now it gets difficult from time to time because you do not have any pockets. So to carry the condoms and the small bottle of lubricant, I have developed 'gangbangers', tie-on ribbons which have a small pocket for a few condom packets and a small bottle of lube hidden behind a decorative set of dangly beaded strings. The ladies tie them on an arm, a thigh, or sling them around their waists. Very handy when moving from bed to sofa to bed to another bed and so on.

They look very jazzy and the men enjoy them.
I may put a pix up in my network photo album showing me in mine.

Serious inquiries only, please.

Next party: Wednesday November 15th at noon.
Put it on your schedules now!

Bed Errors:

1- Leaving your socks, shoes, or watch on.
2- Answering your cell phone.
3- Engaging in small talk.
4- Watching anything other than her.
5- Drooling on her or spitting.
6- Collapsing two seconds after your climax.
7- Mentioning the sexual skills of other women.
8- Turning sex into stand-up comedy.
9- Using infantile pet names for body parts.
10- Forgetting about your physiological differences.

Halloween is about kicking Death, who has been making grabs for our ankles, in the face and saying "Not yet!" We might dress it up in cuteness but this 'harvest festival' has nothing to do with grain. Halloween is about life, death, the flow of time and "Not going gently into that good night." Dance, my minion, dance; tonight we taunt our fears, for tomorrow we might weep.

Halloween is also about
giving the devil his due.
Hence the goth sexual
overtones about which I,
for one, know ALL about.
EG

And here you thought I was
just a 'pretty face'.

10/13/2006

Female Insecurities

allegedly:

QUOTE: 1- You might not call her after the date. 2- You
just want to sleep with her. 3- You're dating other women.
4- You're not that interested. 5- You're cheating on her. 6-
She's not satisfying you in bed. 7- You're not attracted to
her anymore. 8- Another woman is stealing your attention.
UNQUOTE

Not me of course and not every woman because more than
a few of these are, IMO, bogus, and in this context,
hilarious - however:

Let's look at this. Lack of communication is the real issue.
Neither of you is talking to the other. Talk or get over it. It

may surprise you to know that he shares many of the same anxieties. The common cure is communication.

Agree? Disagree? Or should the tarantula stop nibbling the angel food cake?

10/14/2006

If you are tired of jacking off while looking at my picture, and want to get with 'the real thing', meaning me I suppose, you are going to have to do better than to merely inform of that fact, if it is true. Stock emails do NOT work, guys. Do not just cut n paste into an email that 'who you are looking for' section of your profile. Just answer one simple question, dammit! WHY ME?

Oh good! More Males!

"IT PISSES ME OFF YOU HAVE NOT RESPONDED."
and this impacts me how? Some guys don't know when they are better off. You can imagine what my response is likely to be.

10/15/2006

An Email Sequence.

To: EvilEvilKitten1

just getting your attention . . .
utterly alpha very powerful, adept, creative guy spending time in dc experienced, talented at giving pleasure not 6 feet, but intimidating, furry, witty, smarter than you are seeking one special big soft lascivious bewitcher who wants more climaxes herself for extended discreet play, downtown dc will be in town this thursday evening

(name deleted) actually i don't think you're real

> > ------ Profile Attached -------

Lawyer, environmentalist, intelligent, interesting, fit, just moved, live in New York and Aspen, spend time in Washington DC, looking for a very unusual, smart, classy attached or married woman for dinner, scintillating conversation and personal engagement. Love to give oral sex for hours to multi-orgasmic bi-woman or women. Must be complex, love foreplay, take fabulous care of your body and skin, and offer the unexpected.

My Reply:
"smarter than you are"
"actually i don't think you're real"
You are mistaken.

\---

His Return reply:

well, show me
call me
meet me
fuck me
(is that humorous enough?)

\---

My Final Word:
No.

What did I tell you guys about 'busting' on women?

10/16/2006

OK now that the Mash is out of the way - we can get down to some Serious Sexual Play! "Foxy, Foxy what's it gonna be?" Non-bi full swap so if she wants some, she knows what's it gonna be! Leather anyone? OH and watch out for the spikes - they're sharp.

10/17/2006

Yes, yes - you all don't remember my costume - since you haven't seen it, that is not surprising. You'll LOVE it, I promise you! although one person did ask "Where's your costume?" She did have a point. Bikers were all saying "You can ride on the back of my bike anytime, sweety." Oh yeah! I'd rather ride them but that's how it goes. Men line up and volunteer when you're busy and are absent when you aren't.

Please be advised that our little shindigs are 'if he's there and breathing - enjoy him - somehow'. Everyone gets laid! No one goes home 'hungry'. All non-bi because fair is fair and if she is then so are you guys! Heh, heh, heh. No really, I do not permit anyone to be pressured into doing anything they'd find unappealing and I RESENT, putting it mildly, being pressured myself. Don't ask what happened to the last man who spanked me during coitus! grrrrr But I am serious about everyone getting laid.

I don't know, I can dance to Black No.1 and Love You to Death. I lap dance to Clubbed to Death although it is 7 minutes long - he didn't seem to mind. No, no - you mustn't actually touch him - but breathing gently on his neck is allowed. EG Then you scamper off and do the housework! Hahahahahaha! Oh - good to go, peeps! Ciao, babies!!

10/18/2006

Yegods!!
Quote:
"6 Reasons Why Women Sleep Around

1- No time for a relationship
Anyone who's ever been in a long-term relationship knows that keeping it in working order often takes a high level of dedication and willingness on the part of both parties involved. Going out of your way to work through a difficult period in the relationship demands much more time and effort than just calling it quits. This kind of devotion doesn't seem to be something that your average Gen-X woman has the time or patience for. She's probably too busy trying to get her career in high-gear and spending time with her friends to dedicate too much time and energy to a boyfriend. For such women, the investment in time and sheer effort required for a serious relationship just isn't worth their while. They prefer keeping things casual and strictly for kicks, rather than having to deal with the potential inconvenience of a boyfriend. One-night stands are the perfect solution for these women because they get all the good stuff and none of the bad. They get to go on the dates, enjoy the dinners and weekend getaways, and the rush of having sex with a new partner, without having to contend with compromising themselves for another person or what they deem to be annoying male habits.

2- Fear of commitment
Other women choose sleeping around over being in a relationship because they're scared of opening themselves up to a man, and making themselves vulnerable in the process. Maybe they've been hurt in the past and believe that sleeping around is a good way to avoid developing any real feelings for another person, which would create the possibility of them getting hurt again.

3- A fun activity
Some women just love sex. In fact, they love the act more than the guy they happen to be having sex with. For these women, sex is the ultimate pastime and they are going to get it as often as possible. They're hot to trot and want instant gratification. Whenever the opportunity presents itself, they are going to take full advantage of it. Their motto is simply "why not?"

4- For revenge
Like I said before, lots of women believe that men have been playing this game much longer than they have. Consequently, many women have been treated as little more than playthings by some men out there. While some women can learn from such experiences and avoid letting them happen again, other women will seek revenge. But not on the guy in question; every man must pay for the heartache that was inflicted on them by a single one. Instead of understanding that they had one or two bad experiences, they proclaim themselves victims and lump all men together. By sleeping around, they're hoping to hurt other men like they were hurt. But what they don't seem to realize is that in the long run, they're only hurting themselves. But plenty of guys are really happy that there are women who think this way, no doubt.

5- To forget their ex
Some women use casual sex as a way to forget their exes. They sleep with a variety of men in order to get over the hurdle of ending a relationship. They avoid loneliness like the plague and will do anything to fill the void that the breakup has left them with. By not focusing their attention on one person, they're sure not to let any emotions interfere with their desire to drown their sorrow in numerous one-night stands. When they're ready for another boyfriend, they'll usually stop sleeping around.

6- Don't know how to say "no"
It's a fact that many women have a hard time saying "no." They try to be there for their friends and families, their bosses and co-workers, and the list goes on. Sometimes, this willingness to please extends to their personal lives as well, and they find themselves unable to turn down a man's advances. They actually feel guilty turning a man down for sex. They may even go as far as to think that because a guy took them out for dinner and was nice to them, they're obliged to sleep with him. Maybe if they paid their own way, they could avoid such guilt-induced one-night stands. " Unquote.

This article was written by a woman of the 'hearts and flowers' variety wherein you have to have some deep emotional attachment to a man before you bed him. So her not terribly subtle slamming of sexually active women is to be expected. I am esp fond of her attacking the 'revenge' woman by saying she's only hurting herself by her 'sleeping around' - not for her bitterness (the real issue) but for her sleeping around - only hurting herself. Hah! But it is her conclusion that hides the 'kicker'.

"*Although there are many other reasons for why women sleep around, these are some of the most common. Gone are the days of men ruling the playing field. It seems that women are just as capable and willing to be players as men are. So does that make you happy, or does it turn you off?* "

Love those appeals for masculine approval! So what's the message here? It is still okay for guys to play the field, for whatever reason, but not for women?

Love it! The Prepatory Prior Party is an excellent idea! So is the Post Party Party! Anytime sweeties! LOL The Pill is the greatest! Periods of two tablespoons for 1 hour and you're done! Yeeehaw! Who is next? (insert wicked grin here.) Yes, I know - quietly so I don't scare the skittish. Shhhhhh. Shhhhhh.

The reason why we have so many parties this time of year is because we are all trying to stay warm!

Congrats to Cat for passing his cert test. Loaded him up on champers, gave him a cigar, and then I pounced upon him! Poor guy! So 'over-worked'. Sweety! Time to 'clock-in'! purrrrrrrrrrrr Ciao, babies!

10/19/2006

Another email:
"Now, I am too old and to far away from you per your profile and, aside from education, you do not meet mine. But, I am curious: what have you against Alpha males?"

His profile, in the 'What I'm Looking For' portion states:

"My Ideal Person:
Intelligence, confidence, education, and femininity"

This means that he does not regard me as being intelligent, confident, or feminine. Furthermore: he is incorrect on which of my criteria he fails to meet. Yes, he is too far away but his age is not a barrier. He is too short, being only 5' 10" in height.

I have two reasons for exposing him in this way: 1. so he can reap the benefits of said exposure which I am hoping you will help provide; and 2. to show the men who have lately been complaining about the discourtesy of not receiving a reply to their emails might learn WHY they DON'T get a reply.

INSULTS GET YOU NOTHING.
Do you understand?

PLUS: the next issue-
"What do you have against alpha males?"

In any true D/s relationship, it is the submissive who has the power. At a word, the submissive stops the play. Responsible Doms and Dommes know this. Part of the enjoyment of such relationships is the shifting of power between the parties involved. I remind you that I am a soft domme, meaning that I do NOT inflict pain, humiliation, or abuse upon my men. Restraints have their role to play but you need have no fear when you are with me. I will take very good care of you. I promise you, you will have the time of your life. So to ask what I have against alpha males is to expose your ignorance of bdsm and of me.
Furthermore:
Where did he ever get the idea that 'femininity' equaled (in all cases) meekness, timidity, and being weak, frail, or reluctant to have sex? Yegods man! Just as there are various kinds of men so too are there various kinds of women. Just because the woman is 'dangerous' does not mean she is any less feminine than other women. Do you, my lovely readers, get the impression that he just didn't think this through or is it just me?

Another day, another dollar - or three. Slept too long but that is what will happen when you play hearts until 4:30am. SUCH a NAUGHTY kitten and teddybear! Tsk, tsk, tsk. Groceries and dry cleaning today - maybe. Just not terribly motivated to do more than - ahem. Keep it clean, kitten! Ok, ok.

We are on the F portion of the alphabet today.

Sorry to cut this short but it seems I am 'needed' in the shower. Ciao, babies!

10/20/2006

Meeting at 4pm
Party tonight
busy Tuesday early evening
Horse Show Thursday evening
Halloween party Friday night

Busy, busy, busy!
Catch me if you can!

She's 'dating' you and she's 'dating' others and you get upset and say she's cheating, has no integrity, blah blah blah! Okay so you have a boyfriend. And your point is what? You are here aren't you? So what mixed message AREN'T you sending?
Look people there's very little wrong with playing the field or 'sport dating'. If she/he wants to play, let 'em. Your 'rights' are only those she/he chooses to grant you.

Then there are those women who already have a boyfriend and are just looking for women. Okay so I guess you feel that doing women doesn't count somehow? After all we wouldn't want to upset the fellow by introducing another man now would we?

This is not very far-fetched. Reference 3-somes and you get ooodles of FMF info and extremely little info on MFM. Tsk, tsk, tsk. Allegedly it is easier to find men for MFMs than women for FMFs - that's their reason. That elusive bi-femme thing you know; as if you can't have a straight FMF.

No, I don't mind when people, and this includes DSGs, add us to their friends/wishlist. It means someone finds us attractive. Yes, that was a mild poke in the ribs to all of you 'skittish' persons. Honestly, I only want to borrow him. I'll even trade you mine - temporarily. Tis the point, no?

Oooo Halloween's coming! So how many of you have already been nibbling the candy? Hmmmmmmmmm?

The Maids are here blasting through the house and I'm cowering in my office trying to get work done. BTW didn't do any of the errands yesterday so I'll have to do them today and fold the laundry. Then there's a meeting with a lovely couple and then a party from which I might get sent home early - seems something may be up tonight! We Hope So!!! Ciao, babies!!!

10/21/2006

Are you experimenting with sex or is sex experimenting with you?
Answers on a postcard, please to the following address:
Ciao, babies!!

10/22/2006

"7 Things Women Find Boring in Bed
1- Asking for permission
2- Predictability
3- Mechanical sex
4- Not going the extra mile
5- Same location

128

6- Too vocal or not vocal enough
7- Never experimenting"
In certain cases, he had better ask permission! *EG*
Ciao, babies!!!

10/23/2006

Veils:
They have been in the news lately so naturally I just had to comment on them.
Yes I know the history but history by definition was then and this is now.
Burkhas make great disguises and if the gloves are also worn - prevent the leaving of fingerprints which is most useful. So I suggest we equip all pissed off Muslim women with loaded Uzi's and let them deal with their men directly. After all - they are masked. And since they are all in black - who's to say who is whom? Wear a veil and become in effect 'an object' not a person.

For some the veil = treat me with respect (except they don't) while for others that veil = "please don't leave a bomb in my cab, thank you". If they treated you with respect, you wouldn't need a man's permission to do almost everything - which you do.

Therefore the veil and the wearing thereof is a sign of servitude and a rather pernicious form of slavery. Wearing a sack over your head with, maybe, eyeholes cut into it - some have a kind of screen, you know, is NOT empowering.

If you don't wear one - they shoot you.
Yeah, that's VERY empowering. PFFT!
So wear it if you want but DON'T expect me to respect you just for that.

I am putting down the hammer now. If it has tires, testicles or TERABYTES, dammit, you're going to have trouble with it! Currently having troubles with all three items on that list!
PESKY EXASPERATING CREATURES AND/OR THINGS!
Anyone else having a difficult day?

Predictability is good is when he's predictably GREAT in BED!! Like just tonight, for instance!
WHEEEEEEEEEEEEEEEE!
Ciao, babies!!

10/24/2006

How to Juggle Multiple Men.
Begin as you mean to go on so decide up front what role you intend for him to play in your life: husband, FWB, friend w/o B, fuckbuddy, primary, secondary, tertiary, or whatever. Work that relationship out with him - nicely; you cannot beat him into it remember. (Yes I know how tough that can be.)
Relationships do change over time so be prepared to accept change as the relationship develops.
Maintain your private space. No moving in; unless he swings too in which case you two can work it out on your own. Three bedrooms? 1 for you two only then his playroom and her playroom? Bowls of condoms tastefully displayed on the mantelpiece? (Move the left one in a bit more, hun.)
Keep it light!"Relationships, even the freedom-oriented ones, are based on give-and-take and a solid sense of equality. So if you're planning to date several men at once,

don't get all bent out of shape when he dates several women; by playing the field, you're giving him the license to do the same. In fact, it may be in your best interest to actually encourage such behavior... provided it's subtle. You're equals in everything, and if you're going to play around, so can he. It's simply a matter of keeping everything pointed in the right direction."
Fair is fair!

This is offensive:
"The time for the "Menaissance" has come. Although we have granted women their fair share of independence and "empowerment," they still lack the common sense and emotional maturity to handle these newfound freedoms; it's like giving a 10-year-old kid a credit card. So it's up to men to take charge and lead the way. It's up to us to take back our independence from the female gender. And once we do get it back, we can steer the way to a true equality between the sexes."
Women = children? Where do guys get this stuff? Where's my Uzi? Amazing what you find on the web!

Now that my hard drive has been beaten into submission and will actually WORK, you may have a blog entry. Ciao, babies!!

10/25/2006

Perhaps a bigger hammer would do a better job? Now I have no sound - digital output is taken by another device. What other device? Sometimes I hate this damn box!

The Art of Appreciation:
Each woman is uniquely beautiful and worthy of being cherished. This thought is what separates the connoisseurs of women and the mere laymen. Every woman has that

certain something that distinguishes her from everyone else. Picking out the details and acknowledging them, **telling her**, is what will set you apart in her mind.

Think about it: What did your girl wear last night? What did she say? Did you notice the tilt of her head, the mischief she held in her eyes or the way she bit her lip? Any time you feel that visceral tug, the urge to muss and take, **tell her** why and how you feel as you do. Recognize those triggers and let her know what she does to you.

Maybe you noticed how the sun lights up her hair, or the motion of her hand tucking a curl behind her ear. You could have been stirred by the sound of her laugh or maybe you stared transfixed at the lines of her body. She may have taken extra care getting ready for you, and her clothes, hair, and makeup are looking extra sharp. It could be the luscious curves in those hip-hugger jeans, or the soft sweater that clings to her curves -- whatever it is that you're noticing, **tell her** about it.
And ladies, do the same for your men?

Uh-huh - bi women? No. "have you ever tried it?" - Look, I've been at this for 38 years - it would be more to the point to inquire what I HAVEN'T tried. You all might be surprised, but I have no fantasies left. Yeah, I'm still hung up over teddybears - meow! Gotta love 'em! Teddybears are the GREATEST!!!! All of you ladies should get yourselves one! Or perhaps two?

Alcohol has a tendency to limit blood flow. This can work both ways 1. to prevent getting erections and 2. to make erections longer lasting. I also believe that a 'stunned' male only feels about half of what you do to him which also makes his erections last longer - and your 'job' harder? A few drinks = okay but 6 drinks = no, no. Keeping my eyes on the prize! LOL Wanna cum, baby?

We have a date tonight! We have a date tonight! Another Teddybear Fancier and her teddybear- this is going to be a blast! Please excuse the dancing about with glee but it has been so long since a 'new' couple has given me a chance. They like Cat, of course, but me they all shy away from. DEEP SIGH anyway; Ciao, babies!

10/26/2006

Google? yeah well how it goes - but I do periodically check just to see what's out there. I'm not 'skeered' about it. More than one person in this world bears my name.

btw TEDDYBEARS ARE THE GREATEST LOVERS!!!!!! WOW THAT WAS FUN LAST NIGHT!!!

ED and guys getting slammed for using a bit of help. Some women regard it as a slam against themselves - as in they aren't stimulating enough! PFFFT. Personally, although I have been told that I am extremely stimulating, I do not care! You do what you do and I'll do what I do and perhaps we two will meet in the bed! *W* May I have an 'amen'?

Now to assemble my Halloween costume for the M&G party! I had better win too - I have spikes and I know how to use 'em! heh heh heh We will be SERIOUSLY out for a good time!

Heard on my way home last night walking back to the truck from the grocery store - had to buy fish food –
"You have some beautiful legs, babygirl!"
See what happens when you wear a short skirt and stilettos?
Ciao, babies!!

10/27/2006

"There are actually two types of multiple orgasms: sequential multiples and serial multiples. It can be difficult to tell the difference between the two -- even for the woman. Distinguishing one type from the other is a matter of timing: Sequential multiple orgasms occur several minutes after one another, with an interruption in the arousal period in between, whereas serial multiples are separated only by seconds, producing one extended wave of pleasure. The latter is the truly rare form of the two."

"The Grafenberg spot is an area on the front wall (toward the tummy) of the vagina, between the opening and the cervix, generally 2 to 3 inches inward from the opening. Theory dictates that the G-spot can be one of two things: either a bundle of nerves coming from the clitoris, or a gland (or series of glands) that produces lubrication, or both. Now, while all women own a spot with a G, not all of them find G-spot stimulation pleasurable. Just as with the clitoris, some women are more than eager, while others do not like it whatsoever. It is very sensitive. Only time will tell. Insert a finger (or two) into the vagina with your palm facing her mons pubis Gently, bend your fingers frontward so that they lightly stroke the front wall of the vagina. Varying the degree of pressure also helps."
Combine this with cunnilingus and even I will turn pink with pleasure! Try it!

Fondling? Groping? Sorry if you men didn't like it. You should have TOLD ME! How am I supposed to know? I'm not a mindreader! I just go by what Cat does or doesn't like and try it out on you. NEXT time - tell me!

134

getting ready for The Halloween Party tonight! "Nip! New and Improved! Now with More Spikes!" Bwahahahaha!!

If you go to the party today, you're in for a big surprise. it's lovely out at the party today but you won't believe your eyes! For every bear that ever there was will gather there for certain because, today's the day the teddybears get caught by Nip! EG Ciao, babies!

10/28/2006

1. The sex improves upon further acquaintance as he learns you and you learn him and both of you RELAX around each other.
2. Begin by tying one wrist, and when comfortable with that, then tie up the opposite ankle. Slowly go on as comfort and trust develops. If you rush it - you've lost it.

3. Investigate his body, try new things - but always slowly - lightly run your claws in agonizingly slow arabesques over his skin and do the same with your lips, stirring his fur with your breath.

Sex is a nuanced affair to be savored – repeatedly!

The Halloween Party Report - GREAT FUN! Nip got out to play a bit with the teddybears - some of whom enjoyed her evil seductive ways. Even got to dance a bit! Some pix were taken so you will get to see. Cat says he was never groped so much in his life - he LOVED it!

seems some of you have an expectation - just remember the ZZTop song "I Wanna Thank You." - you're what's for dinner!

to answer some questions raised - if you want him, take him. Nothing lights me up like a naked man tied down onto my bed - but it isn't mandatory. The sex improves the more you do it with that person. We deliver what we promise. Now the housework is calling so I must go. Ciao, babies.

10/29/2006

Non-communicative males are horrible! If you cannot talk about it, get the hell over it. After all of this time, one would think he'd damn well know better. If he thinks he's getting out of this alive - he had better think again. I am NOT the most patient of women.

It has been very painful watching you guys self-inflict both online and IRL, so I have written a book just for you. No it is not *"Notes of a Dominatrix"* - that comes later. **Anyone volunteering to edit this one for me?**

10/30/2006

I am ill so it is back to bed for me.
Cancel all of my appointments for this week.
Sorry, darlings.
Ciao, babies.

10/31/2006

Cold not any better. Going back to bed. Ciao, babies.

HAPPY HALLOWEEN

NOVEMBER

2006

11/01/2006
Relapsed:
Returning to my bed now.
Alas, no ministering teddybears!

FACT: The chances of you dying from 'second hand smoke' are equal to the chances of you dying from being hit on the head by a potted geranium plant falling from a third story balcony while you pass beneath it.
FACT: Every smoker pays for their own healthcare AND for two non-smoker's healthcare. You're welcome.
FACT: No one forces anyone to work anywhere. If smoking in bars bothers you, work somewhere else.
People - outside of your property lines, you have no more control and no more rights than anyone else. If you do not like smoking - go where they aren't. No one is twisting your arm to stay.
Healthy workplace? Yeah, bars are notorious for being HEALTHY places. Right. What planet are you from again?

This week's bad emails include:

"Leave me a number"

"I don't know exactly what you're looking for but maybe I help you get it. Maybe you can help me get what I want too ?"

"What's up?"

but the prize goes to:

"HELLO, MY NAME IS S AND MY HUSBAN R, WE ARE COUPLE IAM 45 AND MY HUSBAN 35 YEAR.

WE LIKE TO NOW COUPLES SEXY, HOT WE CAN JOIN TOGETHER,IF YOU WANT INTERESTY CALL O WRITE US. S AND R. "

uh - yeah. I'll get right on that. (the spelling is their's)

Got me out of bed to tell me
thinking of bugging out
Lost my temper - badly.
But said nothing.
Just stood there vibrating with rage.
Situation remains volatile.

Updated my geo site with same as YIM indentifier
love the lengths we have to go through!
y'all know all that by now.
I think my html encoding is coming along nicely!
and I learned it all from books and on-the-job training, so to speak.
also haven't been out of the house for days -
help I'm going nutz!
Ciao, babies!

11/02/2006

Re: Halloween Leftovers

STEP   AWAY

FROM   THE

CHOCOLATE AND NO ONE WILL GET HURT

Something Different:
to wit:
tall, elegant, teddybear fancier with her teddybear seeks same for frolicking exchanges in the early evenings during the week, inquire at Vicarage & Vine, 2nd floor
answers on a postcard, please!
(write you own 'seeking pleasure' ad - must end with: inquire at Vicarage & Vine, 2nd floor.)

The R3, the VEC, the IRS (sssshhhh, they'll hear you), this item and that item, and "whatthehellisthis"?? Hey, I am up to my elbows here!
"To shred or not to shred, that is the question. Whether it is nobler to endure the slings and arrows of the outrageous demands upon my purse from creditors who have assured me they have waited long enough, or to consign said demands for payment into the whirling teeth of the cross-cut shredder? Aye, that's the rub!"
Sorry, but you know how it gets around here when it is time to make a dent in the paperwork - I get giddy - Don't you??

Okay, that's enough. Time to get this illness over with! I have issues to deal with and cannot spend any more time on this cold. Besides which, Cat wants to kiss me.

Oh, Frank!

This week begins The CatNip Winter Schedule wherein Nip is only seen every OTHER Friday, parties excepted. So if you are holding a party and require a VERY fun-loving couple - give us some warning and we'll work it in somehow - not to worry, we have the Polyamorist Scheduling Program loaded onto the mainframe. A bit of differential calculus here. A touch of Probability Theory there. See? Click. Whirrr. Buzzz. Ding! Told you we could fit it in!! Ciao, babies!!!

11/03/2006

Happy Birthday, V. tee heee
Good Luck to my favorite teddybear!
Have fun, today, R-baby! - hugs

So here I am all snug and cozy and filled to the gunnels with cold meds. I must be sick - I am wearing thick wooly socks - men's size 16 and heavy bathrobe over my garments. Stay warm. Stay warm. Stay warm. Drinking even more than usual - yes, even the dreaded cranberry juice!

Not cleaning to day because the maids are coming - they'll make the place clean, shiny, and good looking.
The shop hasn't called about my truck yet. Thanks to FnL for taking it in for me! .
I do have an alternative vehicle available should The Call come. But I'm not grocery-getting until tomorrow so I most likely will not go out today.
Almost done with my paperwork. Then I can begin studying for my next three exams. *crossed fingers*

If you enjoy my blog, you'll LOVE my books - go and buy them, please - make great gifts for 'progressive' persons. *W*

insert coughing fit here

what else... hmmm

have to call some people:
dentist
hairdresser
the other panel participants
Marie
lawyer
the shop if they don't get back to me soon

And that is about it for today!
What do you have to do today?

I am blue because women don't do it for me. Cat's blue because men don't do it for him. We don't care what you do with others. We figure that's your business not ours. Neither curious nor UNcomfortable thank you. As to the age thing; we don't mind youngsters but it is personality-dependent..

Still unwell but improving mightily!

Wish Cat good fortune today! And help him celebrate tonight! I have to stay in but not to worry - there's next week coming! Ciao, babies!!!

143

11/04/2006

My Expedition, called Ganesh, will cost $1,390.00.
Thusly:
Fixing misfiring cylinder #4 and attendant cleaning and re-
programming of computer = $640
Fixing exhaust leak = $110
Replacing worn out front lower ball joints = $625
VA State Inspection = $15
And he says it will be done by this afternoon.
PRICELESS!
HURRAY!

Another book is in the works! This one's for wise infants,
small rogues, and progressive children aged 5 to 13 years.
It continues where Nursery Tales leaves off.

CONGRATULATIONS, DARLING!!!!
LET THERE BE DANCING IN THE STREETS!

зло зло котенок

Lordy, lordy, would ya look at that. Amazingly enough all
of my teddybears are ENFPs. Tis a charming, small conceit
to think it matters and that humans are so easily
categorized. Very cute. But I don't believe a word of it.

She dreamed of a time when she would waken, after a night
of passion, and spend some time with her horses, then an
hour or so looking over the schedule and managing her
affairs, then some time in her garden before lounging naked
by the pool enjoying the day and feeling the heat caress her
skin and warm her aging bones during lunch. Dalliance in
interludes partaken throughout the remainder of the day, as

she wandered doing everything delightful. To have such a life without let or hindrance! Each day presenting its possibilities and each night its delights!

11/05/2006

"I recently read that in Asian countries, that it is common for the woman to be 1/2 +1 or -1 year of their mates age. That means a man of age 40 will likely have a mate of age 19-21 years old. Supposedly, the marriages are healthier and last whereas closer in age marriages tend to fail.
Anyone familiar with this, or have a point of viw to share?"

1. good for the older man since he gets more kids he now has to support
2. good for the older man since he can hold the household rule (no competition)
3. good for the younger woman since she's being taken care of (does not have to fend for herself)

Of course the male could be a serial husband - that is he trades in his youngster every three years for a 'fresher' model, thus making sure he out-propagates all the other males.

Good deal, huh? Betcha Father's Day is a blast. Nice for the guy to be confronted by all his kids at once asking - "so you ditched Mom because why?" I get a kick thinking of such a 'serialist' frantically traveling from city to city trying to make all of those school plays, birthdays, parent-teacher conferences, Little League games, etc., etc., etc.; while trying to make enough money to support them all. You know how well men 'multi-task'. He could use all of his frequent flyer miles to send all of those kids to college too.

So wish him well! He's going to need all the good wishes he can get.

For the fellow who just wants a wife and kids, well, that's different. There remains that biological window of opportunity for women to have kids (in her 20's) so there's nothing else for it. I wish them both well.

As to marriages failing between couples closer in age: as Freud once said "If we could exterminate the male ego, we could drop the divorce rate by 90%" Gentlemen you need that ego for your male to male and business/competitive interactions. Don't bring it home with you. We are all friends and lovers at home. At least, that is the plan.

"It's been many years since I've even had a woman my own age. The younger woman brings out the best in me, I try harder to keep pace with her stamina & libido, give her an evening that will hopefully lead to her wanting more, and understand that older can be better, that experience counts for more than being an eager young pup who's ready again in 3 minutes without the Cialis! That being said, I have plenty of lady friends my age or a little older, just not as my lovemaking partners. It's really sweet when your partner is 20 years younger than you & what you DO know has her panting trying to hang on for your climax to be told to not hold back, to let it go, then have her come her second time as you come with her. That gets looks of adoration afterwards the young pups don't tend to see as I recall from my young pup days. PJ"

gentle ironic laughter

For those wishing to comment on our respect, or lack thereof, for other cultures - how can I respect a culture that

146

relies upon female denigration, subjugation, and commodization? I can't.

For those males who think, as does PJ above, that women in their 40's can't keep up - you may kiss, TWICE!, that portion of my anatomy shown in the accompanying photograph. OKAY. Your turn! Tell me what you think! Go for it!!

My muse is not some kindly creature whispering in my ear..oh no... my muse is a demon gouging my back with its claws, howling write, write, write!!! I cannot do otherwise: not sleep, nor eat, nor live until the demon is silenced.

I can't quite remember the screen name of she who has my Halloween pix but I really do wish she'd send them to me. Pretty please?? Ciao, babies!!

11/06/2006

Seems men are confused about this and have been for a while now. Well, fellas, I don't know that women in general want anything in particular. All I can tell you is what I want. Women are individuals; each one with her own mix of the good, the bad, and the indifferent. What you want is the woman, or women, whose mix blends with your own mix with just enough difference to keep it interesting. Are we having fun yet? When meeting her - focus upon her - this woman, right here, right now. The past doesn't matter and the future can take care of itself. Who is she, really? Find out; but softly, softly so as not to skeer her off. Maintain the social mask for a bit longer.
Tis a dance!
Enjoy it!

I was thinking last night about how some words, and how they are defined, reflect more upon the one who uses them than they do of the person about whom they are used.

For example: Cougar

def 1= "A woman typically over the age of 40 who seeks the company of a young buck...under the age of 25. She usually looks like a bleach blonde hag with all the trimmings of a dried up bird (fake claws, tough skin etc.)"

def 2= "An attractive woman in her 30's or 40's who is on the hunt once again. She may be found in the usual hunting grounds: nightclubs, bars, beaches, etc. She will not play the usual B.S. games that women in their early twenties participate in. End state, she will be going for the kill, just like you."

The same woman seen through whose eyes?

and then there's the word Slut.

def 1= "a woman with the morals of a man."

def 2= "a girl thats fucked so many guys she cant close her legs anymore."

Once again - same woman seen through two sets of eyes.

"Jealousy is a very powerful emotion. Although unchecked jealousy can easily get out of hand, a touch here or there can really fan the flames of attraction. If she thought you really didn't care about the bartender who hit on her or her coworker who has a crush on her, she'd think you didn't care about her at all, and she'd likely find somebody else who did. When you ask the intentions of her close-working coworker or probe into her relationship with her personal trainer, she may chide you for your overactive imagination, but it's certain that she's smiling on the inside. Remember: When it comes to jealousy, a little will go a long, long way, so use it very sparingly. Be aware of its power and allure: She can get really hot over a man who's protective of her assets."

148

To be jealous is to fear losing them to another - which pretty much brands you as being insecure and you might as well write LOSER on your forehead and be done with it.

1st point = To want someone to be jealous - thinking it means they care about you - write LOSER on your forehead as well since YOU are also insecure. That ranks right up there with 'he beats me so I know he loves me.'

2nd point = The only assets of any concern are procreative assets. You want to know whose genes mixed with whose. Other than that - no big deal. So long as rules, needs, and feelings aren't being neglected, there should be no problems. Sorry but this topic STILL comes up!

How to Get Rid of Her:
"1. Being critical.

It is said that a little constructive criticism can be positive. This is the case, of course, for everybody except your girlfriend. Although suggestions are generally considered acceptable, particularly if she asks for them, putdowns and unwarranted negative input are expected from her mother, not her lover. If you correct her, tell her how to dress or generally act as though you know best, she will feel nitpicked and self-conscious. Every smart woman knows that she shouldn't spend her time with a man who doesn't make her feel good about herself. When in a relationship, be kind and generous, pick your battles, and only give her advice if she asks for it. Also, temper your criticisms with compliments.

2. Making it obvious that your career comes before her.

Your job is important to you, and as such, it's important to your girlfriend. She's likely very proud of your successes and wants you to do well. On the other hand, if you start staying late at work every day, if you frequently cancel dates for last-minute business obligations or if you constantly hang out with your coworkers after work hours, she will get ideas about your priorities. Although a woman appreciates a focused and ambitious man, she also expects you to make time for her. Think of it this way: What fun is having a great career and lots of money if you have nobody to share them with?

3. Cheating.
Physical cheating is never acceptable unless you and your girl have an agreement about such behavior. But cheating isn't limited only to sexual misconduct -- there is a second type of cheating that can be nearly as hurtful. In this sense, read the word "cheating" as emotional cheating -- committing to somebody else in a girlfriend-y way. This means having a female friend that you relate to better than your girlfriend, that you spend more quality time with or that you enjoy more. This type of cheating applies to very serious relationships in which your girl would expect full disclosure and sharing. If you're relating that well to somebody else, chances are you're short-changing your girlfriend. This doesn't mean you can't have other friends or even other really close friends -- it just means that your girlfriend wants to feel like you trust her and confide in her. She doesn't want to be second-best. And if she is, she'll notice.

4. Becoming unkempt.
Style is by no means infinitely important, but if you go from GQ to P.U. as soon as you're comfortable with her, she'll be sure to keep her distance. This tells her two things: 1. You were just putting on a facade to attract her, and 2. She's not important enough for you to maintain that facade. If she was attracted to you when you were wearing well-cut suits, chances are that's what she likes, and she may stop being attracted to you if all you wear are sweats and jerseys. If you're into sweats and jerseys, that's how you should go out onto the market.

5. Being snappy.

Now that you and your girl are getting closer, she's around more. And now that she's around more, her habits are becoming less novel and charming. You find yourself lashing out at her every so often and talking to her like she's your little sister. You act as though you're annoyed by her every move. You're not, of course, but you just feel comfortable enough to inform her of your preferences -- bluntly. Unfortunately for you, she probably won't accept this behavior for a very long period. Instead of being short with her, try to realize when you're getting annoyed. Then, decide rationally whether this particular annoyance is worth fighting over or not. If it's not, do your best to leave it alone. If it is, then try to let your girl know calmly. Chances are she'll be glad to know what bothers you, and she may even have a few suggestions for your habits.

6. Being controlling

This one is age-old. Many people in relationships suffer from fanatic controlitis. You get jealous of her guy friends. You tell her not to spend so much time gossiping with her girl friends. You tell her she spent too much money at the shoe store. More than anything, you tell her where and when she should go out. Although women have a reputation for being clingy, they also enjoy their independence. Chances are your girlfriend lived her life pretty successfully before you entered the picture. It is equally likely that she can still manage her own time and money without your help. There are situations in which she may want your input or advice, but otherwise, don't be pushy with advice or demands. Instead of demanding time, ask for it. Unless you want her to duck out when she sees you coming into a room, you have to give her space and let her make her own decisions.

7. Judging her friends and family.
If you find her friends, her sister and her mother annoying, you're going to have an awfully hard time. They're going to be around quite often, and she'll talk about them even more. It's important to try to see what she sees in them. If her posse is a bit shallow, try to find some substance, and if her mother is overbearing, try to realize she just wants to help. You have to understand that these people are her foundation and that she'll be very defensive about them. If you try to see the good things in them, you might actually start to like them. Also, avoid direct confrontation with all her favorite people, even if they egg you on. Do your best to get along with those closest to her because fights with them will translate into fights with your girl. If you can, become their favorite guy; it'll pay dividends in the end.

8. Becoming disinterested.
Men often believe that the way to attract women is to be aloof. Even if that works in the beginning, it is certainly not the case once you become serious in a relationship. Your woman remembers what it's like to be wooed. She's also keenly aware of the fact that if you don't pay attention to her, a lot of other men will. If you stop complimenting her, stop taking her out or asking about her life, she will feel neglected. Recognize that she doesn't have to be around you; you have to make it worth her while. If you want to keep her around, you need to make her feel like she's special. Look her in the eye. Call her in the middle of the day from time to time. When you think she looks pretty, tell her.

9. Not making time for her.
You promised Joe you'd watch the game with him.You haven't been to the gym enough lately. You have to run errands. Although you may want to do all of the things you did when you were a bachelor, you also have to make time

for your girl. It's tough, but sometimes you and your girl will both have to give up time with pals in order to spend time together.

It's all about the small things
If you want to keep a woman around, you should make her feel important, special and competent. Any of the behaviors listed above will indicate that you're taking her for granted -- and if there's anything a woman hates, it's being taken for granted. So make those small gestures; after all, if she's worth keeping, it shouldn't even feel like an effort to you."

Actually guys, it is even easier than that - all you have to do is to contradict everything she says!

Jealousy is a loser's game. Nevertheless I do not ascribe every negative feeling exhibited by others to jealousy.
Some people are just ill-tempered and ill-conditioned louts.

Dealing with Relationship Issues:
Not altogether that difficult, but you do have to be adult about it. No screaming, yelling, fighting, loud voices, slamming doors, etc. None of that. Neither tantrums nor 'the silent treatment' shall be accepted.
1. What precisely is the issue? You have to be specific and clear. No 'you know' allowed. If you cannot articulate it, then it isn't an issue. Get over it. Your partner has every right to ignore it if you cannot specify it.
2. Can you discuss it like a rational yet loving human being? If not, then let it wait a bit until you are cooler but not more than 36 hrs. Always make an attempt to color your statements as if you "may have been mistaken?" Perhaps you didn't mean this when you said that but that is what I heard. If you throw a tantrum or refuse to speak about it, then once again, it is not an issue – get over it.

153

3. Do not hear or respond to juvenile or irrational behavior. Just look at him/her and wait. Do not turn away – for that would be dismissal which would not go over well. But stick to your guns! Changing your mind, or forgiving, or asking to be forgiven, will only encourage further displays of bad behavior. Blackmail will not be tolerated. Withholding sex is a form of blackmail btw.

4. Need I say it? Violence will not ever be acceptable behavior. Throw the violent person out by whatever means, lock them out, and call the police immediately! DO IT.

5. Everyone deserves a second chance – just the one second chance, however! If his/her behavior does not change and you have to throw him/her out again – that's it! Fini! Cut the tie and move on.

Effective communication is required to maintain a healthy reciprocal relationship. Learn how to do it. Any questions? Opinions? Examples? Ciao, babies!!!

11/07/2006

"In other words, no matter how good she looks, she may be somewhat intimidated by younger women. And when a woman feels inadequate, everything falls to shambles, putting you back at square one. Actually, it puts you into the negatives, so pay attention and avoid inadvertent blows to her self-esteem."
I'm so glad the author said 'she may' else I'd have to say something very unladylike. LOL

"You think you want to swing? Do you daydream about having two girls at once? Do you want to see your girlfriend with another woman? Maybe you want to see her with another man while you take on another woman and join in for sloppy seconds?" -first of all you wear condoms so there is nothing sloppy thank you. Why the immediate leap to female bisexual behavior? Guys realize that to most of us the female bisexual idea is about as attractive to us as the male bisexual idea is to you..

"Adding people to the party brings with it different experiences. It is extremely important to understand your wishes, wants and hopes for this lifestyle change. It would be the height of irresponsibility and utter disrespect to your partner if you both did not carefully examine why you want to do this."

- a bit too 'touchy-feely' for me - am just here for the fun, baby. One gets the impression from the article that the author has no actual experience swinging. 'No means no' is the second rule, wearing condoms is the first. You ask permission to join in and everyone's polite and gracious mainly because you are naked and therefore feel a bit vulnerable. BTW it doesn't have to be 'a lifestyle' - a grandiose term, it can be just something you enjoy from time to time. People are so quick to label every little thing a lifestyle. Anyway time for me to scoot!

"We are about doing things safe & legal, so she does NOT swallow and doesn't allow bare back penetration - don't even try, don't ask. In turn he respects same limits for others we meet."

-from the NIH website: "Epidemiological data support the premise that, whereas HIV transmission via saliva is low or non-existent, oral infection with HIV in semen appears to be possible. Animal studies confirm that HIV can be transmitted via the oral tissues. Oral trauma, ulcers, drug use, smoking, co-infection with oral herpes, sexually transmitted bacterial diseases (e.g., oral gonorrhea) or periodontal disease might increase oral HIV transmission."

So while it is possible, it is highly improbable - so swallowing is unlikely to cause any transmission. Of course once semen reaches the stomach it dies. The hydrochloric acid in the stomach is more than strong enough to kill HIV and if it weren't for the lining, it would eat through the stomach itself - ulcers. btw I swallow and I am tested quite regularly - just today in fact.

Okay next week came and we're BUSY this Friday thank you very much. So no M&G for us this week and not for me next week but I'm soo there the following week. Got all of that? Good. I have to call some people.

Vote and please Vote NO on #1 - we don't need an 'except for you' in The Bill of Rights.

Alright single gentlemen....The final vetting will be tonight, see the playtime posting, so get there and say Hi to Princess. I'd say 30 to 50 years and around 6ft would float her boat? She has very kindly undertaken the arduous task of checking men out for one of THOSE parties. You know the kind I mean. Look for the blonde wearing black. Don't leave her there at the front bar all lonely! Ciao, babies!!

11/08/2006

It is with deep regret that I inform you that Amendment 1 passed yesterday. All of those, esp those with bi-wives, who voted for it are kindly asked - what if it had been against you?
Unfortunately the insensitive louts of VA have passed the dreaded, stupid, and totally un-necessary Amendment #1 thus changing our Bill of Rights to the VA Bill of Rights Except for You. As well as completely removing the credibility from The Declaration of Independence's "life,

156

liberty, and the pursuit of happiness" as well as The Constitution of the United State's Bill of Rights.

If you voted for it and you are on this site and/or other similar sites - you should be drug out into the streets and SHOT for a damned lying bastard of a hypocrite. Especially so if your bi or homosexual yourself. And especially so if you're here as a couple with a bi-wife or bi-husband!

EITHER WE ALL HAVE THE SAME RIGHTS OR NONE OF US HAVE ANY RIGHTS.

I make no apologies either.

As a very fine man has said: "Wielding the power of the state to enforce the "Mandates of Heaven" is unacceptable. Doesn't matter to me that the would-be wielders wave Korans or King James Bibles." Sorry, cannot blog today. Ciao, babies.

11/09/2006

Okay I think I have calmed down now. Maybe. Perhaps. Lets just NOT go there. No Politics within the range of Nip's hearing or vision. Y'all don't need the resulting blood loss. Fortunately, she can always be distracted by scotch or sex. "There , there, Nip. It's okay, sweety. Look what I have for you!"

It is fortunate that I, the Feline of Darkness, is easily distracted by scotch or sex, else social conservatives would undergo rapid wholesale slaughter. I do not object to them living their nice, wholesome, white-picket-fence lives. I wish they'd simply return the favor and let me get on with mine. Don't you wish for the same?

wandering off calling "Here, teddybears! Here, teddybears! Look what I've got for you!"

157

In case we find ourselves starting to believe all the anti-American sentiment and negativity, we should remember England 's Prime Minister Tony Blair's words during a recent interview. When asked by one of his Parliament members why he believes so much in America , he said:
"A simple way to take measure of a country is to look at how many want in ... And how many want out." And only two defining forces have ever offered to die for you:
1. Jesus Christ
2. The American G. I.
Not to put too fine a point on it or to sound too 'Rep' - The US remains one of the better countries.

Masculine Qualities Desired - My List
(for informational purposes only)
1. about my age
2. taller than I am
3. furry
4. bright, witty, a bit wicked and yet, essentially kind.
5. sexually experienced
6. possesses a zest for life
7. open to polyamory
8. fully adult
9. strong enough to be my equal
10. loving enough to be my teddybear
Fortunately such men aren't difficult to find.
One simply must use the right bait. *W*
Ciao, babies!!

11/10/2006

That is the nature of politics. The demands of 'the party' or of the position can corrupt or twist anyone involved. And people wonder why some Americans don't vote. Cynical bunch that we are.

158

Bi? Tried it and - yawn. 'Nuff said.

Took the day off. Tired of a great many things just now and not feeling my best. Wish I could just curl up in bed but too much needs to be done. So in with the meds and on with my little white sneakers and off I go! *hack, hack, cough, wheeze* and will someone please get my husband off my case!

Why would a woman want a gangbang?
Quote: "Gangbangs are a kind of mystery to me because they seem to go against everything I know about women. I cannot imagine that a woman would feel special, sexy or desired after having anonymous sex with 4-10 complete strangers. I can understand that being the center of desire of many men must be very empowering and arousing thought but does that really reflect the reality and legacy of being in a gangbang? I know why men like GBs: they get to "use" a woman for their own gratification and they get to live out their "porno fantasies". So why do women want Gangbangs?"
LOL - anyone care to enlighten the poor fellow?

Party tonight so we will not be joining in our usual meet n greet. Kiss everyone for us! *EG* Ciao, babies!!!

11/11/2006

Was I speaking Ancient Greek? Last night at the sex party, I told a prospective play partner that I do not care to be spanked - big surprise, huh?- and he made a point of doing it anyway. So I rolled him over, pinned him down and thoroughly spanked him. Then I got up and promptly forgot his existence. Til then it had been great fun and more fun was immediately in the offing! Why did he have to go and

159

ruin a good thing like that? Leave my admittedly delightful rump alone! Ciao, babies!!!

11/12/2006

A man who didn't study history posted the following.
"Boy, what a bunch of fucking ingrates, most of you have bashed so-called organized religion here. Yet you don't realize that your very existence you may have to thank "organized religion" Our first cultures and civilizations not to mention laws that WE STILL LIVE BY were handed down by ORGANIZED RELIGION! Its unbelievable that the human race just knows so damn little about its history, if we don't know where we came from then how do we know where we are going! And to answer another question posed here, if all people practiced some simple self control then we would neither require birth control nor abortion; Both of which destroy the natural balances in nature, YES by fucking with birth rates and the like the human race is destroying our own future. Look at the last 30-40 years since abortion and birth control have been legalized, has the world gotten better or worse. You can answer that question yourselves!"
Oh yes? Really? And from whence do you think the organized religions got those ideas? That's right! From the Pagans!!! This is a man whose brain should get out more! Why he's on the site is a bit of a mystery too.

Many 'modern' women seem to have a thing against 'putting all of those hormones into my body' with the shot, implants, or by taking the Pill. Ladies, the hormones are the same as you would produce if you were pregnant. All these drugs are doing is inducing your body to believe that it is pregnant now and therefore you do not ovulate. The risks associated with taking the hormones are the same as being pregnant and if the hormones make you ill then guess what, so will pregnancy. Took The Pill for many years without any ill effects. Then had two kids and a tubal ligation. Now without a uterus entirely - no periods! So am free - truly free! Love it!!

This is from a blog about women in business with the issue at hand dealing with sex. I have spent most of my time in the military dealing with all kinds of men in all kinds of situations. Early on, I was 'sexually harassed' once: a male co-worker spanked my rump. The next thing he knew his back was up against the machinery and my hands were around his throat. I told him to never do that or anything like it again. After I let him go. I called his supervisor and read him the riot act. The word went out, apparently, because never again in 20 years was I ever bothered. On the job romances and male team members discussing lap dances were the two situations mentioned in this other blog. The women reported feeling stressed about this. Unfortunately I do not feel free to give them the advice that would really help them for fear that they'd be shocked to the core. I toned it down but I do not think they'll 'get it' somehow. My advice? Lean back in your chair and laugh at them! You know none of them would last 5 minutes with you - frail creatures that they are. So why feel threatened? Tis 'schoolyard' stuff beneath your notice. If asked just say "I don't bite little children."
It does work ladies! When I asked one guy why he and his colleagues never talked 'that way' to me, he answered "because you'd deck me." Being 'dangerous' does have its advantages. *EG*
Any other businesswomen/professional women care to venture an opinion?

The most expensive single malt scotch I have yet found is, drum roll please,
Bruichladdich 40 yr old for $2,400.00 per bottle.

That's right, folks, you heard it here first, $2 and almost one half grand US shipped directly to you from Islay, Scotland. I have no idea how the stuff tastes, and am unlikely to ever find out at that price, but if it is similar to other Islays I have known and loved, Laphroaig and Lagavulin, then it is NOT a scotch for the faint of heart or the uneducated of palate. For those just starting out try Skapa.
Ciao, babies!!!

11/13/2006

There is a skill to this! One has to be extremely sexy and inviting without leaving a sleazy trail of slime behind you. How well do you manage your affairs, sweeties?

Assemble 3 different single malts from three different regions of Scotland. Distilled water. Savory treats and bittersweet chocolate on the side. Use three tulip shaped glasses per person.
The scotches recommended =
Skapa - very light and fine from the Shetlands way up north
Glendronach - red and sweet from the central east
Lagavulin - amber, oily, and rich from the western isle of Islay
All at room temperature, mix with a bit of water, pour shorts - please. Smell then taste.
Eat in between scotches.
Once you find one you like, try that one full strength.

Ciao, babies!!

11/14/2006

Took some time off and switched off the APG at Night color scheme to find white with pale pink and light mint

162

colors - how very 'old lady' of apg. Terribly refined, dahlink! So have been finding my way around again.

"Here teddybears, teddybears! Look what I have for you!"

Female Sex Boundaries
"When you first get together with a girl, it can be hard to figure out how soon is too soon when it comes to certain sexual antics.
1. Making her submissive.
2. Anal activities. As far as anal sex goes, girls who love it love it, and will request it without any hesitation.
3. Fetishes. If you happen to have a fetish, introducing it to your new girl is a big deal.
4. Oral sex on her. This may seem odd, but many women still aren't very familiar with men who love to go down on them.
5. Period sex. When you first get together with a girl, she may not know how to broach the subject of her period. The big question in these situations is, "Do you have period sex?"
What I find interesting is the slant. She has to change to suit him. This is only an excerpt of the full article but you're not missing much. There's no hint of him receiving anal nor of him being submissive or of him relaxing about any of his fetishes. Message received = female sex boundaries are not to be respected but are to be overcome. Where the article did get it right is when it stressed that communication is the key.

Party last Friday was very nice. Lots of lovely naked men roaming about! Played with a few but was not up to my usual speed - took it easy you might say. Almost forgot the scotch too - huge error! Cat tucked me in and scampered out again! Feeling much better now, thanks! Now you

163

gentlemen will have to watch your backs...and fronts! Ciao, babies!!

11/15/2006

I may be in trouble - we shall see. Until that becomes clear - PARTY! Well, and why not? I will dislike it intensely, if it happens, but I will survive nevertheless. So I will clear my desk, perhaps meet some people - I hope so, and generally get on with life.

Never feed me beforehand, it slows me down, - only after.

Thursday - noon 4 men and I will participate in a "Stress Management Seminar". 2 of the men will be Cat Toys and 2 of the men will be new. We will see if a queen size bed can hold us all. Shall I tell you about it? Would you care to know?

My role model is Mrs. Emma Peel as played by Diana Rigg. We all had one or two when we were growing up. This character was mine. "But a little cheating, is expected." Who was/were your role models, baby?

He did the grocery getting. Two packages of hotdogs and a cucumber?!?! I ask you! What were you thinking? Oh, I see. You forgot the list. There were too many cute women in the store, uh-huh. You were remembering recent interludes. Thinking about Thursday too - ok. The world was rotating anti-cyclonically?!?! HEY! Come back here! Don't go dancing off to the bedroom like that! But I'm blogging! Oh, dammit! Ciao, babies!!

11/16/2006

It turned out that my partner in crime "The Good Witch" was well enough to attend! So 4 men and 2 women met for a Stress Management Seminar during which various 'degrees of non-separation' occurred. She was in her regular casual clothes and I was dressed in a semi-power outfit of total black, stilettos, stockings (thi highs) skirt and sweater - with suitable jewelry (this time I didn't lose an earring!) and black lace undies. My undressing seemed to be appreciated - slowly, with suitable pauses during suitable poses. We began mildly enough with all 6 of us on the bed at once with cunnlingus and being kissed and caressed and I got my breasts licked, nibbled, and sucked. Love that! Then She went on with a bit of fellatio and 'from behind' sex with a backrub while I indulged in fellatio with the new guy while the blonde fellow, mmmm, continued cunnilingus. All of those hands and mouths and penises! Fun! One fellow - who arrived late and left early - was particularly caressing! Very nice! We both had him. Then She took the blonde guy to bed while I did the other two on the sofa from behind and fellatio; rotating back and forth so they wouldn't orgasm too soon. Then we posed for photos, some of which you'll see in my network photo album, but during the photo session things went from posing to playing so more sex was enjoyed by all - again! Then the blonde had to leave, she had had sex from him while I had oral from him; leaving the new guy and Her favorite who she took back to bed with her. I just snuggled up on the sofa and chatted with the new guy. she returned all nicely pink and he almost crawled out of the bedroom - seriously dragging! Then we all departed. She and I went to dinner after I picked up Slut2. After dinner Slut 2 and I went back to the suite and had GREAT fun after we fixed the bed. (things had gotten rather exuberant there) I pounced upon the recumbent naked Slut2 and he tried to see if he could induce squirting from that position. He could. Then he handed me my glasses and we were visible in the mirror "Just watch the teddybear." Hmmmmm yes! A bit of a rest for him to recharge and then we went with "standard position no.1" after which he pounced on me and then I fed off of him. We were done then. Tidying up ensued. the bed was a complete mess and there wasn't a dry towel in the place. But we left it as clean and tidy as was possible. The 4 from the afternoon were nice but not furry. So had to have Slut 2, who is nicely furred, later. I cannot say how many orgasms the others had, I could guess, but I had something around 30 during the afternoon and another 12 or so with 2 squirtings with Slut 2 later on. WHEEEEEEEEEEEEEEEEE!!

This party report brought to you by The Wicked Woman Group. Ciao, babies!!

11/17/2006

Regarding the recent post about women in business being made to feel as 'outsiders' when the boys decide to talk sex; I was called by the lady who posed the question. She wanted to know what I meant by 'out-gunning' them.

Here's the answer:

Say something along the lines of "tsk, tsk, you boys must not be getting enough at home" and then immediately follow that with a summation of the last business point discussed.

What was interesting was that this occurred at the vice-presidential level. A bunch of 50 year olds sitting around playing schoolboy games. If you say something like I have suggested, the implication is that you are well satisfied, not the least put out by such tactics, and that you are perfectly capable of handling anything that may come along - all useful skills in the corporate jungle.

I find it interesting that so many women seem so ill at ease with their own sexual prowess that they cannot control such incidents from a superior position. Come on, ladies - it is just sex talk.

Still in trouble - aren't some men just amazing? But WOW had fun yesterday like you would not believe! 5 men and two women - perfect mix! Two were teddybears! So you know I thoroughly enjoyed myself. Cat remains the best, however! Snuggling up with him is always mind-blowing!

Having spent yesterday getting 'spent' - house stuff today - one always pays for one's pleasures in one fashion or another. So it is off to do something non-sexual for once! Wish me luck! Ciao, babies!!

11/18/2006

My Momma Done Told Me..
the following 5 Rules
1. school comes first
2. it isn't love
3. do not get diseased
4. do not get pregnant
5. YOU pick the men
So I imparted this on another website to teens just starting out. WOW, did I catch HELL!
Seems all the girls and guys today are out seeking LOVE in a big way - they're 14 for Christ's sake!
"You should only do it if you really care about the other person."
After being accused of constant one-night-stands, and of only having 'empty' sex, having sacrificed my 'spirituality', incapable of having 'meaningful' relationships, and of being arrogant as well as stupid - had to come here and SHARE it

with you. Forgive me, but I find their attitudes both FUNNY and yet very SAD. Ciao, babies!!

11/19/2006

The National Air & Space Museum: WOW! AWESOME! Today The Boy and I went visiting out at Dulles. We had a SPLENDID time! I cannot recommend it highly enough! You all HAVE GOT TO GO!

For those fearful of injury - do not worry - I can be exquisitely gentle. Push a few of my buttons and I am more likely to be a purry little kitten. Cat does this all of the time. He does a bit of "Here, kitty, kitty" and leaps gleefully for the bed. Some things are just too good to resist!
Ciao, babies!!

11/20/2006

But I knitted my schedule again and I missed an appointment with someone today at 2pm - SORRY!!
Please call to reschedule!

Went to the dentist this morning. (he's cute but no teddybear) Yes, my molar is broken; yes, there's a cavity there; yes, we have to drill out all of the old filling, rebuild the tooth and then put a crown on it. $1300 next Tuesday - after Thanksgiving!
Not sure which hurts more - the tooth or the $1300!

Bought a bed, then waited for an hour while they fussed to find the thing in the store room only to have them tell me it is not accessible and to come back tomorrow morning! GRRRRRRR.
I have a hard time waiting in the first place when the answer's yes - I have no patience when the answer's no.

Naughty people!

Met a new, delicious, and highly skilled teddybear for his test ride tonight! So much fun and rather cute too especially when he's wearing his collar! He admitted to being nervous - not knowing what to expect. But I soon put his fears to rest. EG Now he's all ready and willing to play further! YEEHAW!! Just remember people - BABYSTEPS!

Oooo male hunters! Yummy! They bring TWO kinds of meat with them! KEWL! After they 'feed' me, they can feed me! LOL So, what's on the menu, guys?

Some things you just HAVE to do, ya know? Speaking of which - there's a Cat here! Ciao, babies!!

11/21/2006

Teddybear Testride.
It began sitting side by side on the sofa with him naked. We progressed slowly since he was nervous - not knowing what to expect. *EG* But I laid the training collar out onto the coffee table and let him play with it a bit while I played with him. Then I stood up, faced him and slowly removed my sweater, my pants, and then my bra. (I love that little gasp men make when they see me naked.) I straddled him, facing him, while he sat on the sofa and placed the collar around his neck and asked him what he wanted to do. He opted to suck my nipples, so I led him to the bed, sat on the edge of it, and said yes. Hmmm he was very good. I then removed my underwear (beige lace boy shorts) and he slowly licked down my body and began cunnilingus. Ahh! So nice! I then took his right hand (wrong hand) and he switched to his left and began G-Spot caressing. OMG! The first of many orgasms and he got very wet. I squirt. He seemed to like it from what he seemed to say at the time.

We then played find my birthmarks (I have two; one on each side). He didn't have his glasses on so he had to examine my skin very closely to find them. I love being nuzzled like that. There I was purrrring and he was doing his very best to stimulate every inch of me. Licking, kissing, nuzzling, caressing. Mmmmmmmmmm. It was getting too warm for him so while I put on his condom, he removed the collar. We then slide in and out - he was curved just right. The head of his penis rubbing right there! Oh wow! That was good! then, in the interest of checking off all the boxes on my checklist, we went to doggy style and he came - very loud - very hard. It was terrific! I hugged him until he stopped shaking, kissed him, and then we took a break.

During the break he put on the collar and began caressing me until I took him back to the bed and had him lie down. I then pounced upon him and began exploring him, finding out all of his special places with hands, lips, and tongue. A bit of fellatio and he was more than ready for the next condom (I put on all condoms btw). Then I was up on top of him, thoroughly enjoying myself to the point where I flushed bright pink and ejaculated all over him! He kept saying things - I am not sure just what but he seemed to be enjoying the sight of my enjoying him. Aaaah! Such a lovely man! The collar had had to come off again. Too hot when he's active. Then I rolled off of him, laughing, and he decided to return the favor and pounced upon me. Meow! Some more in and out and I came, he came, we all came. More hugs and then I teased him with the idea of tasting his semen. EG He grinned but said eeeek! I laughed and said too early, huh? He grinned back, he had gotten over being nervous by his time, and agreed - too early. We snuggled up together on the sofa, drank some more (soda) and then went off to shower together. Well, I showered first since I like it much hotter than he does. A warm towel later and he decided to invite me back to his place and some pinot noir next week for some further fun and Teddybear Education since he said he would like to become one of my male Sluts.

I was a very happy Kitten having had so many orgasms and he felt both drained and relaxed. Think he passed his 'testride'?

The Wicked Woman Group
Coming soon to the Metro DC area THE group for group sex and naked partying amongst friends!
This group takes up where the FGBC leaves off! Please come and join The Wicked Woman Group in the fun!

Two points first: buddy - post whatever pix you want; and women do not 'steal' or otherwise compete with other women over men. What would be the point? He should stay with you because he adores you - not because you won't unlock the cuffs. (Let's not go there). So off to get the new bed. Ciao, babies!!!!

11/22/2006

"If a woman gives a guy "attitude" when he approaches her, should he keep talking to her or consider himself "rejected" and move on?
Here's something to think about...
Women often reject men on "autopilot" An attractive woman gets hit on by men day in and day out Pretty soon "rejection" becomes an automatic response. It turns into a screening system, with the initial rejection as a test. Only guys who can get past the initial rejection survive. Now, not all women are like this. But here's a little secret about those who are: These women are used to meeting guys who "can't take the heat." They meet hundreds of men who "wuss out" to every one that "makes the cut." And because

of this, once you get past her initial rejection, she will see you as a rare commodity. To put it simply... you are in. A great example of this took place in the movie Gone with the Wind (go rent this now if you haven't seen it already). Scarlett O'Hara was anything but nice to Rhett Butler, but he took it all in stride because he knew it was just an act... and that deep down she was totally in love with him. Take this same stance when you meet a woman with "attitude." Come from the position that you know what it's like to be her, and that you know she has to weed out the losers somehow, and that you know if she opened her eyes, she'd fall for you in a second. Don't actually voice this to her, but let it shine through in your actions. Give her a second chance to give you a second chance... and soon you... being the rare find that you are... will be the one in control."
LOL Ya think? What did we say about 'male persistence'?

Happy Thanksgiving!! May your blessings be both manifold and manifest!

Okay are you ready for this?
"Premarital sex seems to do damage to someone's ability to trust their future spouse. There is a sense of being used. Even if they both wanted it, there always seems to be a sense of regret and a sense of shame and hurt that they weren't important enough to wait for."
"Premarital sex brings on the guilt. Guilt is a common problem that creates a wedge of blame and shame between spouses. "
"Premarital sex with other partners creates a variety of sexual experience. Some may see this as a plus but in real life it's not. Your spouse may not do things the way a past lover did and then you have frustration and dissatisfaction. You have sexual memories that pop up at inopportune times. There can be jealousy over past relationships or fears over comparisons to past lovers. You don't need to be an

172

experienced lover to please your spouse. You can learn to be a great lover after marriage. Think of it as on the job training. "

"Premarital sex opens the door to disease. You are taking serious risks with your health, your reproductive health (you want to have kids someday?), and even your life. "

"Premarital sex opens the door to greater heartbreak. I know many of you feel you are in love with "the one." If you give yourself to the one you love and then break up before the "I do" you will have a broken heart and will have given yourself to someone that you will never marry. How's that sound?"

"Premarital sex is not like marital sex. There is a certain "naughtiness" and excitement about premarital sex. That "naughtiness" backfires after marriage. If you wait for marriage that sexual excitement becomes a part of married sex instead of being the "naughty stuff" you did before marriage."

"You lose the specialness of first sex on your wedding night."

"And then there are the kids. When you have sex .... drum roll .... you can produce a child!" (duh!)

"Premarital sex makes sex less important than God designed it to be."

Never have I heard such utter rot! These things are not inherent in the sex itself but only in the baggage these people deliberately put in the minds of those who "believe" - for social control.

Ouch, ouch, fuck that hurts, ouch! Did something to my lower back - cannot move - send help! Ciao, babies!!!

11/23/2006

"She can't help herself, dude. But you're going to handle this situation by being supportive and keeping your mouth shut. And when you guys go out, you're going to the gym. Whatever you two do together, it's going to have the theme of getting and staying in shape (and shedding pounds). Whatever you do, you two are going to keep moving. Every time you see her, you'll head to the gym or go running or bicycling together.
You don't do anything else with this lady. You don't go sit in a movie theater and polish off a bucket of buttered popcorn with a side of nachos. You don't go out and eat barbecued ribs. Gene, you're going to be your girlfriend's coach. And if she wants to drop you because of that or she decides not to see you, then fine -- man up to it. But that's what you're going to do. You're going to coach this woman to get on the right track as long as she hangs around.
To you Psych majors, nagging doesn't work. It doesn't work when women do it to men, and vice versa. So don't even be tempted to pick at her, man. Keep your trap closed -- no criticisms or snide remarks or "subtle" suggestions. Keep it light and keep it funny. Your actions are going to speak for you. Every time you see her, this is how you're going to behave. "

I feel that this would work in reverse too. If you care about that sort of thing. I personally prefer my diet and exercize program: don't eat and fuck like crazy. Ciao, babies!!

11/24/2006

How to Meet a Woman Tonight:
Find a target-rich environment It's important that you find those special places that are PACKED with attractive women, places where it's natural to start talking to them

174

and where there's less COMPETITION and distraction from other guys.

Play it cool
When you see a woman you want to meet, pay attention to the situation and approach her when she's not likely to feel "rudely interrupted." It's also a MUST that you eliminate nervous ticks, stilted body language, fast movements, stuttering, and any other signs that show you're uncomfortable. And, of course, look her straight in the eyes.

Practice your approach
It's important to mentally rehearse your first conversations with women. Plan what you're going to say, think about how she will probably respond and what you're going to do in the most common situations.

Use great "opener" on her
(none of those suggested were any good)

Get her talking
A woman loves sharing her opinions, so why not use this to your advantage? Start the conversation by asking her opinion on something.

Get her e-mail and number
Most guys make this step way more complicated than it really is. After talking for a minute or two, just say, "Well, it was nice meeting you, I'm going to get back to shopping/my friends/work/whatever." Turn away and take a few steps… then look back at her and say, "Hey, do you have e-mail? Great, give it to me," then take out your pen and hand it to her. As she's writing her e-mail address, say, "And put your number down there too."

This might work but I'd venture to say you're chances would be better if you met her criteria or her 'weakness'. My weakness is those certain teddybears I'm always going on about. Fortunately, picking up men is MUCH easier! What do you think? Do you have any 'weaknesses' or how to meet tips?

How I Pick-up Men
Active Mode:
1. Look extremely fetching.
2. Flirt with every male in the place.
3. Identify a suitable man.
4. Wander over there and catch his eye.
5. Hold eye contact while moving closer.
6. Kiss him lightly on the lips for 20 seconds while touching him elsewhere.
7. Smile and say "Hello".

Passive Mode:
1. Look extremely fetching.
2. Catch his eye and hold eye contact.
3. Flirt when he stops by.
4. Caress some part of him
5. Say "Yes".
There you have my techniques.

Cat Therapy. Yes, I too have a furry 'carpet tiger' roaming wild about my house. She is a most useful lifeform. Here she is performing therapy for a strained back. Plus, she is too cute for words! Little Miss Ambersandy T. Cat is a grumpy old grandmother cat now being well into her 15th year.

"When the dust settles, Joni Mitchell may stand as the most important and influential female recording artist of the late 20th century. Uncompromising and iconoclastic, Mitchell confounded expectations at every turn; restlessly innovative, her music evolved from deeply personal folk stylings into pop, jazz, avant-garde, and even world music, presaging the multicultural experimentation of the 1980s and 1990s by over a decade. Fiercely independent, her work steadfastly resisted the whims of both mainstream audiences and the male-dominated recording industry. While Mitchell's records never sold in the same numbers enjoyed by contemporaries like Carole King, Janis Joplin, or Aretha Franklin, none experimented so recklessly with their artistic identities or so bravely explored territory outside of the accepted confines of pop music, resulting in a creative legacy which paved the way for performers ranging from Patti Smith and Chrissie Hynde to Madonna and Courtney Love." I quite agree!!! Ms. Mitchell is extremely awesome.

Not one of you came to help! Gee - guess I know who my friends are! If I could get up, I'd whack your shins with my cane. Male teddybear massage therapist wanted - inquire within - naked lady needs help. Damn those trapezes!

Off to see the medics. Somehow. Don't wait - this may take a while.

I'm going out tonight if it kills me! Maybe Cat will carry me up the stairs??? LOL Ciao, babies!!

11/25/2006

11/25/2006

The Wicked Woman Group is looking for more participants. Please join us - adhering to the rules of course.

NUCLEAR CHILI
sear one pound of hamburger in the bottom of a large pot
until most of the grease is gone
add in enough chili powder so you can smell it then add in
smaller amounts of cumin and cayenne
cook and then balance the spices and add a pinch of salt
turn the heat down under the pot
pour in a large can (24 oz size) of kidney beans- drained
mix then add a dash of red wine and enough water to make
it moist - just moist
Cover and warm through approx 30 minutes
serve hot

SAVORY CHILI
brown one pound of hamburger in 1 tsp olive oil in pot
leaving half the grease n the meat
add 1 Tablesp of tomato paste or ketchup and caramelize
the meat (Mallard Reaction).
add in 1 tsp chili powder, 1/2 tsp cumin, and 1/2 tsp
cayenne
add in 1 large (24 oz) can of red kidney beans with the
juice
reduce sauce to one half over high heat add a pinch of salt
serve hot with grated cheese and sour cream on top
Either one should keep you 'warm'!

From Il Cortegiano translated by Sir Thomas Hoby (1561)
"His conversation with women to be alwayes gentle, sober,
meeke, lowlie, modest, serviceable, comelie, merie, not
bitinge or sclaundering with jestes, nippes, frumpes, or
railinges, the honesty of any. His love towarde women, not
to be sensuall or fleshlie, but honest and godly, and more
ruled with reason, then appetyte: and to love better the
beawtye of the minde, then of the bodie. Not to withdrawe
his maistresse good will from his felowlover with revilinge
or railinge at him, but with vertuous deedes, and honest

condicions, and with deserving more then he, at her handes for honest affections sake."
Some things never change!

11/26/2006

DEMON SPAWN is here!! All parties interested in photographs are asked to email me at the ya you know who address.

11/27/2006

Rivals: You know that you really don't have any, don't you? No one is just like you do you see. She/he may be cuter, younger, slimmer, hotter, more or less whatever than you are. Nevertheless - she/he isn't you. Amazingly enough, it doesn't really matter - this outward appearance. Yes, it gets attention but that is not what captures a heart. You know this. There's the gleam in the eye; the half smile of the lip - those elusive things like the slide of a hip. Those things that make you laugh; all that defines you. Those capture a heart. You can therefore be done with jealousy, insecurity, and fear. And just get on with having fun. Here endth the lesson! LOL

The Wicked Woman Group Is where women can indulge their desires for more than one man without fear or apology. The Selection Committee is assiduous in finding, vetting, and making sure that there is at least one male there that will suit your fancy. All women are encouraged to join us and to make her wishes known so we can find the right sort of men for your enjoyment. While it is true that you give every man there his chance with you - you are only required to give him his chance. Every man is obliged to offer you something sexual. Whether that all ends up being a kiss or something else is up to the two of you at the time.

But regardless of how its done, and by whom, everyone gets laid. My parties are woman-centric meaning the individual lady controls the action. This is a 'sensual delight between friends', not some mechanical slam bam affair (unless that's what you require). What you do on your side of the bed is your business. Since this is 'between friends' all males are asked to submit to being vetted beforehand to see if we like you, to see if you are really interested and available, and to judge if your personality and skill level will mesh with the group and please the ladies. You will note that nothing has been said about your appearance, your status, or your age. If that is an issue then perhaps this is not the group for you. Everyone is cordially invited to join in the fun!

I'm not romantic. Sitting on my library deck a summer's evening with you, slowly getting drunk watching the sunset while listening to Janis singing "Summertime".
Lying beside you afterward watching the play of light on your fur and skin; slowly re-igniting then laughing as you mention 'cigarette' in an effort to save yourself by distracting me.
Napping together on a Sunday afternoon, fully clothed on top of the bedclothes while the kids play their video games in the basement.
Sitting in my truck with you, in the dark along some empty hilltop road watching the fireworks in the middle of the night.
No, no - I'm not at all 'romantic'.
Ciao, babies!!

11/28/2006

Men are strongly encouraged to get themselves vetted. The ladies all have different tastes in men and you just might fit her desires! You never know which ladies will be there so getting vetted and volunteering exponentially increases your chances of being invited to play. The Selection Committee tries very hard to make sure that every lady attending has at least one man there who suits her. They can't do this if they don't have you on their list of hopefuls! Get vetted and volunteer!

I wandered by his place. Then I wandered down the hall to his bedroom shedding clothing as I went which he gallantly picked up as he followed me. I laid down naked upon his bed. He then began massaging my back muscles looking for the knotted ones. His nice heavy hands glided over my skin and I began to feel deliciously warm. Kneading, stroking, pressing; he moved at just the right speed with just the right pressure. The slight gritty feeling of the body oil made my skin tingle. Mmmmmmmmmm so very, very nice. I rolled over and we began again. Mmmmmm slowly , ever so slowly he moved toward eroticism. He bent his lips to my breasts and cradled me in his arms as he fingered and caressed me. He slid down my body and licked first my right hip (I quivered) then the left. His mouth felt so good! Mmmmmeow, baby - I purred at him. He didn't seem to mind. Several orgasms later and I was waving my tail at him. *EG* I do sooo adore large furry teddybears.
Ciao, babies!!

11/29/2006

"Start with some passionate kissing and foreplay. Wait until you are both really worked up, then suddenly refuse to penetrate her, get out of bed, and get dressed. Give her a coy smile and tell her innocently, "I'm not that easy, sweetheart, you'll have to wait until I'm ready." You have to clearly show her that you're teasing her so that she doesn't feel like you're judging her or that she did something wrong. Once you're dressed, lean down, give her a passionate kiss and tell her, "I want to wait to make it even more special." Then leave. Women have always held all the sexual power, but not anymore. These techniques will set you apart from all the other guys she knows who just want to score. You'll leave her intrigued and she'll definitely be back for more."

Is he kidding? Leave?!? Buddy, if you left me like that - you're NOT coming back. Intrigued? Oh no. Reaching (figuratively speaking) for the nearest loaded 12 gauge? Oh yes! Justifiable don't you think?

When trying to set up a meeting have several specific date/times and places in mind. Offer a choice of three that fit your schedule and permit her to pick from there. If you wait and/or we do this 'back and forth' routine - well, I tend to lose interest. You get the 'indecisive' box checked which means you may not be alpha. We're all busy, hun so give me something specific to work with here!

What's your main issue with appointments? Other than getting stood up, of course.

You shave, you don't shave - aren't we getting sooooo particular! Once upon a time you'd have killed to get any sex at all and now look at you! Mighty prissy there and sooo metro-sexual. Remember the musical HAIR? Rebellion against the prissy short back and sides. Long may it continue! Here, baby! There, Mama! Everywhere Daddy, Daddy! HAIR!

I do so adore large warm furry teddybears! Especially those whose firm paws give long, slow and tantalizing massages!

The most painful part about going to the dentist yesterday was paying for it! Ouch! Damn that hurt! The wonder is that the card didn't instantly go up in flames. Permanent will be in next week so back I'll have to go. Unlike someone I know - I don't need my paw held. EG I'm staying in this weekend but will be out the one after. Take good care of him! Ciao, babies!!

11/30/2006

Halfway Decent Advice this time! "So, you've dumped her. Or she's dumped you. Either way, once you find yourself single, thoughts soon come around to meeting other women. But getting back in the game, especially after a long-term relationship, can be daunting. The first steps back in the world of dating should not to be taken lightly. You shouldn't attempt to bed new women to take revenge on your ex, whether it's to lure her back with jealousy or as a way to get over her. You should do it because you're a single guy and that's what single guys do. It goes without saying that you have to be completely over your ex before you get back into the game. Women will immediately pick up on it if you're using them to distract yourself or numb the pain. Exactly how long it will take to reach this stage varies. No matter what, it's worth the wait because the single life rules.

Cheer up then gear up

Immediately after the breakup, you're going to be miserable. Somehow you'll be bringing every conversation around to her, you'll find yourself planning how to get her back and generally lamenting the fact that everyone else is happy while you are in hell. Approaching other women with all this going on is definitely a bad idea. Women can smell depression and desperation a mile off, and the scent is not appealing to them. Instead of dwelling on your ex and the relationship, remember the good side of being single: all those late nights with the boys, the freedom to do what you want when you want and, most importantly, with

183

whom you want. When you stop thinking that there's something missing from your life and start to relish the idea of being single, then it's time to start bedding other women. If you're honest, you'll admit that there were times when you were with your ex that you envied those who were single. Well, start smiling again because now you're one of them...

Take a look around

It's time to celebrate. You've mourned the death of your relationship and now you need to toast the birth of the single you. What is called for is a one-night tour of everything you've been missing while you were in the relationship. Gather your friends. After listening to your moaning, they'll be almost as eager as you are for a big night out. Explain that, in one night, you aim to seek out everything that you couldn't do before. Take in a bar crawl, drop a few bets on the dogs and enjoy a strip club or two. The point isn't to hook up with women. We've already noted that desperation is a major turnoff. The night is for the boys doing boy things. It marks you stepping out of the world of relationships and being welcomed back as one of the guys, making a gradual re-entry in the life of the carefree, single guy. Of course, if you find that women are approaching you, don't turn them away.

Change locales

Now that you've been reintroduced to single life, don't stick to your old haunts. The new you deserves new territory. There will be plenty of places, particularly bars, that your ex used to discourage you from going to; usually because that's where the hot, single women go to. Now you can stalk these hunting grounds with immunity. Here you will be a fresh face, where no one knows the history of your failed relationship. The women there won't think of you as the ex of so-and-so, but as the new guy on the scene. These new locales are the perfect place to test out your new pickup skills.

Fill up your free time

Chances are you'll find yourself with more free time on your hands. A relationship takes a lot of time, and it's hard (not to mention unhealthy) to plug that gap with nothing but new bars and flutters at the track. But even this can be beneficial to the newly single man. Your ex did the cooking? Then take up a cooking class. Here, you'll fill your immediate need of edible food, gain access to new women in a nontraditional hookup environment (where their defenses are down), and add "the home-cooked meal" to your dating repertoire. Plenty of activities serve the dual purpose of filling spare time and getting you back in the game. Coed sports, the gym, art classes, and singles holidays are great starting ideas.

The new hit single

The transition from being in a relationship to being single can be hard. But don't worry: It's all for the best. There are thousands of women out there just waiting to be bedded by you. So what are you waiting for?"

This advice works for women too btw. But the author could have been more succinct. He could have also tempered his glorification of the single life as well but he's trying to cheer the newly divorced up I should imagine so I'll let him get away with it. The entire point is to step out, step up, and leave all of your baggage at home - focus upon this woman right here and right now without any expectations other than getting some sign of interest, her name, and her phone

185

number. See how succinct the author could have been? *EG*

Seduced into Sexual Subjugation: He had no idea how absolutely mind-blowing his sexual subjugation would be. But he trusted me. I began by having him disrobe then collaring him and placing cuffs around his wrists. I then attached his wristcuffs to the tethering strap at the head of his bed. I became naked, straddled his body, kissed him then slowly kissed the corner of one eye, nuzzled slowly down his cheek to his ear and then ran the tip of my tongue lightly along his jaw and then over his lips – very, very gently. I kissed the corner of his other eye and nibbled on his ear lobe and licked lightly up the edge of his ear then down to his neck. I kissed his throat beneath his chin then slowly with hands, tongue and body caressed my way further south, tracing gentle arabesques with my claws and fingertips - sometimes ghosting over the tips of his fur, other times using the edges of my claws to tantalize his skin. My breath slid over his skin where I had moistened it causing his nipples to harden. Settling down between his thighs I ran my hands lightly up his legs while gently breathing on, without touching, his cock - his breath caught in his throat. I took his testicles one at a time into my mouth and sucked and licked - flickering with my tongue. He was moaning very softly. Then I swallowed him and loosely - gradually closing my mouth around his cock without pressure. Slowly I increased the pressure and began sliding up an down and around his cock. Teasing the head with my tongue as I sucked and rotated around his cock. Just enough to make him extremely willing and compliant. I rose up and slid him inside of me and began using him for my enjoyment. Up and forward then down and back, faster and faster. Ah! So very nice! I remember that I was smiling. then sitting back on him and scrubbing back and forth rapidly. Repeating the pattern as I had orgasm after

186

orgasm juicing all over him all the while. OMG! was, I think, what he said when he oragsmed. He was still quivering when he tried to follow me to the sofa for a break afterwards. He almost had a double orgasm that night. We'll work on that! BTW - he kept the collar.

Age is just a number until the Alzheimer's kicks in or the Parkinson's or when women start requiring you to bring a note from your cardiologist saying that it is okay for you to be 'actively engaged in sexual pursuits'. Having said that while debilitation may mark those older , vanity marks those younger. Thus spake the ancient, gnarled, and gravely debilitated (this week) Nip.

So how many of you 'set up' your hubbies with cute chicks? Guess it is just me huh?

Another turkey salad sandwich day. Well, it beats eating oatmeal for breakfast. Now if you'll excuse me, I'll just slip my gravely debilitated self (also naked) into the hot tub. Hold all my calls! LOL Ciao, babies!!!

DECEMBER
2006

Dec 1, 2006
Regarding Male Membership in The WWG
Males must be recommended by a member unless they
have been previously vetted and are therefore known to us
or must be Cat Toys or Male Sluts - these men know who
they are.
SEMPER FELINES

Dec 2, 2006
The AFF foundation invitations have been sent to all but
two persons - if you are on the list and have not received
yours please contact me ASAP.
Either that or have your Y IM up tonight.
That isn't an email address - silly peeps!

As part of my continuing Modern Culture Series, I am
ripping some tunes from the latest bands as provided to me
by my slightly unsprung offspring.
Tonight we have:
Three Days Grace
Breaking Benjamin
Panic! at The Disco
and
(of course)
the latest from:
Weird Al
Anyone have any further suggestions?

Dec 3, 2006
Perhaps an 'Honorable Mention' or a 'Thank you for
Playing' but No, I did not win the Sexiest Female Blogger
Award. I appeal to a different kind of audience. *VWEG*

But CONGRATS to STORMY who did!!

Due to the holidays and the importunities of certain pesky males, another vetting opportunity has been scheduled for Monday Dec 4th at Mike's in Springfield at 6pm in the bar with both the Good Witch and I.
This will be for January's Birthday Bash;
which will be followed by February's Birthday Bash.
The ladies whose birthdays fall in those months have a preference for a certain type of male - so come out, come out and we'll see if we can't fit you in somewhere. *EG*
'Nuff said, baby?

Sorry guys but:
Makeup -rarely worn
High heels - when out only
indoor relax clothes = white sweat suit, thick cream wool socks - men's size 16 rolled at the ankles - white flannel bathrobe
Normal outdoor wear - blue jeans, white top, white sneakers - when moderate weather
Sex wear - nothing at all and don't eat my earrings please - thank you
If you desire a 'lipstick' kind of gal - I'm not the woman for you.

Dec 4, 2006
"Fighting is a normal and natural part of any relationship, but the truth is that the faster a fight is over with, the better it is for everyone. There are some ways to keep arguments short -- if not sweet -- while still dealing with the issue at hand."
No, no, no! If you have to fight to be heard, then you're with the wrong person. If you two cannot sensibly discuss something like adults - PFFFT! Grow up or get out. Besides, males should not have opinions, right? *EG*

190

Don't you think so? Feel free to disagree! (Yes, even the males can comment.)

The reason you have my number is NOT so I can bring drama, or more drama, into your life but rather so you can ask questions directly.
Too many people walk around with stuff in their heads that either isn't true or is hindering them. This is why I will, upon occasion, challenge your statements, behaviors, and beliefs. Feel free to disagree- but an unexamined life isn't worth living.
Some sit on the sofa bemoaning their situation while doing nothing to improve it. So I strategically kick where applicable.
Not that I am without my flaws – I can't think of any at the moment, but I'm sure you'll tell me soon enough what they are. *EG*

"Close But No Cigar"
by Weird Al Yankcovic

Jillian was her name
She was sweeter than aspartame
Her kisses reconfigured my DNA
And after that I never was the same

And I loved her even more
Than Marlon Brando loved soufflé
She was gorgeous, she was charming
Yeah, she was perfect in every way

Except she was always using the word "infer"
When she obviously meant "imply"
And I know some guys would put up with that kind of thing
But frankly, I can't imagine why

And I told her, I said
"Hey! Are we playing horseshoes, honey?
No, I don't think we are!
You're close! (Close!)
But no cigar!"

Then I met sweet young Janet
Prettiest thing on the planet
Had a body hotter than a habanjero
She had lips like a ripe pomegranate

And I was crazy like Manson about her
She got me all choked up like Momma Cass
She had a smile so incredibly radiant
You had to watch it through a piece of smoked glass

I thought after all these years of searching around
I'd found my soulmate finally
But one day I found OUT she actually owned a copy
Of Joe Dirt on DVD

Oh, no! I said
"Hey! Are we lobbing hand grenades, kiddo?
No I don't think we are!
You're close! (Close!)
Oh, so very close! (Close!)
Yeah, baby, you're close! (Close!)
So close!
But no cigar!"

(Oh, yeah!)
(Oh, no!)
(Oh, yeah!)
(Oh, no!)
(Oh, yeah!)
(Oh, no!)

(ALL RIGHT!)

[Hand claps, trumpet solo]

Julie played water polo
She wore a ribbon on her left manolo
She had me sweating like Nixon every time she was near
My heart was beating like a Buddy Rif solo

And she was everything I've dreamed of
She moved right up to #1 on my list
And did I mention she's a world famous billionaire
Bikini supermodel astrophysicist

Yeah, she was so pretty she made Charlize Theron
Look like a big fat slobbering pig
The only caveat is one of her earlobes
Was just a little tiny bit too big

I said
"Hey! Are we doing government work here?
No I don't think we are!
You're close! (Close!)
So very, very close! (Close!)
Aaw, baby, you're close! (Close!)
So close!
But no cigar!"

Missed it by that much! (No cigar!)
Ah, yeah! Ah, right! (No cigar!)
Really, really, really close! (No cigar!)
But no cigar!

Don't be too damn 'nice in your requirements', people!
Two reasons, no one wants to have to live up to that and
you aren't 'all that' either, sweety!

Generosity of spirit!

Dec 5, 2006
Kitten & The Five Bears
First a handsome newbie, then the soon-to-be-a-Cat Toy joined us. Even mature men like to exchange reassurances as to what is what. The newbie smokes cigars!!! OH MY!! I might be in trouble here! Then in came a Cat Toy with another newbie who is being invited upon the Cat Toy's recommendation. If this newbie is no good, the Cat Toy will pay. *VEG* (btw Cat Toy and newbie drove up from Richmond to be there.) Then in walked Slut 2. Ah! What a fun evening!
I purrrrr, purrrrr, purrred all the way home!

Dec 6, 2996
Calling All Teddybears!
He'd be taller than I am, male, furry, almost as intelligent as I am, definitely well-read and witty, confident to the point where he can wear only a collar and leash and still be sexually aggressive, have a warm and essentially joyous personality, a HUGE sense of humor that is not malicious, leads when dancing, likes rapacious sexually aggressive women, employed or otherwise decently well-funded, has hobbies and interests in addition to enjoying massive amounts of sex, and is willing to hang out with me - if he adores me that's a plus! Teddybears go to the top of my list automatically. Please note that as long as he's cute, healthy, and clean - what he actually looks like is of little importance to me. Who he is - that's most important.

but

He has to be polyamorous or otherwise willing to share because one man is not enough! I intend to have a nice estate somewhere where it is warm all of the time and stock it with cold champagne and hot men - preferably as detailed above.

Any volunteers!

Actually I think the non-smokers should go outside to non-smoke!
Blaze away my lovelies! *EG*

Dec 7, 2006
Teddybear Party
We began with M and J who were then joined by R and Slut 3. W came in bearing roses and chocolates! Slut 2 wandered in about then, when we were all busy; I with Slut 3 and M, and my partner in crime with W, J and R. We had all configurations several times over switching men back and forth until they were well worked over and the ladies had had more than several orgasms! My bed was soaked! Oh WOW! Was that a great time! I threw J down onto my bed and rode him vigorously and came all over him. He was very wet - audibly so. Slut 2 joined J and I and it was very exciting. Sluts 2 and 3 formally met for the first time. R and Slut 3 made a great team too - extremely erotic pairing. W and J joined forces to make sure The Good Witch enjoyed herself in the other bed. Excuse me while I purrrrrrrrrrrrrrrr. W - you left your towel behind please make arrangements with me for its return.
You all missed a tremendously pleasurable party!!!

Dec 8, 2006
Bureaucracy
John Thomas, a Catholic, in March, 1592 recanted his faith on his way to the gallows. The next day, he recanted his earlier recantation and asked to be hung. The sheriff, a bureaucrat to the bone, said:

"Since you are so keen to be hanged, assure yourself that I should be delighted to oblige you if your name were on my list. But since it is not here, go away."
Perhaps I could use that now if I substituted the work "fucked" for the word "hanged"?
What do you think? Hmmm?

Dec 9, 2006
Sorry, guys but these girls aren't coming out to play any time soon. They need all the support they can get.
Black lace perhaps?? It was bright red satin last night.
I won't tell but I might show you one day. But only in person, and in passing - as it were - on the way to total nekkidness.
Of course there is my profile picture. Stop salivating!!
wiping the drool off my picture You'll ruin the finish!

Dec 10, 2006
So many people are singin' the blues just now, perhaps it is the season, with the fading of the light or the shorter days. Maybe holiday hype has bitten them? Some I know are dealing with breaking up. Relationship issues occupying far too much of their time? It is hard to say precisely. And I am not the one to ask since depression doesn't seem to be part of my personality. My anger focuses outwardly, not inwardly.
So tell me - how do you 'handle the blues' when they come to grab your heart?

Dec 11, 2006
Breaking Up
There comes a time when, well, you just have to move on. Sell by dates. Expiration dates. It happens. Ah yes, it hurts. We've all been there. Some times it just doesn't work out. I usually just walk away; no regrets, no recriminations, little, if any, further contact. After all, he was fun but it was just

time to let go. If he should wander away, ah well. Just not what he was looking for I guess. Face up, 'fess up and move on. I have a ferocious temper but I learned early on to keep my tongue between my teeth (to shut up) and await events. I decide what outcome I wish to have and work toward that. If it doesn't happen, I move on knowing I took my best shot. I do get angry - but, as written herein earlier, just because one feels 'dramatic', doesn't mean one has to act 'dramatic'. You tend to lose credibility if you do.

My prescription: drink 16oz of whiskey in one fell go while listening to Beethoven's Ninth at FULL volume (don't spare your foundations) and then crawl into bed. Then keep your mouth closed.

What do you prescribe?

Bad Advice:
"Regardless of the type of man you are -- strong with bold opinions, moderate with no taste for confrontation, or passive with a gelatinous backbone -- guess what? Unless you're made of wood, you're going to be dating, you are going to get into arguments, and the expectation (at least from the feminine perspective) is that you are going to lose those arguments.

Any type of man could, at any time, find himself in any kind of an argument. Maybe your pants were off when they really should have been on. Perhaps you zigged when you should have zagged, or, despite your best intentions, you just spoke out of turn.

The trick to saving face in a fight is to always be prepared. You wouldn't go out for a night on the town without some cash and a pressed shirt, would you? So why would you head into a relationship battle without your best artillery?

Nobody wants to be that guy in the corner taking a browbeating from his best gal, especially when, whether that beaten man was wrong or right, he could have come out unscathed. Logic is frequently abandoned when arguing with your girlfriend for one reason: They will not admit they are wrong. Ever. Not going to happen -- so put it out of your head. No matter how compelling you may be, or how wrong she might be, fair is not the name of the game. The trick is this: proving to yourself that you're right, while making her believe she's right as well.

Different men have different expectations about winning arguments, but the art of war is the same. Take all arguments with your ladies with massive grains of salt and remember; you can always win by letting her believe what she needs to believe. That should be clear about four seconds in.

Where we stumble is when we need to prove to ourselves that we can win no matter the contest. Don't forget that it is in our nature to protect what we believe. If we spent all our time getting along, there would be no such thing as make-up sex."

There is nothing wrong with getting along all of the time! Make-up sex is not worth the preceding drama either. Why waste my time and energy arguing anyway? Just walk. Say goodbye and walk away. Life is far too short to spend it with contentious persons.

And what's this "she'll never admit she was wrong" stuff? Grrrrrrr.

Dec 12, 2006
"The idea of living without regrets is a mantra for the ages. Despite this, it's too easy to live by the status quo and try to fix your mistakes as you go through life. What is regrettable varies from person to person, and some things that cause regret are beyond control. But if you find yourself trying to patch up your life, chances are you'll find yourself regretting more and more of the things you didn't

do. With this in mind, make a solid plan for your future endeavors. It doesn't need to be too detailed; it just needs to put into writing your major long-term goals, such as travel plans, getting a raise at work or finishing that book you've been intending to write. Once you write them down, post the list somewhere visible or somewhere you can review them often.

As you pin down each long-term goal, break it down into smaller units. Big tasks are often daunting and may leave you without enough motivation to tackle them. You're more likely to fail and wear yourself down if you leave a big task on the shelf for an extended period of time. Stop this cycle by breaking it down into more manageable units for the shorter-term.

Take charge and plan your social occasions. If you don't have plans for the big holiday weekend, make your own plans and get all your buddies on board. The only way to make memories is to do stuff, and the only way to ensure that you're doing stuff is to take responsibility for planning your own social calendar. Relish in what you've accomplished to make your life fuller and less regretful. As you see yourself accomplishing your own goals, you'll be motivated to tackle even more. When you do something that causes problems or slips, treat yourself as you'd treat an employee at work; with sensitivity and constructive criticism. Harboring negative feelings about your failures is akin to being hard on somebody at work, and you'll resent and discourage yourself.

Be a good student and learn from your mistakes. If you have a nasty experience, don't let it discourage you; rather, let it teach you a lesson of what to be wary of or what to tweak in your own behavior. If you consistently fall into the same, bad situation, take a moment to analyze what brought you there. Take note of the things that you could have avoided.

Make a vow to keep in touch with people who are important to you. It may not seem like a big deal now, but in your later years, the dissolution of personal relationships may be a really big regret. Devote a morning or an evening each week to make that one visit, meet for a coffee with that one friend or make that long-overdue phone call. Each time you touch base, you'll be working toward the further goal of maintaining friendships. Keep one eye on what you're doing, and the other on your future self. It's really easy to get caught up in the moment and do things you'll wish you hadn't. Occasionally, we all suffer from a bad temper, impulse buying or other actions of passion, but try your best to keep these moments of weakness to a minimum.

If you have doubt about how you should deal with a particular situation, think about how you want the story to go in the future, and act accordingly. This way, instead of burning bridges or wasting time, you'll be preserving the right opportunities and ensuring that more will come along. Each experience should teach you something as both accomplishments and failures carry their own lessons. Pay attention, look around, and learn from what you see. Each time you do something great, pat yourself on the back and remember what got you there. Better still; learn not only from your experiences, but from those of others around you.

Most people deserve a second chance when they screw up; however, there are others that, for one reason or another, just are not good for you. Some try to use your good nature to further their goals, while others are a roadblock on your way to your achievements. Don't waste your time with toxic people. If there's somebody who always brings you down, it might serve you well to burn that bridge and never look back. However, be frugal with those relationships that you choose to ditch, as those who drive you crazy now may be very good for you later on. It's divine to be fair and forgiving, but if you get burned more than once by the same guy, it may be better to leave him to his own devices.

Keep little reminders of what you want all around you. They don't need to be embarrassingly obvious, but they do need to remind you of your priorities. If your anchors grow stale and you ignore them, move them to a new place (you'd be surprised how much you'll notice them again) or get new ones. Life is lived in the everyday, so use your anchors to help you aim high in all that you do.

Living a great life on your own terms is an enviable goal; it's also a very accomplishable goal if you set your mind to it. It's important to realize that achieving your goals should be rewarding every step of the way and not just at the end. Make sure that as you're mapping out your future, you're also relishing in the present. There's nothing that causes more regret than letting the good times slip by. Keep your eyes open to the world around you and immediately use the opportunities that come your way. Never lose sight of your goals and remember that balance is the key to success."

Whatever you want your life to be - do it.
Finally, some good advice, no?

The Hunt
"For many, the English countryside is hallowed ground; its idyllic grandeur and pastoral beauty has been celebrated for centuries and serves as one of the UK's most envied icons.

In the midst of this legendary territory is the county of Leicestershire, which enjoys a long and distinguished association with the English hunt. In fact, here and across the UK, hunting does not merely constitute a rich heritage stretching back generations; the hunt is also a vital component of the local economy.

The narrative of the fabled fox hunt is told across generations in the fence and the soil, in etiquette and custom, in hoofs and hounds, by royalty, gentry, and sportsmen alike. Despite this, the hunt was dealt a blow in 2004 when Parliament passed the Hunting Act, which made hunting with dogs a criminal offense. As such, it has divided animal-rights groups and hunting advocates nationwide. Fortunately for the country's hunt enthusiasts, the act has as many holes as Blackburn, Lancashire.

Thus the hunt continues, if slightly compromised. You, the newcomer, will probably not know the difference; and while you may not experience the thrill of a fox flushed to guns, you can nonetheless experience and appreciate this fantastic aspect of traditional English culture.

The hunt is part athleticism, part thrill, part personal experience, and certainly part social gathering. You will be hard-pressed to find a hunt that doesn't fully embrace newcomers and express a genuine desire that you learn and appreciate this long-held tradition. Feel free to ask questions, to chat it up with others, and simply to have a great time being a part of this folkloric and sporting English experience."

There's just something about blasting through the landscape not knowing where the hell you're going or where you'll end up that 'speaks', ya know?

From a very special and very dear friend:
"You are an amazingly erotic woman."
Thank you.

Dec 13, 2006
An Exercise in Eroticism for Men
Try this: close your eyes, hold you hands out and think -
your hands are slowly gliding down her back - how does
that feel? Smooth, silken, soft, warm, furry? Now do that
for every part, you don't have to specify - let us guess
where you are - just how her skin feels beneath your hands,
nothing else.
Now, Write it down herein.
Ladies, feel free to contact your favorite writer!

Dec 14, 2006
Male Slut Rules:
1. Any woman, any time, any way she wants you.
2. But you must inform your primary first - this is not
seeking 'permission' but just to keep the scheduling straight.
3. And condoms will be used with everyone other than your
primary.
4. Testing will be done at least annually.
Violations of the rules will be dealt with as they occur.
Violations of the rules may result in being quietly dropped
from the circle of friends.
Now you know.

Blue
lying lizard-like
sweated, sand-caked
before that endless ebb
before that rising flow
on the cusp of blue oblivion

my ice-cold chrome-plated steel heart
bone muscle flesh
my blood roaring
eyes blind

so smooth sleek
gasping for breath
incandescent skin

slopes and angles
oblivious to all else
must, must have
him

Dec 15, 2006
Reprint: Interview: EvilEvilKitten1 Meows
Here's a few questions I threw at EvilEvilKitten1 , she was gracious enough to answer them and tell us about her interesting life!

Q: What are some of your hobbies?
A: I have far too many hobbies to mention them all but MEN ranks right up there!

Q: What sort of things have you written?
A: How To books with topics ranging from gardening to sex and two kid's books as well as books on financial topics.

Q: How did you loose your virginity?
A: This other teenager and I got together when I was 11 - mind you, when I was 11 I was 5'9" tall, weighed 150lbs, and had a 36" chest - pretty much what I am now. We did it twice. He said the first might not be so good but that I'd enjoy it from then on. He was quite correct! *EG*

Q: What was the best sex you ever had?

A: OMG! Let me think - there's been so many superb times! Each time is different you realize even if with the same person. No. It is just to difficult to choose which one time was best. Hey, its been 38 years of wild and wonderful sex! Impossible to choose!

Q: You have group sex, tell us about that lifestyle?

A: I'm not sure it is a 'lifestyle'. For me, for us, it is more of something we do like some people have dinner parties - we have sex parties. Group sex is heavy sensory input more than relationship development although you can make friends on the sheets just as well as you can over drinks. You can tell the difference between men since each has his own style of play. And that is how we regard group sex - as play between consenting adults. It does take some courage, however; you have to let go of any insecurities and prejudices you may have. Abandon your fears and leap on in - that sort of thing. There are a few variations but that is generally how group sex works.

Q: What does being polyandrous mean to you?

A: Have serious intimate relationships concurrently with more than one man. I do mean serious. Emotional ties very much in evidence. You can be formal with agreements and contracts, etc. or informal. You can all live together or not. I have a primary relationship and two secondary relationships. I am those secondaries' secondary since they have their own primary relationships as well. Interlocking intimate relationships in a network of mutual support and deep affection.

Q: Tell me about being a Dominatrix? What types of things do you do ?

A: I am a soft domme - no pain, no abuse, and no humiliation. I seduce alpha males into subtle sexual subjugation. This means that I direct and control. There are some trappings of bondage -collars and so forth but nothing beyond where he is willing to go. It is more about men accepting a passive role and being compliant than anything else.

Q: What do you think the other person gets out of it?
A: He gets three things out of it. First, he gets a vacation. He's not in charge. He's not responsible. He doesn't have to think, wonder, or worry. He gets to let go. Second, he gets all of my attention focused intently upon him. Since I am responsible for all outcomes, I am going to make sure that he has the time of his life. Finally, he learns about himself. Men spend so much of their time trying to get women into bed, trying to please women while they're in bed, and then trying to keep the women in the bed that they have no energy left to think about themselves. I explore his nuances with him. All he has to do is accept and let himself feel.

Q: Have you ever been harassed or stalked here?
A: Oh, yes. But I have my methods. One of which is publicly outing them. So if I say 'so and so' is a stalker - no I am NOT kidding nor am I making it up nor am I a 'woman scorned' or 'jealous'.

Q: What's the strangest offer you've gotten here?
A: LOL There have been a few. Since these are very individual, and your blog is widely read, no I am not going to say.

Q: Would you let yourself get into a long distance relationship?
A: There would be no point so no. Chat buddies excepted.

Q: What's the most number of men you've slept with in one day?
A: 15 men. There was this party.... It would have been more but two men could outrun me and did.

Q: What are some of the things that really piss you off ?
A: Men I have never met telling what I 'need' or 'want' or 'like'. Pain, abuse, and humiliation. Disrespect including implied insults.

Q: Have you ever played Mrs. Robinson to a virgin?
A: OMG NO!

Q: When's the last time you had sex?
A: Last night.

Q: Who all gets in your network?
A: People I like. People who need to know what I look like. I do delete some from time to time.

Q: Your profile says men only, are you sure you wont make one exception?
A: Sorry, but I remain MEN only! You bi-girls run off and leave your men to my tender mercies! *EG
(reprinted with permission)

I have written a few books this year. Here's the list of those available to the public.

Children's Books:
Nursery Tales for progressive children under 5 years of age
The Rogue's Handbook for progressive children from ages 5 to 13

General how-to books:
Financial Basics how to manage your money
Basic Gardening for the absolute beginner

Polo Tailgating (including recipes)
Introduction to Classical Music and a cd of the music on the Recommended Listening List

Professional Book:
Practice Management Procedures-2007 a professional manual covering how I run my practice

Mature Audience books:
Chat first year on the Internet
Sex Education for Laypersons just the facts
WOMEN a primer for men about their favorite subject
The Polyamorist for women about men
beguile the subtle art of sublime sexual subjugation of men
Wicked Woman a business idea - humor
Notes of a Dominatrix the basics for beginners

All are available for purchase.
Yes, I do get enough sleep, thank you *EG*

In 2007, I expect the following to become available.
Children's book:
Escape Velocity for progressive young adults aged 13 through 18

General books:
Designs & Scribbles art and beauty
National Air & Space Museum our collection of photographs thereof
Aunt Agatha's Answers covering a wide range of topics from the perspective of a wealthy British matron of a certain age - humor
Householding how to almost everything about a house

Mature Audience books:
Further Chat second year on the Internet

my ice-cold chrome-plated steel heart poetry & prose of an unfettered woman

Don't expect to see them in your local library...yet.
I still get enough sleep thank you *W*

BANNED!
"several of us are weary of your rudeness, sarcasm, condescension and braggadocio."
I assure you - all of my erotic posts are entirely true. So I do not see how 'braggadocio' enters into it.
Yes, I can be 'rude, sarcastic, and (I suppose) condescending' but since they are all subjective - well, just not the group for me.
I know of one other who was also banned from the same group - he wasn't upset - the group was boring - his word not mine. So I am in good company!

An Exercise in Eroticism for Men
RESULTS
First Place = J
Second Place = W
Third Place = w
J - I'll buy you a drink! When and where?

Dec 16, 2006
Attitude = halfway to bloodthirsty
You won't be hearing from me for a while as you all do not need to deal with it. It is bad enough that I must.
I'll be out vetting tomorrow and will honor those few commitments I already have for the coming week. After XMas I cannot say what I'll be doing - other than running over the odd puppy, putting my fist through plate glass windows as they make themselves available or spitting.
All souls brave enough to YIM or call - please.
(the above options refer to a previous post herein)

Dec 17, 2006
Why Men Like Playing with Alpha Kittens
other than she's fun....
1. If she says Yes to a first encounter - he is sooo getting laid.
2. If she says Yes to subsequent encounters - he must be DAMN good!
or am I missing something?

Dec 18, 2006
An Exercise in Eroticism for Men - Part Two
Describe precisely your reaction to the following passage using ONLY 5 words - and make it sing, baby! *EG*

"You are sweating with the effort needed to control yourself. You have to keep from cumming for as long as is possible. You have begun to pant as I continue to circle and caress you with hands, lips, tongue and claws. "Please fuck me." You are getting louder and more insistent. "Shhh, baby, shhh." I whisper back. You must learn to relax and enjoy the attention your mistress gives you. Learn to relish the agony of your desire. Feel the lust overwhelming your brain, flooding out all thoughts. You can smell my special perfume. It only adds to your frustration. You are almost weeping at being kept waiting for so very, very long. "Now." I quietly say as I take firm hold of your penis with my right hand and your testicles in my left."

May the best man win!

Now that I have acquired Slut 3, whose day is Monday, my Mondays are no longer blue - but rather OMG SO DAMN HOT!!! You would NOT believe how I rode that man tonight!!

210

Dec 19, 2006

For those 'just in case' opportunities:

Men -

They have things similar to cigarette cases that look good, are of metal and hold three condoms and several packets of lube and fit in one of your pockets.

Have one lady's bathrobe in your closet.

Several unopened toothbrushes, a hairbrush and comb, some 'for sensitive skin' unguent, and several ponytail ties in your bathroom.

and something decent to drink.

Women -

Slip a small bottle of lube into your purse.

Have one man's bathrobe in your closet.

Have a man's razor and shaving cream available. And those unopened toothbrushes.

and something decent to drink.

Just trying to be 'helpful'! Anyone wishing to add to this list?

Dec 20, 2006

Things I am Doing Wrong

Yes, you heard me w-r-o-n-g! Not merely incorrectly but out and out w-r-o-n-g. So I'll have to work on them and get it 'fixed' if 'fixed' is at all possible.

This weekend should provide me (us?) with the perfect opportunity.

Thanks to all who IM'd and helped this past week. I'd swear you want me to stay married! Trying to 'save yourselves' are you? Hmmmm. Perhaps I'm drawing too many inferences.

I'll let you all know how it goes.

Dec 21, 2006
-from The Economist a letter from Scott in Fairfax, VA

"The Dating Game

SIR- I found your article on the fashion for purity in America to be, well, quaint. As an evangelical Christian man who, in keeping with his religious convictions, has remained chaste before marriage into his 40's, my experience with women, including Christian women, has been that they care not one jot about pairing with a spouse who is chaste. In fact, I have had a few instances where a chaste woman actually preferred a fellow to have a resume', especially if he was a little older. It does not mean that an otherwise attractive buckaroo is taken out of the rodeo, but being chaste does not appear to move one from the runner-up category to the leader board. Christian guys go down in flames in the proverbial dating dogfight. Until women care about their partner being chaste and use it as a criterion to select a spouse the concept of chastity will remain drivel, fantasy, and wishful thinking."

As it should be? What do you say, ladies?
Opinions on a postcard, please!

The winner of An Exercise in Eroticism for Men - Part Two is......R!!
with P and J rounding out the field.
You guys did very well! Thank you for playing!
R gets to select his own prize.
Anyone care to guess what he'll pick?

Next Vetting
This Fri, Dec 22nd, at the Taj Palace on Lee Jackson Mem Hwy in Chantilly, VA aft 9pm.
EEK1 presiding.

Dec 22, 2006
Please join us in supporting the cause.
Today is Global Orgasm Day!!
However you do it - DO IT!!
WHEEEEEEEEEEEEEEEEEE!!!

Dec 25, 2006
Merry Christmas!!
May your stockings be filled with delights
and your heart love with the strength and wisdom of 10.

Dec 26, 2006
Year-End Clearance
1. Everything's fine, thank you. Relationships all continue well.
2. Yes, I have an ego. Amusingly enough, my manner is both lauded and deplored. It depends upon who you ask.
3. My time remains limited - call this week for an appointment next week and the 'Winter Schedule' is in effect until June of 2007, when the 'Summer Schedule" will take effect.
4. I do like to dance although I'm not terribly good at it. If it is a slow dance - you'd better have a firm grasp, steel-toed shoes, and for god's sake -lead.
5. I'm a rock-n-roll, heavy metal "chick" so if it doesn't have a back-beat and a high energy level, I'm probably am NOT going to be interested. "Slow dances" and classical music excepted.
6. If we're going to be engaged in sexual congress, the earlier the better. I do have time constraints so lets chat later; okay, baby?
7. I work/live/fuck like a speeding locomotive and I smoke like one too. Get over it or move on. Or give me something else to do. *W*

8. If you really don't want the answer, then don't ask the question. I might try to be tactful but ... sometimes it may not turn out that way.
9. From the masculine point of view, I am demanding, rapacious, and overwhelming.
10. Ladies: friends only.
Meow, meow people!

Dec 27, 2006
For those who cannot read my profile:
Me:
Tall, lithe, and elegant domme' who bewitches alpha males, and only alpha males, into becoming willing cat toys

as they succumb to their own desires.
My Ideal Person:
Those whom the gods love....who also bleed freely, heal quickly, and need not answer for marks left upon them.
Males must be at least 40 years of age, 6ft tall, furry, witty, able to withstand my ardor, kneeling, and nearby.
Please note that 3 somes and 4 somes are preferred.
If you do NOT meet the criteria - ALL of them - for one-on-one as written above - do NOT call me.
He MUST like cats!!
Thank you.

The Metaphysics of Sexuality
"Our moral evaluations of sexual activity are bound to be affected by what we view the nature of the sexual impulse, or of sexual desire, to be in human beings. In this regard there is a deep divide between those philosophers that we might call the metaphysical sexual optimists and those we might call the metaphysical sexual pessimists.

The pessimists in the philosophy of sexuality, such as St. Augustine , Immanuel Kant, and, sometimes, Sigmund

Freud , perceive the sexual impulse and acting on it to be something nearly always, if not necessarily, unbefitting the dignity of the human person; they see the essence and the results of the drive to be incompatible with more significant and lofty goals and aspirations of human existence; they fear that the power and demands of the sexual impulse make it a danger to harmonious civilized life; and they find in sexuality a severe threat not only to our proper relations with, and our moral treatment of, other persons, but also equally a threat to our own humanity.

On the other side of the divide are the metaphysical sexual optimists (Plato, in some of his works, sometimes Sigmund Freud, Bertrand Russell, and many contemporary philosophers) who perceive nothing especially obnoxious in the sexual impulse. They view human sexuality as just another and mostly innocuous dimension of our existence as embodied or animal-like creatures; they judge that sexuality, which in some measure has been given to us by evolution, cannot but be conducive to our well-being without detracting from our intellectual propensities; and they praise rather than fear the power of an impulse that can lift us to various high forms of happiness.

The particular sort of metaphysics of sex one believes will influence one's subsequent judgments about the value and role of sexuality in the good or virtuous life and about what sexual activities are morally wrong and which ones are morally permissible." by Alan Soble, ed.

I am one of the metaphysical sexual optimists. But I also feel that there is more to it than just that. Contrary to what may be popular belief, WHO he is matters much more than almost anything else since sex begins in the mind.

Tell the truth now; which are you, baby? Pessimist or optimist?

Dec 28, 2006
Step Into My Dungeon
Some people have expressed some concern for their safety - but really - you should have known that my dungeon would not be like anything you ever imagined.

Friend's Dilemma
I gave her a copy of Chat for Christmas and she called me up today to ask "How much of that is true or is it just 'chatter'? LOL well, actually........I'll just leave that up to you to decide. *W*

Dec 29, 2006
Trying on Dresses
First: the bath! Sliding into a tub of steaming hot water; scrubbing all over with rose scented soap using a mild
skin brush; rinsing off then rising toward a nice big fluffy towel.
Then Dress 1: a strapless black sheath of something taffeta-like - perhaps a trifle too big in the bodice?
Then Dress 2: the one with the opera neckline with the shirring on the sides made from black jersey knit - fits like a glove!
Then Dress 3: the black sweater dress with the v-neck - a trifle loose. Might be too large but it is warm!
Hung them all up, put them back into my closet and put on blue jeans and a white long sleeved t-shirt - and I'm running about in my bare feet!
Sorry, guys but you missed the glamour show!

Dec 30, 2006
The tree, the lights, the ornaments - time to put it all away in preparation for the new year to come!

It isn't all sadness however. The year did have its "up" moments *W* after all. As you prepare your resolutions and map out your plans - look forward with courage and delight like this frisky little alpha kitten!
What are you looking forward to this coming year?

Dec 31, 2006
We all begin with good intentions but..well, you know what happens. So have a plan and live you plan is all I can recommend! We will all try it this coming year!

EEK's Resolutions for 2007
1. be nicer to my husband
2. *****
3. @@@@@
4. #####
5. increase savings
6. $$$$$
7. no tickets at all
8. finish coursework
9. %%%%%
10. keep all of my current men happily by my side
(Resolutions edited for your safety)
What have you resolved to accomplish this New Year, Sweeties??

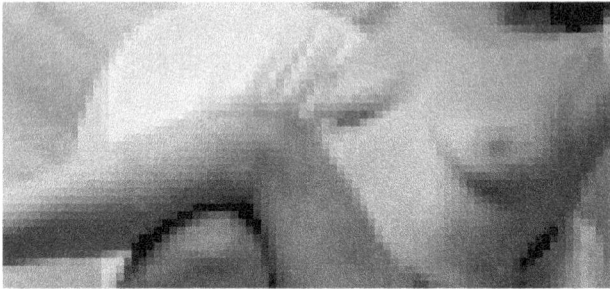

2007

JANUARY
2007

Jan 1, 2007

HAPPY NEW YEAR!!!!

Jan 2, 2007
The January Blues: except that it is nice outside! WTF? 60 some odd degrees in Jan? HEY! I'll take it! Trust me - this beats slogging through sub-artic blizzard conditions (been there, done that)! Nothing so erodes the joy out of life more than freezing!
Therefore-
Anyone wanna hot tub it? I have some champers left!
Do you like winter? Have you this thing for snow?

Who gets offended and why?
"People who are hypersensitive"
Hypersensitive people have been around forever, but their numbers have increased in the wake of political correctness. They get offended because they see life as having a certain set of rules. For example, knock-knock jokes are fine, but jokes about women's knockers are out. It's not that the joke or topic offends them; it's just that they play by the rules, while other persons get away with saying what they think. And then there are those who just have this thing against women like me.

"People who think all comments are targeted at them."
You know them; they're egomaniacs. It's one thing to be a little neurotic, but it's something else entirely to think that the world revolves around you. Most of the time, these people get offended about comments that couldn't possibly be directed at them, but because they think the whole world is talking about them all the time, they believe every comment must be about them.

"People who don't read properly."
I'll only say this once: You've got to read the whole post. If you don't read all of it, don't complain. But take that extra step to understand what you've read. That way, you won't fly off the handle without justification. If the post is unclear - ask!"

What do they get offended about?

"Everything and nothing."
You name it, it will offend someone. With my luck, I'll be at a party complaining about traffic (a topic you'd think most people could agree on), only to find I'm talking to the one guy who works for the department of transportation. Does he say: "Yes, traffic is bad, we're working on it," or just laugh along with the others? No. He goes off on me for two hours about how I don't understand the complexity of the problem.

"Personal reasons."
Let's face it: I can't know everything about you. If I had known that your sister lost her eye opening a champagne bottle, I probably wouldn't have made that joke. But I didn't know. There's always some guy out there who becomes outraged for personal reasons (even when your comments couldn't possibly be construed as malicious) or who gets upset for someone else (even when the other person isn't personally offended).

"Touchy topics."
Sex, relationships, racism, religion, death, and politics are all serious topics, and they're all guaranteed one-way tickets to offending someone, and that's too bad. We should be able to talk about these things, but the people who are easily offended when someone offers a different point of view stifle the conversation. And for the record, teasing

someone about losing a relative is mean, but making a joke about death isn't taboo because, let's face it, it happens to everyone."

I'd advise: Take it easy.

"Don't jump the gun."
You might have guessed by now that I've offended more than my share of people. But I'll tell you what almost never happens: I seldom get to finish my thought. My advice to those who are busy drafting their angry responses while reading this is to chill. Take a second and ask yourself if perhaps you're being a little too sensitive, and therefore missing the point.

"Find a middle ground to react."
Disagreeing with someone is par for the course in life. But telling another person what she/he can and cannot say goes too far. If you disagree, wait for her/him to finish and then react logically and sensibly to her/his ideas. Don't just bark out your own notions of what people should and shouldn't say.

"Read things in context."
Remember that not everything that is written or said is directed specifically at you; it's usually for the public at large. Everything happens within a context, even your reaction. It's the context that shapes the meaning of a statement. So consider, among other things, who the statement was directed at, what came before it and the speaker's perspective.

"Have a sense of humor about it."
Humor can diffuse most situations - the 'class clown' rarely gets beaten up. But even so: those who can quickly exercise

some wit can have the whole audience rolling - and the awkward moment passes.

"Ignore it."
If all else fails, it sometimes pays to simply ignore the comment. Life is too short to argue with everyone over every little thing. You've got better things to do... I hope. My advice is to try to let things slide. If they're really so bad, don't lend them credibility by talking about them."

I generally opt between the last two: laugh or ignore.
Got any other ideas on how to handle this?

Jan 3, 2007
If you really want to know, you'll have to ask me. Quizzing others will not do you any good. But before you do that, consider:
1. do you really NEED to know?
2. is it any of your business?
3. do you want the TRUTH?
4. what are you going to do with the answer?
You see, I may decide to be tactful but then again, I may not. So if you cannot handle the blunt, trenchant truth perhaps you shouldn't ask the question.
Fair Warning!
So what did you want to know, baby?

Yesterday
If wishes were granted,
we'd sleep side by side.

"This week's Business Week features Margaret McGlynn, President of Merck Vaccines, a woman clearly on track with many of her goals. Having joined the company out of college in 1981, McGlynn, 47, could easily emerge as Merck's CEO in the future, having been refreshingly sited

223

by one boss as having "an ability to argue her case in a relentlessly logical and wonderfully intense way." Among other things, she is focused on the launch of Gardasil for females aged 9 to 26, "hailed as a breakthrough because it prevents some forms of human papilloma virus (HPV), a leading cause of cervical cancer." All of us know someone, a sister, friend, colleague who has been diagnosed with and potentially died due to cervical cancer. "Merck has been lobbying state legislators to mandate the vaccine for all young girls." "

As a HPV survivor, I have encouraged my daughter to get this vaccination as soon as possible and I hope all parents of daughters between ages 9 and 26 will do the same!

Note:
Please do not bruise the male. Return in good condition. I promise to do the same. Thank you.
EG
Do you promise?

Jan 4, 2007
Before she erases it since I sincerely doubt she will post it.
"I'm on the sidelines and so get to hear all sides of this drama. Interesting how people's perceptions of the same events differ. It is unfortunate that you felt the need to insert one particular line in your story. Goodbye."
People, keep me out of your little dramas. I hear all about them, but really, this isn't high school. If it doesn't work out, it doesn't work out. Move on with some grace.

Risk vs Reward
This stock market concept also applies to relationships albeit in a somewhat skewed fashion.
Each person has their own personal 'balance sheet' of assets and liabilities. If your liabilities - such as being an axe murderer - outweigh your assets - you're cute - then there's

too much risk for too little reward and that relationship isn't going to happen. Usually. One always has to make allowances for human perversity.

You do not have to quantify each item. This is not accountancy. But as in the example above, you can make reasonable judgments of the relative worth of each item.

Just let me finish adding up here.......carry the one.....Oookay.

Oh how nice! I am happy to announce that I'm below the curve meaning that the rewards out weight the risks. (As long as I'm not driving a moving vehicle in such a way that I attract the attention of the police.)

So tell me true - are you a 'good value' or are you not?

Being 'Picky'

I do not agree that not meeting people (men) means that you are 'picky'. Why? Because until you actually come out from behind your computer and go and meet someone, you do NOT know them at all. Profiles and blogs and chat and emails - they all are just electrons through the wires - without substance. But meeting - ah! there's no place to hide then. The chemistry happens or it doesn't. No harm, no foul. And you have another business card to add to your collection!

Time may be misspent but it is never wasted so meeting people is never a waste of time. Human interaction, if civil, has a value even if that value isn't immediately apparent. Besides - its just lunch.

Therefore: come out, come out from wherever you are!

Jan 5, 2007

How to Break-up

Move your things out. Firmly and calmly meet in person and say goodbye. Endure the emotions, if there are any. Do not hesitate. Do not apologize. Do not give out any sops of 'kindness'. Then leave. Do not look back. From that point

on - nothing. You are both free to do whatever with whomever. Take a deep breath and move on.
Adults do not air their dirty laundry in public.
This is a public service announcement.
My relationships remain happy and whole, ty.

Be careful what you say in your emails to me, guys.
"Are you brave enough to meet your final destiny? EEK...you may seem like a tigress to others, but you know you will be a kitten under my touch...William"
"Even your autoresponse is wimpy. Bow down before your new master and honor hin. W"   (his spellings)
Oh really? Since when does a true alpha male need to strut and posture in such a way?
Go and attempt to annoy some other woman.

Jan 6, 2007
If money were no object and the police would look the other way - no your other other way - that's it - that way- over there!
Murcie'lago LP640 Roadster
Now if only it could out-run radar!

My next house will be my dream house, if all goes according to Plan A.
Plan B is to sleep in my car, on a back road, over the next hill, by the second tree on the left.

Loud and good rock n roll both modern and old from top of the line artists. Good single malt scotch. Smoking. Big dance floors. Lots of happy D/D-free happy people who are ready to have a good time. Comfortable seating that doesn't require 6 people to move out the way so you can get out. Reasonably muted lighting. No televisions. No food. Don't care what you wear. Open 24 hrs.
Know you of such a place??

226

Or one that comes close?

I have yet to hear of a coherent reason why couples tend to go with FMF's rather than the much easier to arrange MFM's. Given the female capacity for multiple orgasms and greater sexual stamina one would have supposed that MFM's would be preferred. Logistically if nothing else. Usually the woman comes up with something on the order of 'one dick is enough' - which isn't true, really - see dildo sales figures. So if it isn't the penis - it must be something else.
Just wondering. *EG*

"Evil Angel"
For to see my depth of sorrow
You are not allowed to follow me
Into this town square
And then run away

Evil angel with your cleft tongue
When you kissed me
On this town square
All the lights came on at sunset
Thought you'd stay

Evil angel bearing apples
When you kissed me
On this drawbridge
As the boats do
How was I to know you'd flee

Tear down these monuments
Bury the coat of arms
And build for me a factory

Evil angel when you're faced with hatred's

Daggers in my honor
You're no match no scratching hearts that no longer bleed

Oh Evil angel tear down the monuments
Evil angel Bury the coat of arms
And rebuild for me these memories
For to see my depth of sorrow

- Rufus Wainwright

Jan 7, 2007
Global Feminism
It is an interesting dilemma. The Islamic male's honor is bound up with the 'virtue' of all the females in his extended family. Thus, he seeks to control these females to ensure his honor, his 'face'. It really is impossible to completely control another person. Thus he feels insecure. To assuage these feelings and to increase his control, he represses these females - dress this way, do this, don't do that, 'virginity exams', 'honor killings' and the holding over his wife's head that he can ditch her and their kids at any time and take another wife at any time - up to a total of four. He can also divorce her merely by saying so. He can rape the maid, be a sexual predator and so on and she can do nothing to stop him lest she and her kids be cast into poverty and the grey area of being a divorce wife and mother living on the bounty of her birth family. Yes, I understand that The Quaran may say otherwise. Yes, I understand and admire the past glories of your cultures. But those glories are past and it is time to 'step up' and 'face up' to the ills of your world and cultures. It is true that the West shares some of those ills. But blaming others is not acceptable unless you are also willing to bear the burden of your own guilt. You are not children. The fears and insecurities of your culture are holding you back. It is time to change. The essence of life is to move forward. Therefore: rise up and walk!

"Hundreds, if not thousands, of women are murdered by their families each year in the name of family "honor." It's difficult to get precise numbers on the phenomenon of honor killing; the murders frequently go unreported, the perpetrators unpunished, and the concept of family honor justifies the act in the eyes of some societies.

Most honor killings occur in countries where the concept of women as a vessel of the family reputation predominates, said Marsha Freemen, director of International Women's Rights Action Watch at the Hubert Humphrey Institute of Public Affairs at the University of Minnesota.

Reports submitted to the United Nations Commission on Human Rights show that honor killings have occurred in Bangladesh, Great Britain, Brazil, Ecuador, Egypt, India, Israel, Italy, Jordan, Pakistan, Morocco, Sweden, Turkey, and Uganda. In countries not submitting reports to the UN, the practice was condoned under the rule of the fundamentalist Taliban government in Afghanistan, and has been reported in Iraq and Iran.

But while honor killings have elicited considerable attention and outrage, human rights activists argue that they should be regarded as part of a much larger problem of violence against women."

-Hillary Mayell
for National Geographic News
February 12, 2002

Warning Signs of an Abusive Personality
It is sometimes possible to predict the likelihood of the person you are currently or are about to become involved with being abusive. Below are a list of behaviors and traits which are common in abusive personalities. These are commonly known as Warning Signs.

While not all abusive people show the same signs, or display the tendencies to the same extent, if several behavioral traits are present, there is a strong tendency toward abusiveness. Generally, the more signs are present, the greater the likelihood of violence. In some cases, an abuser may have only a couple of behavioural traits that can be recognized, but they are very exaggerated (e.g. extreme jealousy over ridiculous things).

Often the abuser will initially try to explain his/her behaviour as signs of his/her love and concern, and the victim may be flattered at first; as time goes on, the behaviours become more severe and serve to dominate, control and manipulate the victim.

Jealousy
At the beginning of a relationship, an abuser will always say the jealousy is a sign of love. He/she may question you about whom you have spoken to or seen during the day, may accuse you of flirting, or be jealous of time you spend with family, friends, children or hobbies which do not include him/her. As the jealousy progresses, he/she may call you frequently during the day or drop by unexpectedly. He may be unhappy about or refuse to let you work for fear you'll meet someone else, check the car mileage or ask friends to keep an eye on you. Jealousy is not proof of love, it is a sign of insecurity and possessiveness.

Controlling Behaviour
Controlling behaviour is often disguised or excused as concern. Concern for your safety, your emotional or mental health, the need to use your time well, or to make sensible decisions. Your abuser may be angry or upset if you are 'late' coming back from work, shopping, visiting friends, etc., even if you told him/her you would be later back than usual. Your abuser may question you closely about where

you were, whom you spoke to, the content of every conversation you held, or why you did something he/she was not involved in. As this behaviour gets worse, you may not be allowed to make personal decisions about the house, clothing, going to church or how you spend your time or money or even make you ask for permission to leave the house or room. Alternately, he/she may theoretically allow you your own decisions, but penalize you for making the wrong ones. Concern for our loved ones to a certain extent is normal - trying to control their every move is not.

Quick Involvement
Many victims of abuse dated or knew their abuser for less than six months before they were engaged or living together. The abuser will often claim 'love at first sight', that you are 'made for each other', or that you are the only person whom he could ever talk to so openly, feel so at home with, could understand him so well. He/she may tell you that they have never loved anyone so much or felt so loved by anyone so much before, when you have really only known each other for a short amount of time. He/she needs someone desperately, and will pressure you to commit to him/her or make love before you feel the relationship has reached 'that stage'. He/she may also make you feel guilty for not committing yourself to him/her.

Unrealistic Expectations
The abuser may expect you to be the perfect husband, wife, mother, father, lover, and friend. He/she is very dependent on you for all his/her needs, and may tell you he/she can fulfill all your needs as lover, friend, and companion. Statements such as: 'lf you love me, I'm all you need.', 'You are all I need.' are common. Your abuser may expect you to provide everything for him/her emotionally, practically, financially or spiritually, and then blame you for not being perfect or living up to expectation.

Isolation
The abuser may try to curtail your social interaction. He/she may prevent you from spending time with your friends or family and demand that you only go places 'together'. He/she may accuse you of being 'tied to your mother's apron strings', not be committed to the relationship, or view people who are your personal friends as 'causing trouble' or 'trying to put a wedge' between you. He/she may want to live in the country without a phone, not let you use the car, stop you from working or gaining further education or qualifications.

Blame-shifting for Problems
Very rarely will an abusive personality accept responsibility for any negative situation or problem. If they are unemployed, can't hold down a job, were thrown out of college or University or fall out with their family, it is always someone else's fault, be it the boss, the government, or their mother. They may feel that someone is always doing them wrong, or out to get him. He/she may make a mistakes and then blame you for upsetting him/her or preventing him/her from doing as they wished to.

Blame-shifting for Feelings
The abuser will deny feelings stem from within him/her but see them as reactions to your behaviour or attitude toward him/her. He/she may tell you that 'you make me mad', 'you're hurting me by not doing what I ask', or that he/she cannot help feeling mad, upset, etc. Feelings may be used to manipulate you, i.e. 'I would not be angry if you didn't ...' Positive emotions will often also be seen as originating outside the abuser, but are more difficult to detect. Statements such as 'You make me happy' or 'You make me feel good about myself' are also signs that the abuser feels you are responsible for his sense of well-being. Either way,

you become in his/her mind the cause of good and bad feelings and are therefore responsible for his/her emotional well-being and happiness. Consequently, you are also to blame for any negative feelings such as anger, upset or depression.

Hypersensitivity
Most abusers have very low self-esteem and are therefore easily insulted or upset. They may claim their feelings are 'hurt' when they are really angry, or take unrelated comments as personal attacks. They may perceive normal set-backs (having to work additional hours, being asked to help out, receiving a parking fine, etc.) as grave personal injustices. They may view your preference for something which differs from their own as a criticism of their taste and therefore themselves (e.g. blue wallpaper rather than pink, etc.).

Cruelty to Animals
The abuser may punish Animals brutally, be insensitive to their pain or suffering, or neglect to care for the Animals to the point of cruelty, e.g. not feeding them all day, leaving them in areas he/she knows will cause them suffering or distress. There is a strong correlation between cruelty to Animals and domestic violence which is still being researched.

Cruelty to Children
The abusers unrealistic expectations of their partner are often mirrored in their attitude toward children. He/she will think of children as 'small adults' and blame the children for not being responsible, having common sense or understanding. He/she may expect children to be capable far beyond their ability (e.g. is angry with a two-year old for wetting their pants or being sick on the carpet, waking at night or being upset by nightmares) and will often meet

233

out punishments for 'naughtiness' the child could not be aware of. Abusers may tease children until they cry, or punish children way beyond what could be deemed appropriate. He/she may not want children to eat at the table, expect them to stay quiet, or keep to their room all evening while he/she is at home. Since abusers want all your attention themselves, they resent your spending time with the children or any normal demands and needs the children may have. As above (cruelty to Animals), there is a very strong link between Domestic Violence and Child Abuse.

'Playful' use of Force in Sex
He/she may pressure you to agree to forceful or violent acts during sex, or want to act out fantasies where you are helpless. A male abuser may let you know that the idea of "rape" excites him. He/she may show little concern about whether you want to have intercourse and uses sulking or anger to manipulate you into compliance. Starting sex while you are sleeping, demanding sex when you are ill or tired, or refusing any form of intimacy unless you are willing to go 'all the way' can all be signs that he/she could be sexually abusive or sexually violent. Forcing you into sexual behaviors and situations with which you may be uncomfortable.

Rigid Sex Roles
Abusers usually believe in stereotypical gender roles. A man may expect a woman to serve him; stay at home, obey him in all things---even things that are criminal in nature. A male abuser will often see women as inferior to men, more stupid, unable to be a whole person without a relationship. Female abusers may expect the man to provide for them entirely, shift the responsibility for her well-being onto him or heckle him as being 'not a real man' if he shows any weakness or emotion.

Verbal Abuse
In addition to saying things that are meant to be cruel and hurtful, either in public or in private, this can include degrading remarks or running down any accomplishments. Often the abuser will tell you that you are 'stupid', could not manage without him/her. He/she may keep you up all night to 'sort this out once and for all' or even wake you at night to continue to verbally abuse you. The abuser may even say kindly things to your face, but speak badly about you to friends and family.

Dr. Jekyll and Mr. Hyde
Very rarely do abusers conform to the stereotypical image of a constantly harsh, nasty or violent person, either in public or in private. More frequently the abuser portrays a perfectly normal and pleasant picture to the outside world (often they have responsible jobs or are respected and important members of the local community or Church) and reserves the abuse for you in the privacy of your own home. Nor are abusers always overtly abusive or cruel, but can display apparent kindness and consideration. This Jekyll and Hyde tendency of the abuser serves to further confuse the victim, while protecting themselves from any form of suspicion from outsiders. Many victims describe "sudden" changes in mood - one minute nice and the next explosive or hysterical, or one minute happy and the next minute sad. This does not indicate some special "mental problem" but are typical of abusive personalities, and related to other characteristics such as hypersensitivity.

Drink or Substance Abuse
While neither drinking or the use of drugs are signs of an abusive personality, heavy drinking or drug abuse may be a warning sign and do increase the risks of abuse, especially violence, taking place. Often an abusive person will blame

the drink for his/her abuse. However, a person who, knowing there is a risk he/she could be violent when drinking or on drugs, chooses to get drunk or high, is in effect choosing to abuse. The link between substance abuse and domestic abuse is still being researched, and it is apparent that while neither alcohol nor drugs necessarily cause violence, they do increase the risk of violence.

History of Battering or Sexual Violence
Very rarely is abuse or violence a one-off event: a batterer will beat any woman he is with; a sexually abusive person will be abusive toward all his intimate partners. Situational circumstances do not make a person an abusive personality. Sometimes friends or family may try to warn you about the abuser. Sometimes the abuser may tell you himself/herself that he/she has hit or sexually assaulted someone in the past. However, they may further go on to explain that "she made me do it by ..." or in some other way not take responsibility and shift the blame on to the victim. They may tell you that it won't happen with you because "you love them enough to prevent it" or "you won't be stupid enough to wind me up that much". Once again, this is denying their own responsibility for the abuse, and shifting the responsibility for the relationship to remain abuse-free on to you. Past violence is one of the strongest pointers that abuse will occur.

Threatening Violence
This would obviously include any threat of physical force such as "If you speak to him/her again, I'll kill you", or "If any wife of mine acted like John's did, I'd give her a right seeing to". But can also include less obvious threats, such as "If you leave me, I will kill myself". Threats are designed to manipulate and control you, to keep you in your place and prevent you making your own decisions. Most people do not threaten their mates, but an abuser will

excuse this behaviour by saying "everybody talks like that.", maintaining he/she is only saying this because the relationship or you are so important to him/her, tell you you're "over-sensitive" for being upset by such threats, or obviously want to hurt him/her.

Breaking or Striking Objects
The abusive person may break your treasured object, beat his/her fists on the table or chair or throw something at or past you. Breaking your things is often used as a punishment for some imagined misdeed on your part. Sometimes it will be justified by saying that now that you are with him/her, you don't need these items any more. Breaking your possessions also has the effect of de-personalizing you, denying you your individuality or literally trying to break links to your past. Beating items of furniture or throwing objects will often be justified by saying you wound him/her up so much they lost control, once again shifting the blame for this behaviour on to you, but is actually used to terrorize you into submission. Only very immature or abusive people beat on objects in the presence of other people in order to threaten or intimidate them.

Any Force during an Argument
An abuser may physically restrain you from leaving the room, lash out at you with his/her hand or another object, pin you against a wall or shout 'right in your face'. Basically any form of force used during an argument can be a sign that actual violence is a strong possibility.

Regardless of which side of this equation you are on - get immediate help NOW!

Jan 8, 2007
John Kay

Steppenwolf leader/founder John Kay is perhaps the most overlooked early contributor to the musical style that would become heavy metal and hard rock. Kay was the first rocker to use the phrase heavy metal in a song, in one of metal's first great anthems: Steppenwolf's 1968 classic "Born to Be Wild." Born Joachim Fritz Krauledat on April 12, 1944, in the section of Germany that was once known as East Prussia, it was the American rock & roll that he heard on U.S. Armed Forces radio after his family moved to East Germany that fueled his interest in music. After "relocating" to Toronto, Canada, in 1958, Kay became even more transfixed by rock & roll -- leading to Kay picking up the guitar, writing songs, and playing in local bands.
One of his best songs was "The Wall" about his trip to the west as a child.

"The Wall"
Crossing the line in the dead of night
Five years old and on the run
This ain't no game, boy, don't make a sound
And watch that man with the gun
Say a prayer for the ones we leave behind, say a prayer for us all
Come take my hand now and hold on tight
Take one last look at that wall

Think of the shattered lives, think of the broken hearts
Think of the battered dreams, of families still torn apart
Wall of bitter tears, wall of crying pain
Wall of chilling fear, you will never keep me here
For I, I shall crawl right down through that wall
I will crawl right on through that wall

That fateful night I was one that got away,
A young and restless renegade
Chasing my dreams, still on the run,

I had some moments in the sun
Years flew by like a speeding bullet train, I sang my songs
to one and all
Then came the day when I had a chance to pay
My respects to the names on that wall

I saw the wooden crosses, saw the bloody stains
Saw the gruesome pictures of all the ones that died in vain
Wall of countless victims, wall of endless shame
Had just one thing gone wrong I might have joined that list
of names
And I cried for all who died there at the wall
I recall weeping at the wall

"Freedom has many difficulties, and democracy
is not perfect,
But we've never had to put a wall up to keep
our people in...
While the wall is the most obvious
demonstration of the failures of the communist system,
We take no pride in it...for it is an offense
against humanity, separating families,
Dividing husbands and wives, brothers and
sisters and dividing a
People who wish to be joined together...
All free men, wherever they may live, are
citizens of Berlin
And therefore, as a free man I take pride in the
words "Ich bin ein Berliner".

(Excerpts from John F. Kennedy speech at the Berlin wall
June 26, 1963)

Turned on the news in November '89
I could not move, I could not speak
Something was burning up in my eyes,

Something wet ran down my cheek
All those laughing faces, all those tears of joy
All those warm embraces of men and women, girls and boys
(cheering crowd sounds)
Sisters and brothers dancing, all singing freedom's song
God, if only I could be there to shake your hands and sing along
Oh I, I would climb right up on that wall
And join you all dancing on the wall
Standing tall walking on the wall
(sound of pickaxes)
Tear it down, right down to the ground
Tear it down, right down to the ground
- John Kay

The Berlin Wall was heavily guarded and around hundred people were killed and many more were seriously wounded trying to cross the wall. The last person to be killed was Chris Gueffroy on the 2nd June, 1989.

The picture shows the final incarnation of the Wall with both the West Berlin side of the Wall and the Death Strip on the East Berlin side of the Wall. The Wall surrounded the entire city of East Berlin. Berlin itself was in central East Germany.

And a Bit of Silly Drama
"You still don't get it dude, I flattered you!!!"

"I think I'll leave my other post on a few more days. There are a couple comment posts I did not approve. They were offensive and/or hostile, when I never offended the posters."

It isn't for you to say whether or not you offended anyone - that is up to them. All you can say is whether or not you MEANT to insult/offend others.

"I doubt you'll find many neutral people who read that quite long blog post, and essentially conclude there was disrespect to you."
Also not the point. Whether other people recognised it or not - I concluded that there was disrespect shown to me; one who has had nothing to do with you prior to this drama of yours.

"You keep begging for attention, when I have so much else on my mind."
So I am to respect your 'feelings' and your time when you do not respect mine? No. Life doesn't work that way. All you had to do was go back in and edit out the offending line. A lady would have.

"Judging from your opinion, yes, the blog was unnecessary. I don't care about your opinion. It is merely one opinion, you know. Not that it coming from EEK makes it anything more.
Judging from dozens of people, the blog was either relevant, important, and/or an excellent read, oh, and dignified too. I get it in chat. I get it in private."
You get disapprobation in chat, on your blog, and in private too. But since those opinions are not 'flattering' you just discount them.

"EEK, you are so dying to be in this story and all your comments, which are not posted, have to do with this marginal line.
You don't tolerate disrespect, so what are going to do about it? That is assuming this was disrespect.

I write well. That was the description I chose of S. By the way, again, it's not about you, and hardly him. Few people recognized who he was, or paid attention to that one line."
"Marginal, check out dictionary definition, has a role and is not redundant nor unnecessary.
I was describing each character, setting a mood.
I have been printed in the NY Times and have authored three books.
I am not posting any of your comments anymore. And, obviously, I will not be responding either.
You are self-centered. I never heard anything about the whole story. You could have at least taken sides against me. But you sure make a good pimp and love your toys. How's that for disrespect?"
You disrespect yourself by the above comments. I deliberately did not take sides against you in your drama and still don't. That is your business. But this small part of it you chose, and continue to choose, to make my business. As for being an author - to whom do you imagine you're speaking?

As for being 'self-centered', pray tell, based upon the following quotes, what are you?

"The whole thing came about, by the way, because it was the only avenue left to me to speak, whether to say good bye or good luck or thanks or sorry or whatever more, which I had a natural right to, at least once."

and

"I'm pretty, witty, sophisticated, and H/W proportionate. I am told that I have beautiful eyes, a kissable mouth, nice legs, and a presence. I am a nice 36 C/D (very sensitive there). I would enjoy the sex better with some sort of non-physical rapport. I enjoy most types of music but particularly classic and alternative rock. I like reading literary fiction, the New York Times. I am a swimmer, a dancer, go to the gym, and practice yoga. And last but not least, I am sensuous and uninhibited, but only when I choose to be. I don't enjoy time with uneducated people, boorish people, fat, ugly, ungroomed people, or right-wingers."

also

"I am one of the best looking women among the Nova people who go to M&Gs, the others work behind the scenes through email mostly. I don't mind saying it and looking immodest. It is a reality that has been proven to me."

Even the title of this post, taken from more of your writings, indicates a self-centeredness bordering on the pathological. Since your sense of etiquette is faulty, I shall explain. If you find you have even perhaps inadvertently offended someone - just to establish a mood for your story- you apologize and remove the offending sentence and rewrite as necessary to re-establish the mood if that is even required.
As to what I intend do about it. Just this. Thank you for confirming your opposition's opinion of you.

Jan 9, 2007
Emotional Intelligence
"Simply stated, emotional intelligence is your ability to perceive your emotions, clearly identify them, understand them, control them, and use them to assist thought. It's the ability to stay focused when confronted with emotions and remain in control. It's understanding the role your feelings play in your daily life and how you deal with others.

Answer yes or no, as honestly as you can, to the short quiz below:

1.Can you clearly express your feelings with the three-word sentence "I feel..."?
2.a Can you differentiate various feelings?
2b. Can you identify why you feel the way you do?
3.Do you respect and accept yourself the way you are?
4.Do others know you have a good sense of self?
5. Are you living up to your potential?
6. Do you feel satisfied with your accomplishments?
7. Are you able to let go of regrets and grudges?
8. Do you feel in control and consistent in the way you act?
9. Are you emotionally independent from others?"

Unlike IQ, EQ can be significantly raised. But it takes effort and a great deal of introspection. You need to be willing to rewire your brain and how you perceive and react to situations.

Here's a rough beginner's guide to becoming emotionally savvy.

1- Identify your feelings
Constantly tell yourself how you feel, with the three-word sentence "I feel..." If you feel mixed emotions, try to single them out, and rate their intensity ("I feel disturbed" or "I feel enraged"). Don't exaggerate or minimize them.

2- Take responsibility for your feelings
Don't look for external explanations for how you feel or make yourself the victim. Recognize that they're your feelings and try to understand why you feel this way.

3- Anticipate your feelings

Learn to recognize how you will feel after a certain event or action. Avoid doing things that you know will inspire negative feelings. Do this not only for yourself, but for others.

4- Ask people how they feel
You want to be able to tell how people feel without asking them. However, you have to first understand them before you can empathize with them. Listen to them without making judgments. Don't try to dismiss or invalidate their feelings.

5- Be less defensive
If someone says something about you that you disagree with, don't get defensive or attack them -- these kinds of reactions demonstrate that you can't handle criticism. Instead, thank them for their honesty and focus on the validity of their comments.

6- Put problems into perspective
When setbacks happen and you feel the urge to get angry, think about how serious the setback really is. How much will the issue matter in 10 years? In 10 weeks? In 10 minutes?

While having a good handle on your emotions is a great tool for success, in the end, it's just another way in which you can improve yourself. People are quirky and unpredictable by nature, so having a complete mastery of your feelings may not be possible. But that doesn't mean you shouldn't try."

Not bad advice, but after we've been through this and that self-improvement program, we tend to being a bit skeptical. Try it and see what you make of this, is all I can say.

Question:
Is one's importance intrinsic or does it only come from our interpersonal relationships or our 'good works'?

Jan 10, 2007
It is The Passion for Life!
Either you have it in your blood, or you don't. The boundless joy of life that though it may ebb and flow nothing can quench! Akin to enthusiasm - from the Greek *en theos* - "the god within", fortunate are those for whom life is a Grand Adventure. Exuberance!

Jan 11, 2007
"You appear in the Friends Network for (handle omitted). This man is married and his wife will be using his profile in her divorce proceedings against him. If you do not wish to be named in this lawsuit, please remove him from your Network."
Oh how nice! So although I have never actually met the man, she's going to use me as a weapon against her erring husband. (BTW I did report this as abuse.) Such a sweet lady.

Jan 12, 2007
How to Buy a House
You should always try to 'underbuy' when it comes to housing. This doesn't mean getting less than what you need but getting what you need for less than you can afford so you can still eat.
1. Take 1/3rd of your monthly net income as the maximum you can spend on your housing.
example: take home is $3,000 net per month so $1,000 per month is all you should be paying for ALL of your housing costs - this includes utilities, HOA fees, insurance and so on.

2. See the banks, etc., and compare the terms to make sure that you stay well under your maximum figure as found in step 1 above. The banks will usually say you can afford some outrageous amount - do not believe them.
3. Keep your realtor to this figure as well when hunting since he/she will try to use the bank's figures instead of yours.
4. Negotiate with the seller through the realtor.
5. Buy the house.
If there's any fixing to be done - try to do it before you move in. This may not be possible but try to anyway as working while trying to unpack and continue being gainfully employed is a hassle.

Jan 13, 2007
What do Men Want?
Men want pretty much the same things women want. Their priorities differ a bit but generally the same things you want are what they want. They basically want someone to give a damn about them. They like to be appreciated for what they do and for who they are. They want to have your respect. They care if you like them or not. They would really like it if you loved them. Try this now. Just go up to your man and give him a big hug while saying something like "Love you, baby." That wasn't so hard was it? Of course it works better if you and he do still love each other. If you have filed for divorce, or he has, it is too late and it is just best to move on.

Jan 14, 2007
Someone Asked Today
what my latest testimonial referred to. Well, if you want to know my techniques - ------------------- I'm not going to give them away. Lets just say that my sexual aim is to explode a man's mind by giving him abso-fucking-lutely incredible orgasms again and again and again and..........

247

Kitten's Dream Date:
Cunnilingus then male superior coitus, fellatio and from behind coitus, body worship then female superior coitus - smoke break. Some cuddling. Repeat until he's a puddle of quivering, but smiling, protoplasm.
checking my list
I think that about covers it. Any questions?

Fair Warning!
do NOT want to hear any more nonsense about how St. Valentine's Day is just another 'Hallmark holiday' etc. and so forth.
Because, it isn't some hyped up bit of fluff.
This is the day when Men are off the leash!
Now if you boys cannot think of something to get up to...don't blame Hallmark!

Jan 15, 2007
Kitten's Dream Date - Part Two
The previous detailed the 'mechanics' - the reality is I tend to pounce, laugh, and roll around on the bed having a great deal of fun!
I exhibit a lot of affection as well! I'll caress you, hug you, and mess up your hair! I'll tease you, do strange things to you, and lure you to your doom!
You'll enjoy it!

Questing for Truth and Happiness?
It is right in front of you.
It pulses through your body.
It lives in your mind.
All you have to do is
to reach out and grasp it.

Jan 16, 2007

248

Liquid Latex
If you aren't allergic to latex, this can be fun! Keep it away from hair and clothing and use a brush - it works better than fingers. Dries fairly quickly if you use a light coat. If you want something more substantial you can reapply - adding more layers after the previous ones have dried.
I prefer abstract designs but you can experiment.

Kitten's Decorating Process
ONE COLOR - for walls, ceilings, fabrics
ONE METAL - in appearance
ONE WOOD - once again, in appearance
The wood trim can be in another color.
I prefer leather furniture capable of supporting large males in comfort.
I also prefer warm colors like amber, orange, gold, yellow; in saturated medium tones.
If you don't have a focal point - make one.
Natural focal points include:
fireplaces
televisions
beds; esp king size beds
those monster kitchen ranges with 6 burners
desks
dining room tables
Minimal knick-knacks.
You have to have BOOKS!
Something in the room should be black.
One lamp in the house should be ugly - so ugly that you love it. Like a gargoyle.
It is a house but not a home until you have a cat.
Meow. Meow.

The Blog Awards!
Are on again. Go here, golden busty globe awards..., and get your nominations in!

Some one nominated me me for erotic picture!
Very nice of them.
I nominated:
Most All Around Outstanding Blog Award-
male- X
female- Y
(handle's omitted)
Hurray!

Jan 17, 2007
Insert Porn Here?
My readership is falling off again....tsk, tsk.
So perhaps it is time for me to relate another of my adventures?
I could do as some other bloggers have done and institute a regular feature such as "Playtime With Teddybears" which would be posted every Wednesday. What do you think?
But now you'll have to excuse me - I have to go - I'm practicing my lap dance technique by giving them. More of the Wicked Woman Product Development testing - ah me! My work is never done!

Teddybear's Lap Dance
I wore black leather gloves, black leather
wristbands with silver spikes, my black leather and silver chain outfit and black stilettos.
My tunes were "Evil Angel" by Rufus Wainwright, "Clubbed2Death (Kurayamino Mix)" by Rob D and "Lucky You" by the Deftones.
Sitting in the chair in the center of his living room rug, music begins and I slink about oozing around him in a slow circle getting closer and closer - sneaking up on him in time to the slinky music. When the song ended I was behind him and covered his eyes with my gloved hands until the next song came on. This song's a real hip-swinging tune so I was moving and undulating up close and personal, straddling

his legs, undoing his shirt buttons, breathing on the side of his neck, in and out, and around and back but with energy and fired with dark purpose. Then back to covering his eyes for the next song - back to slinky again. This time I gently trailed the spikes along his arms and thighs as well as stalking him in a feline manner. He was very stoic and didn't move an inch, something else did, but then he wasn't sweating so I must need more practice.

Another Book!
I have finished "MEN" a primer for women and it is now being edited and proofread. So it will be out very soon. I also did the cover. Very Tasty!

Jan 18, 2007
I Made the Cut!
Go to nominations for sexiest female blogger-vote now! and nominate your pick!
There are LOTS of sexy lady bloggers out there!

Flirting!
"When men and women spend a lot of time around one another, flirting becomes a means of communication and entertainment that can make everyday interactions more fun and exciting. Just like other interpersonal activities, though, each person flirts and accepts flirtation differently. While some people flirt constantly, others reserve this affectionate type of interaction for expressing genuine feelings that extend beyond friendship.
Either way, it can sometimes seem impossible to tell when flirtation is just for fun or when it's an invitation to take things to the next level. If there are true feelings behind the flirting, it's important to be able to recognize them in order to avoid any awkward or destructive situations. Sometimes a flicker of the eye or a brush on the arm can reveal volumes about the underlying relationship. Read on for tips

on how to read her flirtatious activities and figure out if her interest extends beyond playfulness."

Level of attention

Flirtation that's just flirtation will tend to be flippant and fun. Friends who don't harbor a real attraction for one another will play, and then move on to the next thing. They have nothing invested because there are no feelings involved. If a gesture or a touch is prolonged, however, it could mean that she's trying to get your attention to push things farther than the status quo.

Exclusivity

Some women are just flirty. If she's scooting around giving everybody in the vicinity a wink and a nudge, there's likely nothing special in the look she throws your way. In other words, if she uses casual flirting to throw a twist into an otherwise boring day, there's probably nothing more behind it. If, on the other hand, she pays special attention to you, there's a good chance you've been singled out for a reason.

Intensity

The key to friendly flirtation is lightheartedness and subtlety. Two people who flirt often will likely have a rhythm to their interactions; it's like a routine. Or she might start surpassing your regular physical boundaries by putting her hand on your leg or your hand when she's sitting beside you. If her actions become more serious or obvious, you may have an admirer on your hands.

Eye contact

Eye language is a very important indicator of the feelings between two individuals. Think of how you interact with your friends, male or female. Most of the time, eye contact is made during face-to-face conversation, but it is casual and frequently broken over the course of the exchange. If she makes prolonged and sustained eye contact, on the other hand, it could mean that something beyond friendship is afoot.

Duration
Flirtation is something that's fun and entertaining, but if it isn't serious, it usually passes with time.
Intimacy
Flirting involves a broad range of activities, from conversation and mockery to gestures and touch. These actions can either be playful or extend to a more personal level. If flirtation began at -- or has progressed to -- a more intimate level than most friendships, you can take a hint that there's probably more to it. "

Bottom line: If she flirts you , you have a chance with her!

Jan 19, 2007

It is a testament to the essential kindness of women that most men remain unstrangled.
More than that - I will NOT say.

Vetting Op
During the week Jan 23rd, 24th, and 25th - you may get vetted - BY APPT. So tell: when and where, guys.

Jan 20, 2007
I am delighted to report that everyone thoroughly enjoyed themselves, and each other, at today's Buff Birthday Bash! We had great group this time! The room was a trifle small but that meant there was no escape for the few newbies - who came up to speed very nicely *W*!
There's no better way to celebrate!!

Jan 21, 2007
Groups
Please note: that this is more of an 'intense' experience than an 'intimate' experience. Some might find it too rich for their blood at first. If you relax, however, you will find

intimacy, affection, and true friendship with the other participants.

Meow, meow people!

Jan 22, 2007

Unfortunately:

"All day long, girls are locked in pitched combat with one another. Is she prettier than me? What's she got that I don't? Who does that slut think she is? So making a point of telling your girl that she's beyond the reaches of both time and skank alike, well that ranks right up there with the highest of compliments. Girls are in the cutthroat business of cutting one another's throats."

SOMETIMES this is true. And women should stop it immediately. Until you are married to him, you have no rights over him other than those he gives you - and vice versa. If you are insecure - that's YOUR problem.

Remember, you are a unique person with your own special charm, therefore you have no rivals and there's no need to compete. And if you are married to him, then you have full legal rights over him and he over you - so no need to compete then either.

Each relationship has its own beauty so again there's no need to compete because what you enjoy with him is not exactly the same as what you enjoy with your other men - and vice versa.

Jan 23, 2007

My Bar:

Is actually the top of one of my kitchen cabinets - the one with the glasses in it just to the right of the kitchen sink. Yes, that one - see the bottles?

Up there you will find:

Jack Daniels Black Label

Jose Cuervo

Laphroaig

and a few other sundries used to make such dishes as "Drunken Chicken".
The champers and the pinot noir are in the pantry to the right of the frig. The extra case of Budweiser, in bottles, is in the dining room.
Beer and wine currently 'in use' are in the frig itself.
I keep trying to fit the extra beer into the pantry but someone, the SRM, keeps putting it in the dining room for some unknown but no doubt odd reason. Strange man.

Jan 24, 2007
Playing With Teddybears:
It Begins
I had a certain 'agenda' in mind for him tonight. I shall experiment with him over the course of our encounter. We will move from the familiar to the new gradually so as to not make him uncomfortable. Naked, there in the candlelight with music playing, first we cuddled and then coitus with him up. Then I tied him down onto the bed with the straps and cuffs. Kneeling on the bed between his spread legs, hiding the vibe between my thighs, I began doing body worship moving from his face downward with excruciating slowness. Exploring him and his sensitivity. Slowly, slowly, slowly kissing here, lightly licking there, a little nibbling, little nuzzling - mmmmm fur. Sliding by, I moved to the ankles and ran slowly up each leg, one at a time. Easing up to his scrotum, taking first the one side, then the other sucking and licking while I activated the vibe which I then gently placed beneath his scrotum onto the peritoneum, I then began fellatio with the vibe held against him with just the right amount of movement and pressure. Up and down and twisting and licking and sucking both upward as well as downward and with the vibe having its stimulating effect- he didn't last very long. I released him and was engulfed in a huge bear hug which ended up with me sitting astride him and riding him vigorously. He and

255

the bed got very wet. This lasted for some time as the sight of a woman thoroughly enjoying herself stimulates him. He never wants me to hold back. He begs for my full, for all of my sexual responses. I have not yet given those to him. Soon, very soon now he will receive them.

In any human endeavor, one has to compare the reward one is likely to achieve or gain with the risks one has to chance. This is as true in relationships as it is in any other area. Is the reward you get commensurate with the risk you run? In some areas the answer is clearly seen. In others, the change in the risk/reward balance is so rapid and so subjective that accurate judgments cannot be made.
So you do the best you can.

Jan 25, 2007
I Used to Have a Dream
that I would live in a house
on the empty beach
along a forgotten shore
quite alone

and now

I live in a house
surrounded by others
in a metropolis
and I am alone

One may think, given the number of men I have known, that they would all become just a blur - an endless sea of faces and other body parts. This is NOT the case. I may not remember them clearly, but each one had salient individual characteristics that firmly root them into my memory. For example, should you come to my home, you will see a wind chime hanging on my front porch. This was a gift from my - he was the older brother of one of my classmates. He was a charming ginger hued teddybear of a man about late 20's - a male nurse at a psychiatric hospital and he drove a white BMW. He was also a sweetheart who enjoyed cuddling.

I've had many adventures in my life and periodically it has also been graced by men who treated me with kindness and consideration - perhaps that is why I love men now. I can only hope that they remember me with equal fondness.

Jan 26, 2007

I attract with my *joie dans la vie* and my high energy. I repel with my domme attitude.

But to those in the know...........I'm a cute little fluffy-bunny *EG* LOL

Jan 27, 2007

Proposed Rule Change:

RE: The Blogs/Pix Awards (voting currently underway)

Each person may only be nominated, and possibly win, in ONE category.

Though you may love them dearly we do wish to keep this from becoming too like the Oscars.

Please vote for me! I'm falling behind! LOL

pun completely intended

Tell me all about your......

Favorite Color:

Favorite Food:

Favorite Month:

Favorite Song:

Favorite Movie:

Favorite Sport:

Favorite Season:

Favorite Day Of the week:

Favorite Ice Cream Flavor:

Favorite Time of Day:
and I'll tell you mine!
You go first!

Jan 28, 2007
It has been said that I am not explicit enough when I write about my adventures. Gentlemen, I do that on purpose. If I were to be more explicit and descriptive there wouldn't be any room for you.

I do not know you and you can dimly picture me - but the idea of a dark-haired, queen-of-the-night, Feline of Darkness straddling your body and enjoying you repeatedly should not be totally beyond your powers of fantasy. Make no mistake. I do enjoy him. One cannot have as many orgasms as I do and yet try to get him to believe otherwise. I turn pink, I make a lot of noise, and everything gets very wet. Even so, I have been holding back. Should I give full rein to my desires or not? What do you gentlemen think?

Thanks to all of you who nominated me and or voted for me in the Blogging Awards!
I appreciate it!

Jan 29, 2007
Nota Bene:
If you're scheduled to meet me/see me/visit me this week - kindly write and tell me so.
I may, just may, have double-booked someone.
And we can't have that!
Plus I have to fit in another naughty shopping trip and one more teddybear - possibly two as one of my men comes off the injured list this week! HURRAY!!!
Also there's that four-letter word that begins with W.
Don't you find that W%$# interferes with a good sex life???

Please post if you are coming to the February Buff Birthday Bash and Red Undies Party on Feb 22nd herein. Thank you!

Jan 30, 2007
All I will tell you is give me men with experience! OMG, these men are incredibly good lovers! Courage, sensitivity, and the ability to 'listen' to a woman's body - they have all the talents! and that's ALL I'm going to tell you....til tomorrow! I am THE most fortunate of evil kittens!

"Why Open Relationships... Usually SUCK.
When you sleep with a woman and tell her that you are also sleeping with other women, what often happens is you de-validate her. She wonders why she isn't enough to satisfy you, and so on.
And while it FEELS like they "love" you because they are chasing you, they actually DO NOT care about YOU as much as they care about validating their own sense of self-worth.
They are simply trying to "tame the player" and, as you know, if you let them "tame" you, they will suddenly become bored and walk off! No more challenge.
Now, I have lived through the old Pick-Up-Artist "open relationship" stage of my life, and I'm a better man because of it. I needed to go through that to learn some tough love and life lessons. But now that I've gone through it, there is no way that I will ever go back. To me - and this is just a personal choice - BISEXUAL WOMEN is the only way for me. This way, I get the best of both worlds.
I've spent most of my life trying to answer the following question "How do you truly and completely satisfy a woman?" In my experience - and this is just MY experience - you can
NOT satisfy a woman. No man ever could. She needs a girlfriend too. I've seen it with my own eyes, and let me tell

259

you, there is nothing more beautiful than seeing 2-3 girls laughing and communicating and vibing together in ways that men will probably never understand.
Why screw around ON your girlfriend when you can screw around WITH HER?"
My take on the above:
Once again: the yes and no pertains. While I personally do not believe that sex can ever be totally 'meaningless', one can make poor choices, and fall into the habit of making poor choices - an endless loop of retreating back to familiar behaviors no matter how 'unsatisfying' due simply to their familiarity. This repeated pattern of behavior will stunt your growth. But when he goes off into bisexuality, only for women mind you, he errs. How do you satisfy a woman? - well, in my case, give her three "teddybears" and see what happens! Each woman has her own 'thing' and a wise man notices and delivers this. In a way, his opting for FMF only shields him from masculine competition and masculine cooperation which might indicate insecurity. It also limits him to a certain type of woman instead of opening up his relationship to all women. Part of the whole bisexuality for women thing is the idea that 'only a woman can completely satisfy another woman' which is piffle. You can just as logically say that 'only another man can truly satisfy another man'. So lets just let that 'who can truly satisfy whom based solely upon gender' idea die. As to final statement "screw around with her" - I can only say HELL YEAH LET'S DO IT! LOL

Jan 31, 2007
Playing with Teddybears
Ah! I am the most fortunate of evil kittens! Not only was he eager for my attention but he also displayed a deep appreciation for me. We began with body worship. He is truly a most gifted lover! Tonight was a slow and most intimate adventure. Then he was in me. Very, very nice!

260

Felt so good. Several orgasms later, we moved to the end of the bed and I leaned over it with him behind and in me. Also very good! I ran my claws gently up the backs of his legs and he learned another thing about himself. Tracing thin lines with the edges of my claw-tips makes him quiver with ecstasy. We both enjoyed an orgasm and then, laughing with sheer joy, I fell onto the bed, rolled over and he began cunnilingus. Oh my! With mouth and hand he brought me to more orgasms! Wonderful! His turn came next as I straddled him and came repeatedly all over him. He loves the sensations, sights and sounds of a wild tumultuous kitten enjoying herself. Then we enjoyed the most intimate of activities – we curled up together and napped. There is no greater indication of trust than when a woman naps within the comfort of your arms. I stirred and then was petted awake for more fun and then we returned to napping. So sweet. He is tremendous fun!

February
2007

Feb 1, 2007
Sexual Trivia
1. A Lapp girl of Finland would show her interest in a suitor by:
a. unharnessing his reindeer
b. bringing him his dinner
c. wearing a flower behind her left ear
d. catching fish for him

2. True or False: Don't speed up when she starts to moan.

3. A woman's biggest mistake in foreplay is:
a. no foreplay
b. having an orgasm before penetration
c. false innocence
d. not fondling the penis

So how much do you know? Answers after we have 10 persons responding!

Feb 2, 2007
"Do you see yourself as others do? Are you reflecting what you had hoped to? How well do you think you get to know another in this medium? How well do you think others know you?
Here's the challenge. Describe me or what you think you know about me in one word. Just one. As the game progresses you cannot use the same word that another has already used. You can comment as often as you like, but each comment must contain only one word. And each word must be descriptive in nature. I will comment by posting the one word that I think best describes you.
Then post this, if you dare, in your own blog and see how others respond."

To Be or Not to Be
-- included.
Next vetting op. is this coming Tuesday, at noon, at Kilroy's off Braddock Road.

Feb 3, 2007
I'll crack the super secret code and find out which Busty Award was won by whom. Y'all couldn't just post a list? Anyway, this is housekeeping day where the house is dusted and vacuumed, the linens are changed, the laundry done, and the trucks detailed. Every Saturday this happens. Do you have a 'designated housekeeping day'?

Feb 4, 2007

"Make a Wish"
You can close your eyes it's over now
It's over now
You can close your eyes it's over

Baby, baby, baby
Make a wish
Tell me have you ever been afraid like this
(It's over now)

I've seen it watching me
That misty thing
Without a face
It weaves my thoughts
Lined them up in black lace
It buries my shape
And leaves no trace

Tomorrow I will have no shame
And I will start again

Make a wish
Tell me have you ever felt alone like this
(Over now)

Better do it, sure
Just wishing
I could move in some more

Tomorrow I will have no shame
And I will start again
Make a wish
You can close your eyes it's over now
Baby I have never been afraid like this
You can close your eyes it's over now

Make a wish...

I took off my shoes
I took off my face
And then I undid the buttons on my dress
(I will start again)

Make a wish
You can close your eyes it's over now
Tell me have you ever been exposed like this
Maybe we could savour that now
Baby, baby, baby
Feels like a kiss
You can close your eyes and start again
I bet you never thought that I could feel like this

Tomorrow I will have no shame
Tomorrow I will have no shame
Make a wish

Conjure One, sung by Poe

265

Make a wish!!

Feb 4, 2007

"Center of the Sun"

When I close my eyes
I am at the centre of the sun
And I cannot be hurt
By anything this wicked world has done
I look into your eyes and
I am at the centre of the sun
And I cannot be hurt
By anything this wicked world has done

exerpt, Conjure One, sung by Poe

If Vetted: the open enrollment period ends Feb 10th so get your name on the list now!!
If Not Vetted: last chance for Feb, this Tuesday, lunch, Kilroy's in the bar.

Feb 5, 2007

I am a ruthless weeder of lists. I have recently removed from my YIM and from my Friends lists, those I no longer care to speak with or be seen by. Sorry, but if you had wanted to get with me, you would have gotten with me. When I cull, I cull.
Good luck and good hunting to those I have removed.

Feb 6, 2007
"The road gets a little bumpy when your partner has something critical to say about you. After all, no one wants

to hear complaints and bad news, especially when it is about them. And if it happens often, probably because you're not well-practiced in the art of listening, it can be interpreted as nagging. Despite how uncomfortable it may make you feel, it is smart to listen to the bad news.

Whenever you're confronted with this situation, just tell yourself that complaints and criticism are gifts. Instead of dumping you and taking her love elsewhere, your partner is sticking with you and alerting you of a potential problem. Effectively, she is giving an opportunity to rectify the problem.

There's one more important trick that will help you receive complaints and criticism more graciously; complaints are based on compliments. For example, if your partner complains that you're not spending enough time with her, the hidden compliment is that she wants to spend more time with you.

If she complains there isn't enough sex in the relationship, she's telling you that she wants more of you. If she complains that you're not lasting as long as she'd like during intercourse that means she wants more intimacy or you to be inside of her longer. These are serious compliments, even though they may come across as something else."

The above is using she/he as the example but this works BOTH ways.

Agree? Disagree? Answers on a postcard, please!

Are we all clear on where we're having lunch today?

Feb 7, 2007
Nothing

it means nothing,
the blood,
let it go;

searing, searing, searing,
it means nothing,
anguish tears pain,
it means nothing,
let it go;
let it run through and through,
it means nothing;
I am the absolute biggest,
fucking goddamn fool on the planet;
breathe deep,
nothing matters,
until my heart turns to,
fucking stone so I won't feel;
I won't feel, I won't feel,
anymore;
but it means nothing,
it all means,
nothing.

Well, sweeties - my blog post most likely has nothing to do with you. My muse claws my back and her screams careen around inside my head - no way there's any of this come back and write later stuff! There's a lot going on in my life. I do, I really, really do say what I mean to say. Sometimes, the mischief may come out and I get cryptic but that's rather rare actually. But if you don't "get it" by all means ASK! Just email me here. All smartasses who play "Shot Your Fox" in the post's comments are greatly appreciated. Ok what was the last comment. I know there were three of them. Hmmmmm. Well, when I remember it, I'll let you know, ok? The edtor of my current book sent me the first 10 editted pages - seems he bled all over it. *sigh*

There's no Playtime With Teddybears feature today because the teddybears are being recalcitrant!!!

Bad, bad Teddybears!

Feb 8, 2007
Friday Feb 9th at Kilroy's off of Braddock Road at noon in the bar.
The list goes to The Selection Committee on the 10th.

Rejection
Not being accepted hurts. For this reason, most women try to decrease the pain by being nice and trying very hard not to say no outright. Most men find this confusing. Men then accuse women of sending mixed messages. Please; if the woman does not say yes outright, then accept that the answer is no, thank you. Should it be the woman who is asking, a "sorry, darling" from him will have to be accepted with grace. If the chemistry is not there, it is not there. But no one is going to tell you that accepting rejection is easy.

What you cannot do is simply disappear from view. If there was no abuse, then the relationship must be ended in person and with regret. Emotional storms are unacceptable no matter how devastated you may feel. All feelings of relief at being free should also be muted. Goodbye is never good and it certainly is never easy. We are social beings so expect a need to recover from the effects of saying goodbye. A period of introspection may be called for especially if you have a history of failed relationships behind you. Learn from your mistakes but do not get a PhD in making mistakes. All relationships have their problems but when even the thought of the other partner becomes soul destroying, it may be time to call it quits. The choice is one between do you still want to be with him/her or do you not.
What do you think? How do you handle a bruising of the heart?

Feb 9, 2007
I have written a few books this year. Here's the list of those available to the public.
Children's Books:
Nursery Tales for progressive children under 5 years of age
The Rogue's Handbook for progressive children from ages 5 to 13

General how-to books:
Financial Basics how to manage your money
Basic Gardening for the absolute beginner
Polo Tailgating including recipies
Introduction to Classical Music and a cd of the music on the Recommended Listening List

Professional Book:
Practice Management Procedures-2007 a professional manual covering how I run my practice

Mature Audience books:
Chat first year on the Internet
Sex Education for Laypersons just the facts
WOMEN a primer for men about their favorite subject
The Polyamorist for women about multiple men
beguile the subtle art of sublime sexual subjugation of men
Wicked Woman a business idea - humor
Notes of a Dominatrix the basics for beginners

All are available for purchase.
And while you are there at LuLu scoping out these, please check out those written by my good friend zz_Todd2!!!

Feb 10, 2007
I'm going to get into trouble here but oh well!

You all know of my seemingly endless desire for male teddybears with brains, skills, and wit who are within 10 yrs of my own age; correct?
Well, men have their preferences too. Check his preferences beforehand when considering your options/plans. Consider both the packaging and the person. For example, if he's really into short, cute blondes - I'm NOT going there! If he's a dom, I'm NOT going there either. Why court rejection like that?
Doesn't seem very sensible to me - and you know I'm ALWAYS sensible, right?

Feb 12, 2007
He sent me this:

"I see your postings, picture and comments everywhere on this site. You obviously like to party. I noticed that your tits are kind of saggy though and want like to contribute to your breast enhancement.... it would certainly better your chances of getting with someone other than the trailer park crowd you're use to. Just let me know where to send my twenty bucks." (his spelling)

Now his profile says:

"I am a successful, well adjusted professional looking for a sexy woman for constant sex. No strings, no expectations, no rules ...... just a satisfying phyical relationship. I live alone and am flexible with time. No rules means I am open to all types of desires and fantasies. Must be somewhat in shape with no drama. Lots of percs and benefits. Contact me for a chat as many great relationships start that way.
My Ideal Person:
I'm looking for a woman who is sexy, comfortable eating dinner in her underwear, physically fit and loves to explore her fantasies. BBW are most desirable but not essential. I

271

am best with happy, well adjusted people without problems. No strings, just fun and pleasure."

This very sad sort of fellow seems to have a few problems keeping his head on straight! He certainly had trouble with 'focus' as well as with spelling. Some men are their own worst enemies! The poor, poor brainless man in this case is Darwin Award material.

Feb 13, 2007
I posted that and I got this:

"(closing eyes and concentrating real hard) -I wish for 72 virgins BEFORE I die (and enough time/energy to train em up!)"

LOL
So I want you all to close your eyes; concentrate real hard; and tell me your wish!
Meow, meow people! It is almost time!! Are you ready??

Feb 14, 2007

PARTY!!!
TODAY WE CELEBRATE MY CONTINUING
TRIUMPH OVER THE FORCES OF DOOM!!

image of a naked and gleeful kitten pouncing upon a pile of willing naked teddybears WHEEEEEEEEEEEEE!!!!

Feb 15, 2007
"Have a Good Time"
Yesterday it was my birthday
I hung one more year on the line
I should be depressed

My life's a mess
But I'm having a good time

I've been loving and loving
And loving
I'm exhausted from loving so well
I should go to bed
But a voice in my head
Says "Ah, what the hell"

CHORUS: Have a good time,babu
Have a good time, child
Have a good time, baby
Have a good time!

(Edited)
by Paul Simon

Tee heeeeeeeeeeee!!
Who can tell from whence, and by whom, this fictional
telegram came?

"I AM AT TOLNBRIDGE STAYING AT THE CLERGY
HOUSE PRIESTS PRIESTS PRIESTS THE PLACE IS
BLACK WITH THEM COME AND PLAY THE
CATHEDRAL SERVICES ALL THE ORGANISTS
HAVE BEEN SHOT UP DISMAL BUSINESS THE
MUSIC WASN'T AS BAD AS ALL THAT EITHER
YOU'D BETTER COME AT ONCE BRING ME A
BUTTERFLY NET I NEED ONE WIRE COMING NOT
COMING PREPARE FOR LONG STAY GERVASE
FEN"

There is a prize for the winner - the first person who gets it
right.

Feb 16, 2007
"Mardi Gras"
C'mon take me to the Mardi Gras
Where the people sing and play
Where the dancing is elite
And there's music in the street
Both night and day

Hurry take me to the Mardi Gras
In the city of my dreams
You can legalize your lows
You can wear your summer clothes
In the New Orleans

And I will lay my burden down
Rest my head upon that shore
And when I wear that starry crown
I won't be wanting anymore

Take your burdens to the Mardi Gras
Let the music wash your soul
You can mingle in the street
You can jingle to the beat
Of Jelly Roll

Paul Simon

What to wear, what to wear?? Any ideas?

Feb 17, 2007
INVITATIONS HAVE BEEN SENT!
Please RSVP with your first name, handle, and cell phone
number!

Feb 18, 2007
"Men it's my new obsession

Men it's not even a question,
Men on the lips of your lover, 'cause
Men is the love you discover

Men it was love at first sight, its
Men when I turn out the light, and
Men get me high as a kite
And I think everything is going to be all right
No matter what we do tonight"

Sorry, Aerosmith and zz_todd2 but I simply HAD to do it.

Quite simply, the Male G-Spot is the prostate, or more specifically, the prostate-perineum. What are they? The prostate is the male prostate gland, and the perineum is a dime-sized soft spot between the anus and scrotum. The important nerves that control the sexual organs, including those controlling erection, orgasm, and ejaculation, converge at the prostate and the perineum area. This means that this area is essentially a man's "command center" for sexual pleasure. The tissue that forms the urethral sponge, or G-spot, in female anatomy forms the prostate, which you can think of as the male G-spot (or the "P-spot") in male anatomy. Gentle massage of the prostate gives him intense orgasms.
buzz, buzz I have a toy just for you!

Feb 19, 2007
I recommend to you the following authors:
Rita Mae Brown - fox-hunting
Gerald Hammond - shooting
Most of us have very limited exposure to the natural world and the creatures therein. While these authors write in the mystery genre, each of them does so with an insight into and a delight in the countryside around them that will prove

beneficial to all by reconnecting you to that 'other' world beyond concrete and digital clocks.
Besides which, they really are very, very good storytellers.

Janis Lyn Joplin (January 19, 1943 – October 4, 1970) was an American blues-influenced rock singer and occasional songwriter with a distinctive voice. Joplin performed on four albums recorded between 1966 and 1970 -- two as the lead singer of San Francisco band Big Brother and The Holding Company, and two released as a solo artist.

"The greatest white female rock singer of the 1960s, Janis Joplin was also a great blues singer, making her material her own with her wailing, raspy, supercharged emotional delivery. First rising to stardom as the frontwoman for San Francisco psychedelic band Big Brother & the Holding Company, she left the group in the late '60s for a brief and uneven (though commercially successful) career as a solo artist. Although she wasn't always supplied with the best material or most sympathetic musicians, her best recordings, with both Big Brother and on her own, are some of the most exciting performances of her era. She also did much to redefine the role of women in rock with her assertive, sexually forthright persona and raunchy, electrifying on-stage presence. Joplin was raised in the small town of Port Arthur, TX, and much of her subsequent personal difficulties and unhappiness has been attributed to her inability to fit in with the expectations of the conservative community. She'd been singing blues and folk music since her teens, playing on occasion in the mid-'60s with future Jefferson Airplane guitarist Jorma Kaukonen. There are a few live pre-Big Brother recordings (not issued until after her death), reflecting the inspiration of early blues singers like Bessie Smith, that demonstrate she was well on her way to developing a personal style before hooking up with the band. She had already been to California before moving there permanently in 1966, when she joined a struggling early San Francisco psychedelic group, Big Brother & the Holding Company. Although their loose, occasionally sloppy brand of bluesy psychedelia had some charm, there can be no doubt that Joplin — who initially didn't even sing lead on all of the material — was primarily responsible for lifting them out of the ranks of the ordinary. She made them a hit at the 1967 Monterey Pop Festival, where her stunning version of "Ball and Chain" (perhaps her very best performance) was captured on film." -by Richie Unterberger

The National Association of Women Business Owners is a mutual-help association dedicated to helping eachother succeed.
If you are a woman who owns a business, please check them out. If you know a woman who does, please pass the word along.
"get by with a little help from my friends..."

Feb 19, 2007
It was a particularly good time not only because of my birthday, my sweety, and being out - but also because I received my first check from Lulu for the books I had sold! I am an author!
May I have a Hallelujah?

Feb 20, 2007
I am happy to report that the teddybears have ceased being recalcitrant and are now ready, willing, and able!
So this week you will get another episode of Playtime with Teddybears!

Sexually Aggressive Women
"Men are used to initiating everything -- from the first contact to sex to proposing marriage. Guys are the ones who have to do all the hard work while women sit around and wait for wonderful things to happen.

It must be difficult being the one who always has to do the pursuing rather than being the one chased by an admirer. But what if the tables were turned? Do you think you'd be thrilled if your woman always did the chasing when it came to sex?

Now before you jump into an enthusiastic chant of "Hell yeahs," keep in mind the famous maxim: "Be careful what you wish for, you just might get it." Would you know how to keep a sexually demanding woman happy?

The female orgasm is no longer a shot in the dark; now, most women expect to orgasm virtually every time they make love. And if you can't get it right, they'll teach you how to do it by taking over the situation.

And look around you: Virtually every television commercial, movie, music video, and billboard ad displays sexually aggressive, um, I mean, assertive women. Therefore, women are quickly picking up on the fact that being sexually aggressive does not necessarily make them tramps.

Unfortunately, many women will not let on about their sexual aggressiveness until later in the relationship for fear that their partner might think they've been around.

But if your woman was raised in an environment in which sexuality was not shunned or treated with disdain, she'll likely be very comfortable with her own sexuality. This can result in a woman who may very well have you limping out of the bedroom once she's through with you.

The wonderful thing about a sexually aggressive woman is that she's completely in tune with what she enjoys when it comes to lovemaking. She has no qualms about letting her lover know what makes her tick.

As well, she'll always be up for a sexual escapade with you, and she'll likely be bold in and out of the bedroom. You can rest assured that she's not shy or uncomfortable about discussing fantasies and naughty little ideas.

The best part of having an aggressive lover is that you won't always have to be the one who initiates; she won't hesitate to take off your clothes and sit on top of you.

This is the kind of woman who could make love to you with slow-motioned sensuality or enjoy some sexual frolic made up of animalistic intuition.

And the fact that she goes in search of her own orgasms takes away some of the pressures that most guys feel when it comes to having sex. Now you don't have to worry about making her climax because she'll ensure that the both of you do.

Is there a downside to women like this?

Although most guys swear that they would do virtually anything to land a woman who would tell it like it is and treat them like sexual prey on a nightly basis, reality dictates otherwise for some.

I talked to several guys who had the advantage of dating such women, and many discussed their fears. Jim revealed, "I became irrationally jealous. I always envisioned her treating other men this way and would become enraged, which ultimately led to petty fights."

Harold admitted: "I was afraid that if there was one night that I simply was too tired or just not in the mood, she would lose all interest in me and go find herself a virtual racehorse that was young, dumb and full of [expletive deleted]."

As well, most guys I spoke to admitted that they sometimes stopped desiring sex as much simply because they knew it was so readily available to them. Because there was no challenge involved in getting the pie, they sort of lost their appetites.

But fear not: The good definitely outweighed the bad, and although there were some complaints, most guys wouldn't trade in their mates for anything in this world. They simply learned a few tricks of the trade and made the best of their situation.

If you happen to be one of the lucky guys who has the pleasure of making love to a woman of this genre, here are a few ways to ensure that she'll be satisfied for good.

Keep her coming

Stay mysterious and always ensure that she desires you. Just as men get turned on by the thrill of the chase, so do women. Don't always give in, and when you do, bring her to immeasurable heights.

Order her around

Obviously, no one likes to have a drill sergeant barking orders at them in the sack, but talking to her while you're making love -- as well as telling her what you want her to do -- will likely excite her more than usual.

Take control

Because she's used to having complete control in bed, imagine how enlightening it would be if you took absolute power and had her at your sexual mercy (willingly, of course).

Initiate sex

Before she gets the chance to make any moves on you, start the foreplay by approaching her from behind and grabbing hold of her breasts while sucking on the back of her neck. Your spontaneity will turn her on immensely.

Okay, so maybe you're not surrounded by aggressive women who enjoy making love wherever and whenever. But keep in mind that sometimes it takes a little time for a woman to open up in that department, as most women are still afraid of being looked upon as trashy or promiscuous. And if you want to make your woman more aggressive when it comes to lovemaking, talk to her about how she feels when you initiate sex. Explain that just like she enjoys being desired, you also need to feel those emotions every now and again."

Yes, The Feline of Darkness is a sexually aggressive woman. I know you are not surprised. But what may surprise you, and is omitted from the above article, is that sex is a lot of FUN!
I find it so. Don't you?

Feb 21, 2007
Playtime With Teddybears
Office Visit
Your hands on my skin, massaging and caressing, such nice strong hands - purr. So nice to have you come by. Warm up with some coitus. Oh my! It has been awhile so you came rather quickly. We shall have to do more of this. A small break and then lie down, sweety, and let the evil kitten have her way with you. I think I may have left a few marks this time. I love riding you! Oh yeah! I cum all over you and get you all wet. This time I am not holding back anything. You get it all this time. There's the desk. Shall we try that? Yes! Now it is your turn to cum. Wow!! You have to stop by my office more often! A naked man in your office makes work much more delightful!

The man with whom I have been previously associated, for 3 years, has found another woman who is more suitable.
Slut 2 is no more.
I wish them every happiness.

Feb 22, 2007
"Scars"
I tear my heart open, I sew myself shut
My weakness is that I care too much
And my scars remind me that the past is real
I tear my heart open just to feel.

-Papa Roach

was told more than a year ago that this is 'my song' vis-à-vis Slut 2

Feb 23, 2007
I hate being blindsided.
I dislike silence when there should be talk.
This was NOT a good time for this to happen.
Other than that - I'll be okay, thank you, since there was, eventually, talk.
Sorry, but this is as 'dramatic' as I get.

Stephanie Lynn "Stevie" Nicks born May 26, 1948, is an American singer and songwriter, best known for her work with Fleetwood Mac and a long solo career, which collectively has produced over twenty Top 40 hits. She is one of the few rock artists to maintain a solo career while remaining a member of a successful band. As a member of Fleetwood Mac, she was inducted into The Rock and Roll Hall of Fame in 1998.
"Famed for her mystical chanteuse image, singer/songwriter Stevie Nicks enjoyed phenomenal success not only as a solo artist but also as a key member of Fleetwood Mac. Stephanie Lynn Nicks was born May 26, 1948 in Phoenix, Arizona; the granddaughter of a frustrated country singer, she began performing at the age of four, and occasionally sang at the tavern owned by her parents."

I am only interested in a discreet LT fwb R with a sincere and suitable man who is committed to "the lifestyle". Mildly evil, cute, witty teddybears without other commitments preferred.

- trying to return to a more social life with the one man in the Cyrillic Post (no it wasn't ABOUT you) - we used to be more social you know. But it will be difficult. Broached the subject earlier tonight, we will see what transpires. Now it I can just keep him awake past 7:30 pm.....

Feb 24, 2007
Notes:
Lives on Silverbird Lane
over an industrial space
a work/live condominium
a writer in a sculptor's place
bookshelves crammed with various books
a working scholar's library
with other works on other topic interspersed
an old mahogany bar
Bought at auction
serves as a smaller chef's kitchen
with an AGA
along the back wall
doesn't eat
one oriental of advanced age
covers the entire floor
room warm with incandescent light
from the industrial fittings overhead
there is a tabby
battered leather lounge chairs
at the elbow tables of a decent size
sofas
one large desk

a tantalus on the side table
under the mirror
on the other side wall
stairs wrapping an elevator
½ bath
laundry
door out to the back terrace
and separate garage
smokes
walks her Scottish Terrier
might drink
from the bottles
displayed on the back bar
home most of the day
gets out at night
monochrome dress
fitted, classic
little jewelry
stands up straight
is straight
though her spine is not
an excellent shot
mixed oils
attar of roses, tabac, and myrrh
scents the immaculate
very little art
but choice
in naked hallway and foyer
sleeps in a large bed
sometimes not alone
has a steam shower
TV projected onto a wall
computer controls
in a closet
all is amber upstairs
she likes it warm

drives a Landrover
a new one
computer
the latest monster
publishes more than enough
if not 'bestsellers'
saves
invests
dreams
listens to the night
no fireplace
candles
black leather
with silver fittings

comments welcomed

Feb 25, 2007
This week will be a hectic one. I have set up lunch meetings for the end of the week - I'm back hunting again, you see. I'm also studying for my test, Monday, in preparation for taking it on Tuesday. Also on Tuesday I will be enjoying my remaining teddybear. Yes, you may get a Playtime with Teddybear post this Wednesday. We will see if I feel like it. But that might depend more upon the test results - I do have to pass this one. Also the book, MEN, is finished and off to the publishers so I might get the proof copy back this week. There are these other contracts to worry about as well. Then there's the SRM issues and my truck needing to go back into the shop. I also have to transcribe the month of February into my other book in progress.
Ah me!
How is your week looking?

Avoiding the Gross-up Rule, IRC Sec. 2035(c) .

When making taxable gifts in excess of the unified credit deduction, the planner should make the donor aware of the possible reversions to the estate and of the three-year rule, under IRC Secs. 2035 through 2038. Gifts which revert to the estate include the proceeds of life insurance policies if the policy was gifted within three years of death. Also all gift taxes paid within three years of death are included in the estate of the donee. This is known as the "gross-up" rule. If, however, the donee outlives the three-year period, the payment of gift tax effectively reduces the estate tax base which, in turn, will reduce the estate tax payable at death.

Do you see?

Feb 26, 2007 1:10 am
Mood: cheerful, 313 Views
Tall, lithe, and elegant domme' who bewitches alpha males, and only alpha males, into becoming willing cat toys as they succumb to their own desires.

My Ideal Person:
Those whom the gods love....who also bleed freely, heal quickly, and need not answer for marks left upon them.

Males must be between 45 and 55 years of age, 6ft tall, furry, witty, able to withstand my ardor, kneeling, sincere, nearby and possess more than half a brain.

I am only interested in a discreet LT fwb R with a sincere and suitable man who is committed to "the lifestyle". Mildly evil, cute, witty teddybears without other 'commitments' preferred.

Founding member of The Wicked Woman Group

I am a soft domme and do NOT do pain, abuse or indulge in humiliation. Basically I want wild, rampant, skin-on-skin, full body contact sex on my terms.

-posted here for those who cannot otherwise access it.

Any suggestions?

Feb 26, 2007
Grace Slick (born Grace Barnett Wing, October 30, 1939 in Evanston, Illinois) is an American singer and songwriter, who was the lead singer of the rock groups Jefferson Airplane, Jefferson Starship, Starship and also as a solo artist, for nearly three decades, from the mid-1960s to the mid-1990s.

"Slick is considered to be one of the most important musicians in bringing the 1960s psychedelic rock to mainstream appeal. She is known for her witty, influential, thought-provoking lyrics, and her powerful contralto voice."

Lots of people moving in - So; When are the house-warming orgies??? Come on, people! Tis a cause for celebration!
Isn't it??

But one simply cannot do more than just catch a glimspe when the test-ride lasts only one hour.
What was there was not very good.
Next!

Feb 27, 2007
That didn't go well at all. Fortunately it will only require further funding to fix it. Then I will try that again. Y'all should have wished me luck or something.

287

Please exercise caution when sitting on the furniture, next time, buddy!!
No, it wasn't booby-trapped!!

The shop called and they haven't found the necessary parts yet. DRAT. DRAT. DRAT. So I may have to reschedule everything unless I can get some wheels. Pesky situation! Some days are just like this, ya know?

Feb 28, 2007

"For What It's Worth"
There's something happening here
What it is ain't exactly clear
There's a man with a gun over there
Telling me I got to beware

I think it's time we stop, children, what's that sound
Everybody look what's going down

There's battle lines being drawn
Nobody's right if everybody's wrong
Young people speaking their minds
Getting so much resistance from behind

I think it's time we stop, hey, what's that sound
Everybody look what's going down

What a field-day for the heat
A thousand people in the street
Singing songs and carrying signs
Mostly say, hooray for our side

It's time we stop, hey, what's that sound
Everybody look what's going down

Paranoia strikes deep
Into your life it will creep
It starts when you're always afraid
You step out of line, the man come and take you away

We better stop, hey, what's that sound
Everybody look what's going down
Stop, hey, what's that sound
Everybody look what's going down
Stop, now, what's that sound
Everybody look what's going down
Stop, children, what's that sound
Everybody look what's going down

-Buffalo Springfield

Playtime With Teddybears
UNCOLLARED
Lying on his bed in the candlelight wrapped in each other's arms and lips. What began languidly became a torrid, wild banshee fuck where each orgasm led to six more as an uncollared teddybear displayed his aggressive nature. What big strong arms you have, baby! He deployed all his 'arts', and earned a few claw marks, but the demands of the day made this first round quicker than most. One thing always leads to another with me and the sight of a naked teddybear lying face- up on his bed is more than I can ignore. Pouncing upon him, I nuzzle down his body then up his thighs - very slowly. Caressing his body with my hair, a breast, a leg, lips and hands; all flowing and wrapping around him as I move lower and get into position. I gently breathed along the length of his cock and took up the head in my mouth without closing my lips upon it; just lightly flickering the tip of the head with my tongue. Then I swallowed him whole in one motion, closed my lips and wrapped my throat around him and came up with a twisting

movement. Up hard and strong with a twist while also pressing my tongue against the base of his penis as if trying to bend it backwards; down gently and soft - repeatedly. Wheee! Up on top and moving and getting him all soaking wet as I cum again and again until straddling him and hugging him fiercely, he too orgasms. This break I spend it wandering around sideways while he chuckles and tries to not walk sideways himself while steering me to the sofa. La la la, giggle. Naked teddybears should never lie down on their beds when I'm in the vicinity. Even if they are lying face-down. I laid on top of him and began nibbling on his ears and breathing on the side of his neck. Then as he brought his shoulders up, I bent his head down slightly and passionately, firmly, kissed the nape of his neck. His responsive quiver shook his entire body. I slid around him, while 'feathering' him and we ended up with me on my back at the edge of the bed with him standing there, my legs (ankles crossed) over his one shoulder, having more orgasms. This time he didn't make it to the sofa but sat on the floor with his head back so I could kiss him some more.

**March
2007**

Mar 1, 2007

Truck is STILL in the shop! Will NOT be able to make my appts! I was soo looking forward to meeting you!

Later that afternoon:
Now he calls and says my truck is done! Why couldn't he have done this earlier when I really needed to go to lunch! The fates are conspiring against me lately!

How have the fates been treating you?

And I have just published Shakespeare: the short course.

Mar 2, 2007
To A Lady, in A Letter.
by John Wilmot, 2nd Earl of Rochester
(April 1, 1647–July 26, 1680)

Such perfect bliss, fair Chloris, we
In our enjoyment prove:
'Tis pity restless jealousy
Should mingle with our love.

Let us, since wit has taught us how,
Raise pleasure to the top:
You rival bottle must allow,
I'll suffer rival fop.

Think not in this that I design
A treason 'gainst love's charms,
When following the god of wine
I leave my Chloris' arms:

Since you have that for all your haste,

At which I'll ne'er repine,
Will take its liquor off as fast
As I can take off mine.

There's not a brisk insipid spark
That flutters in the town,
But with your wanton eyes you mark
Him out to be your own.

Nor do you think it worth your care
How empty and how dull
The heads of your admirers are,
So that their bags be full.

All this you freely may confess,
Yet we ne'er disagree:
For did you love your pleasure less,
You were no match for me.

Whilst I my pleasure to pursue,
Whole nights am taking in
The lusty juice of grapes, take you
The juice of lusty men.

LOL More good stuff! Rochester also serves as a grave warning to those who would follow the 'wild life', dying as he did at age 33 from heavy metal poisoning which he took, in vain, to cure venereal disease. As witty as he was, John Wilmot wasn't wise.

Shakespeare: the short course
"Read the following and answer the question" is the format of the book. Three plays: one tragedy, one history, and one comedy; plus a select series of sonnets named "The Dark Lady" sonnets.

The Plays

Macbeth
Richard III
Measure for Measure

"Therefore I lie with her, and she with me,
And in our faults by lies we flattered be."

This is good stuff, people!

Mar 3, 2007
I shall focus upon housework - eeewwwwww - but it must
be done, babies. You know it must. So here I am in my
ratty jeans and a T-shirt - no I never wear them out of the
house - doing this and that. Vacuum with the left hand
while the right hand dusts. Pausing a moment to rotate the
laundry through the machines. Then it is folding the dry
stuff, and making up the bed.

After this: it is doing my claws and fluffing my fur and off
to the big Mardi Gras party!!!

Expanding my social circle, you know.
Kitten in the library with a goup of comely, willing, and
able teddybears!
Sounds good to you?
Later:
Y'all missed one hell of a party!!!!!
I had a MARVELOUS time!!
And that's all I'm going to tell you - such a tease!! LOL
But, oh, how I danced!!

Mar 4, 2007
"Foxy Foxy"

He who gets slapped and he who gets saved,
He who brutalizes the timeless stage.
He is the mongrel, he wants it all,
He lives for relics, hang on the wall.

Don't you wanna ride it?
Educated Horses
Don't you wanna ride it?
Educated Horses

Foxy, Foxy, what's it gonna be?
Foxy, Foxy, what's it gonna be?
Foxy, Foxy, what's it gonna be?
Foxy, Foxy, what's it gonna be?

She who looks back, and she looks away,
She internalizes the motion wave.
She is the butcher,
She wants the air,
She hides the scars under her hair.

Don't you wanna ride it?
Educated Horses
Don't you wanna ride it?
Educated Horses

Foxy, Foxy, what's it gonna be?
Foxy, Foxy, what's it gonna be?
Foxy, Foxy, what's it gonna be?
Foxy, Foxy, what's it gonna be?

Don't you wanna ride it?
Educated Horses

Don't you wanna ride it?
Educated Horses

Foxy, Foxy, what's it gonna be?
Foxy, Foxy, what's it gonna be?
Foxy, Foxy, what's it gonna be?
Foxy, Foxy, what's it gonna be?

Don't you wanna ride it?
Educated Horses
Don't you wanna ride it?
Educated Horses

- Rob Zombie

Kinda reminds you of The Doors, doesn't it?

Mar 5, 2007
"Having a little jealousy can enrich relationships, spark passion and romance, and strengthen a couple's devotion to each other. Therefore, you shouldn't panic if your partner shows some signs of jealousy. As long as you don't feel scared, stressed or like you're walking on eggshells, you don't have to worry."

"Dr. David Buss, author of The Dangerous Passion, says, "Jealousy is as important as trust in keeping couples together." He notes that "... jealousy evolved to fill that void, motivating vigilance as the first line of defense and violence as the last. The paradox is that jealousy -- an emotion evolved to protect love -- can rip a relationship apart. On the other hand, your own actions could be contributing to her insecurities and spawning that dreaded green-eyed monster. Sometimes, without even realizing it, men add fuel to their women's flames."

Stop it. As the red highlighted areas betray, jealousy is NOT about love but about fear (insecurity). And it works both ways, men being just as insecure as women. If you're insecure - fix it, don't inflict it. Try a little trust, then a little more trust. There's this entire high school mentality that equates 'sharing' with 'sloppy seconds'. PFFFT. If your relationships are all about propping up your sagging ego - you don't have a lover - you have a 'crutch'; an 'enabler'.

Next there's the "I deserve better" train of thought. Why do you deserve better? Who are you and what have you done to deserve better? Not to knock a healthy ego, but seriously - are you really all that? We are all just people here. Most of us are a mix of the good, the bad, and the indifferent trying to do the best we can. And most likely - you are just like the rest of us.

Would I feel and say the same if I were alone? Actually, yes. I spend most of my time alone and have for years. I know what it is like to be awake at 2 or 3am yearning for the touch of another, in my case male, human being. I have missed 'my designated/chosen companion' for the major holidays - in one case from Halloween to Valentine's Day. I was military remember. I had to directly face 'fear of loss' and 'fear of being left alone in the world'. Not pleasant, but I'll survive and live to smile and love again.

Jealousy is a huge waste of time better spent having fun.

There's a male cardinal perching on the beam supporting the front of the deck and the Heather is budding out. Soon it will be a mass of pale lavender flowers. Then it will be time to prune the many Roses and rake away the mulch. The Scotch Broom will need to be restaked and the Pyrocanthra will need trimming. You would not believe the lushness if you saw the garden now. But it will happen once again. The riotous tumbling of plants in my garden reflects my own exuberance for life.

"So, you want a boyfriend. You're sick of the singles scene and ready to move right past "Go" and settle down with someone who will carry you straight into your happily ever after. Well, hold it right there, Miss Antsy-Pants! Before you go tango into the sunset with Mr. Right, you have to take a few spins around the dating dance floor with a few Mr. Right Nows. Dating different personality types is the most effective way to find out your likes, dislikes and deal breakers. In fact, spending time with the wrong guys -- namely these five -- can actually make you a better package when Mr. Fabulous comes along.

1- Mr. Nice Romantic Guy
He'll show up with flowers, leave cards around your apartment and quote Keats on a whim. Think old-fashioned courtship where you're being wooed instead of sitting by the phone wondering if he'll call.

Celebrity counterparts: Cary Grant, Johnny Depp as Don Juan DeMarco

What he'll teach you: This affectionate man will show you a softer side of our male counterparts (what a relief to have someone fawn over you for a change!), all the while raising your expectations of how you wish to be treated. After realizing that there are guys out there who understand the importance of a random note or kiss in the moonlight, you'll be less likely to stay with someone who degrades or ignores you in the future.

The catch: Most of the time, these guys are in love with the idea of love. This means they will come on strong but lose momentum in the long haul as the reality of a relationship

298

sets in (i.e. disagreements, uneventful days), but that doesn't mean you shouldn't date him and enjoy the experience. Just keep a level head while he floats around you.

2- Mr. Big Shot
He dresses sharp, talks slick and has the perfectly coiffed looks of a man straight out of a lad mag. One look at him in his tailored suit and you're toast -- which is exactly why he wears it.

Celebrity counterparts: Chris Noth as Mr. Big, any Bond

What he'll teach you: From sending your nether regions to Brazil (Mr. Big Shot doesn't do granny panties) to the proper way to age a Cabernet, you're in for a crash course in the finer way of life. Dinners will be four-star and the conversation will be witty. You'll walk away from this relationship more sophisticated and well aware of your own inner vixen.

The catch: As the 007 of romance, he's going in for the kill. He knows exactly what he's doing and the effect it's having on you -- and every other girl around him. The odds of this guy slipping out of his suit and into a comfy relationship are low, but that doesn't mean you shouldn't enjoy the smooth ride around the town while it lasts.

3- Mr. Sexy Older Guy
He's old enough to have settled into his skin and has been involved with enough women to know that you require much more than dinner and a few martinis to get into the mood. Best of all, he never makes you late for dinner because he's playing Xbox.

Celebrity counterparts: Sean Connery, Antonio Banderas

What he'll teach you: He has a lifetime of experience to share (in and out of the bedroom), which will likely keep you on your toes (and curling them, too!). Plus, he'll show you how to see life in a different way. No matter how long it lasts or how it ends, you'll walk away worldlier -- and will never settle for a measly five minutes of foreplay again.

The catch: Despite what Demi and Ashton might say, age is more than a number. If you are just starting to get comfortable in your skin and he's shed his several times, there is a good chance you'll have issues with long-term compatibility. Sure, he's hot now, but how will you feel in 10 years? Give one another a thrill, then move onto someone you both can relate to.

4- Mr. Man's Man
He carries your bags, will defend your honor and would rather swallow glass than shave his chest or take hot wax to his eyebrows.

Celebrity counterparts: Frank Sinatra, Russell Crowe

What he'll teach you: This rough rogue will have you relishing in your femininity like no other. Why? There is something about raw masculinity that brings out the damsel in all of us. Dating this bruiser will show you how fun it can be when he shows you who the man is (think Rhett Butler when he scooped Scarlett up those stairs). Dating him will do one of two things: make you squeal with delight or appreciate your ability and right to wear the pants sometimes. Regardless, be sure to play Scarlett at least once -- trust us.

The catch: You're dying to be wined and dined, but he's already made plans to meet you down at the pub. This is the guy who gets inspired by Braveheart and cries only "out of frustration." He's also prone to affairs… with his favorite sports teams. Oh, and forget about asking him to hold your purse while you do anything -- he wouldn't dare.

5- Mr. Fun Social Guy
Whether he's out with friends or meeting the family for brunch, one thing's for certain: He's going to be the life of the party.

Celebrity counterparts: Will Farrell, Vince Vaughn

What he'll teach you: There is something very attractive about a man who's always ready to have a good time. You'll laugh a lot and learn how to go with the flow and let things slide. These types are often quite spontaneous, which means you should be ready for anything from a quickie to a quick dash to Vegas.

The catch: Most people are social because they like the company of others, but Fun Social Guys are social because they love to be the center of attention -- and they love the excitement of something new. This poses an issue for long-term loves because: A) Who wants to be an audience member 24/7, and Let's face it: Relationships can get dull at times -- what will he do then? Enjoy the roller-coaster ride, but don't be afraid to walk away to more stable ground."

Yeah. Like it is THAT easy to categorize anyone! Sometimes you just have to laugh!

I will be heading south for the birth of my next grandchild. This time, I will be alone as my mother battles once again

for life. There is no joy without sorrow and no sorrow
without joy.

Mar 6, 2007

Be careful what you wish for!
There are few things more disconcerting than screwing up
only to find she hasn't been paying enough attention to you
to notice and/or breaking up with someone only to have her
say "Okay, thanks." and wander off shedding you like last
year's skin only to have her later say "Who?". "Oh, yes.
Tall guy, had a parrot, eye-patch, and walked with a limp."
when you were short, walked straight, and hated birds.

The Soft Parade
By The Doors
When I was back there in seminary school
There was a person there
Who put forth the proposition
That you can petition the Lord with prayer
Petition the lord with prayer
Petition the lord with prayer
You cannot petition the lord with prayer!

Can you give me sanctuary
I must find a place to hide
A place for me to hide

Can you find me soft asylum
I can't make it anymore
The Man is at the door

Peppermint, miniskirts, chocolate candy
Champion sax and a girl named Sandy
There's only four ways to get unraveled
One is to sleep and the other is travel, da da

One is a bandit up in the hills
One is to love your neighbor 'till
His wife gets home

Catacombs
Nursery bones
Winter women
Growing stones
Carrying babies
To the river

Streets and shoes
Avenues
Leather riders
Selling news
The monk bought lunch

Ha ha, he bought a little
Yes, he did
Woo!
This is the best part of the trip
This is the trip, the best part
I really like
What'd he say?
Yeah!
Yeah, right!
Pretty good, huh
Huh!
Yeah, I'm proud to be a part of this number

Successful hills are here to stay
Everything must be this way
Gentle streets where people play
Welcome to the Soft Parade

All our lives we sweat and save

Building for a shallow grave
Must be something else we say
Somehow to defend this place
Everything must be this way
Everything must be this way, yeah

The Soft Parade has now begun
Listen to the engines hum
People out to have some fun
A cobra on my left
Leopard on my right, yeah

The deer woman in a silk dress
Girls with beads around their necks
Kiss the hunter of the green vest
Who has wrestled before
With lions in the night

Out of sight!
The lights are getting brighter
The radio is moaning
Calling to the dogs
There are still a few animals
Left out in the yard
But it's getting harder
To describe sailors
To the underfed

Tropic corridor
Tropic treasure
What got us this far
To this mild equator?

We need someone or something new
Something else to get us through, yeah, c'mon

Callin' on the dogs
Callin' on the dogs
Oh, it's gettin' harder
Callin' on the dogs
Callin' in the dogs
Callin' all the dogs
Callin' on the gods

You gotta meet me
Too late, baby
Slay a few animals
At the crossroads
Too late
All in the yard
But it's gettin' harder
By the crossroads
You gotta meet me
Oh, we're goin', we're goin great
At the edge of town
Tropic corridor
Tropic treasure
Havin' a good time
Got to come along
What got us this far
To this mild equator?
Outskirts of the city
You and I
We need someone new
Somethin' new
Somethin' else to get us through
Better bring your gun
Better bring your gun
Tropic corridor
Tropic treasure
We're gonna ride and have some fun

When all else fails
We can whip the horse's eyes
And make them sleep
And cry

-Jim Morrison
almost totally incomprehensible lyrics but it is a great song

Вам нужно не иметь никакое претендуйте с мной темная повелительница на темная лошадка не для злейшей крайности vile ни плен но отпуска от претендуйте освещено от позади солнцем звезды поманить все еще расширенную свободу руки предлагая сердца, котор вы льнете к предположено хотя оно не служило вам добро темные езды повелительницы на самостоятельно жить в сновидениях других людей

Dovete non fare fingere con me una signora scura su un cavallo scuro non per l'estremo diabolico di durance né vile ma il rilascio dal fingere illuminato dal sole le stelle la libertà d'offerta ancora estesa della mano del cuore che aderite a che cosa è previsto anche se gli non ha servito il pozzo i giri scuri della signora da solo sul frequentare i sogni di altri uomini

-set to Beethoven's Moonlight Sonata, the Adagio
this is an experimental sonnet
doesn't quite work

Mar 7, 2007

Rewards
Back beneath his collar and kneeling at the end of his bed, fondling and kissing my breasts while sliding his hands up and along my legs and thighs and periodically wrapping

306

one arm around me he then moved on down, kissing my body until he began cunnilingus while still caressing me. Several orgasms later, mmmm I love orgasms, I gently pulled on his collar and put my crossed ankles onto his left shoulder as he entered me. Oh yes, right there. Yes, Just like that. My back arches and I lightly run my claws down the front of his thighs as he moves inside of me. He then began climbing onto the bed, one knee, then the other as I wrapped my legs around him. He came, as I did, when I gently bit his shoulder. I love hearing him cum. But I don't' let him stop there. I squeeze him and continue to move, doubling him. Now it is time for his massage. I begin on his back. This is a real massage suited to the heavier musculature of men. I put my full weight into it, working his flesh into submission. As his body relaxes shoulders and wrists down through his legs, I begin gently drawing arabesques onto his skin with my claws, kissing, him, licking his skin, touching him with my lips, hair, and body; sliding up and down along his length. Kissing the nape of his neck I whisper that it is time for him to roll over. He does and I begin again with my heavy handed techniques then move up and begin gently licking the corner of his eye with the tip of my tongue, then over his lips and kissing at the point of his jaw moving from side to side, then down his throat, his chest, his stomach. Then I breathe onto his cock without touching him. Slowly, ever so very slowly, I take him into my mouth. And begin attempting to remove his brains from his skull via his penis. Resistance is futile. Men are so cute when they cannot move afterwards and when they regain movement they tend to walk sideways which is also cute. Please don't fall down. You're too big for me to lift. Snuggling on the sofa until he's gotten his breath back. I lie diagonally onto his bed and he scoops me up into his arms, kisses, mmmmm, and then I slide him in oh yes, more, more, more. Without missing a move we go into scissors and then his reward. I slyly move his cock out and back a bit and we're spooning but at a 90 degree angle and I slide him up into my ass. Moving together he soon orgasmed and we lay there with him still inside for several minutes. Mmmmm, you're welcome, baby.

See you tomorrow.

Mar 8, 2007

"What should I do if a woman asks if I'm a player?
She asks: "Are you a player?"
You answer: "Are you trying to hide the fact that YOU are?"
One key in situations like this is to NEVER give a woman a direct answer. Use your Cocky & Funny skills to come up with five good answers and try them out on women.
Maybe say, "Yes, I play sports... what do you like?"
As you can see, I like to turn questions and accusations around and guess what they're trying to hide; that what they're asking about is actually something that is wrong with THEM.
Just don't answer directly and most women will give up.
If you get defensive and say, "Oh, no... I'm not a player at all...," most women won't believe you anyway -- even if you're NOT a player."

Don't answer directly and yes, most women will know you're bs-ing them and take no further interest in you. You're off her list, buddy. Think of it this way: either you have cojones and tell the truth or you don't have cojones in which case why should she waste her time?

Mar 9, 2007

In order to live with any kind of grace, you have to learn to appreciate the ironies of life. Even when they hurt. You should also try to learn from them. Some find this difficult to do. It is both amusing and heart-wrenching to watch the same fruitless patterns of behavior being repeated.
I do it even as I try not to.
Tell me - are you guilty too?

Too many 'newbies', only one of whom was really any good. Ah well! Perhaps we should stick to our own parties. It was nice to get out, however.
Organization and partner selection - keys to a good party.
Don't you think so, too?

One of my Editors: a very sweet man, stopped by the other morning to pick up a manuscript. He also me wonderful birthday gifts! Two books and a bottle of scotch that came with two glasses! THANK YOU, SWEETY!

John Wilmot, 2nd Earl of Rochester; Much of his work is an exercise in shockingly portraying the shallowness and degradation of his life. He wrote about what he himself could not escape much as Shakespeare did in his Dark Lady sonnets, though Shakespeare was the greater poet. This same pattern, of writing about what you yourself cannot escape, is also clearly seen in De Quincy.
I'm sure you could also add more names to this list.

Mar 10, 2007

There's a bet on:

1. if he does it - then I have to go out to dinner and actually eat dinner including vegetables *shuddering*

2. if he does NOT do it, then I get to hear him and his group play.

Should be fun!
We shall see how it turns out!
deadline: 10 June 2007

No matter how narrow a woman's life might seem on the outside, there is in every one an internal life of fantasy and joy. Do you not agree?

Mar 11, 2007

I am not a domme' seeking 'a night off', thank you. You may stop writing and sending me 'challenging' emails designed to dare me into forming some sort of relationship with you. Save the electrons.
I find such behavior juvenile, and therefore boring, at best.
You would find me disconcerting because any 'taming' you would undertake would have no effect. It is likely that I would be taking mental notes and writing a scathing critique of your methods, attitude, and poor candidate selection procedures.
The last one who tried, many years ago, found me dancing The Charleston (very poorly but I was blindfolded at the time) instead of adopting the preferred submissive pose and attitudes.
Terribly sorry, babies.
But, your desired outcome is just soooo not happening.

Spring Point-to-Points
All those wishing to accompany me are requested to let me know. Most begin at noon. BYOB and I do the driving!
EG
March 17th, Saturday, Airlie Race Course, Warrenton.
April 29th, Sunday, Glenwood Park, Middleburg

310

and the Championship meet:
May 27th, Saturday, Morven Park, Leesburg
There are others so if you cannot make these or if you'd like more information, just ask.

Mar 12, 2007

Just a few 'very good friends' is how this all began. Then one thing led to another and another. Well, I'm going back to my original premise.
Therefore: I am only interested in a discreet LT fwb R with a sincere and suitable man who is committed to "the lifestyle". Mildly evil, cute, witty teddybears without other 'encumbrances' preferred. No 'agendas', please.
More than that cannot be guaranteed.

Kitten-cisms
1. when the desire overcomes the fear - you're ready for sex/relationship.
2. similarly, if the pain outweighs the pleasure - you'll stop/change the relationship.
3. he/she steps-up or you step-off -quietly demand your due.
4. be unstinting - live the life you wish to live wholeheartedly.
5. you get what you give - the old thing called "karma" as well as be reciprocal in your relationships.
Those are mine - what are yours?

Mar 13, 2007

Hi Ho, Hi Ho; It's Off to.... Court I go.... but I have to leave soon so as to NOT have to speed to get to traffic court to answer for speeding. Ироничность.
Wish me luck, please! I am going to need it! It is also a long walk back!

STROKING THE BONES

Hmmm come and pet me, baby, with those long light touches you do so well all up and down my body, one hand caressing the front of my hip, the other hand stroking the back of my leg as your lips kiss and nuzzle just beneath one buttock until your hand finds my G-Spot and your tongue finds my peritoneum. Oh yeah! Feels so very good! Then it is quickly into our favorite position of you standing at the edge of the bed with me on my back and my crossed ankles onto your shoulder with you deeply inside being squeezed as you move in and out. I love hearing you cum as much as you love hearing me. Now that the preliminaries are over, I have two new things for you to try. You kneel on the bed staying upright, your back to me and with greased hands I begin caressing you while pressing my lips on the back of your neck, nibbling your ears, and breathing on the sides of your neck as my hands slowly and firmly slide all over your body. Accept the pleasure you feel. Enjoy it; suspending all thought. One hand sliding down the front of your throat while the other caresses your testicles from behind. Then up your spine while caressing your penis. Always three points of contact for while my hands are busy so to is my mouth or my body sliding along your skin. Slowly. Repeatedly. Building but never enough to bring you to orgasm. Lie down onto your back. I begin fellatio then bring the vibe up underneath and behind your scrotum slowly moving it down and back until I find your G-Spot with it. How you love it! Your penis deep in my throat, my hand holding your testicles and that vibe gently moving just so. But your orgasm is mine to control and you are not permitted to move. Accept the pleasure you feel. Let it run freely through you. Up, down, in, out, twisting, hard, soft, gentle, rough - over and over again. Leaving the vibe where it is at, I sit on top of you and take you inside me. Now. Yes, now! A short wild ride as I cum all over you and you cum inside of me. Yes!! I get up and pull on your legs, stretching you a bit as you relax. Feels so good. I tidy up leaving you time to recover from your first male G-Spot orgasm. Deep slow breaths, baby - there's more to come. Now we're going to enjoy sex with strength. It is my own original technique called stroking the bones. There's nothing light and tantalizing here. Now it is just controlled masculine strength and ardor as you with heavy hands ignore the usual erogenous zones and instead focus on the bones in my body. Sliding down the arms, across the shoulders, along the ribs, around the shoulder blades. Your greased hands holding and moving me as you exerting all of your strength. Then the spine from the back of the skull slowly down all of the way to my coccyx. Oh that feels so overwhelming! Again and again! Aah!! Then the pelvis and the down the legs. I had been kneeling at the edge of the bed, now I rotate to face you as you kneel there and wrap myself around you - totally ignited. One hand firmly holding me to you as your mouth seeks my breast and your other hand finds my G-Spot again. Then I am kissing you violently while clawing your back and rump. Biting your shoulders. Highly erotic wild power sex as I rotate again and stand before you bent over and you enter inside. Yes, now! Go! WOW!

Never fear to cut loose, sweety. I will not break.

Mar 14, 2007

There really is an "International Ask A Question Day", and it's today!
I'm observing it by Opening myself up for questions from you. I haven't done this in 6 months, and probably won't do it again for another 6 months. So put your thinking caps on, and ask me...!! Can I ask you a question too?

313

"Make no mistake about it, I don't think it's a good idea to act like a jerk to other people. But I DO think it's a GREAT idea to tease women, bust on them, be Cocky & Funny, and play hard to get. Now, the reason most guys treat a woman they like extra nicely is because they're AFRAID of doing the things that could build attraction because to do that would mean RISKING REJECTION. It's safer to be nice to her because how can she reject you when you're being nice? But if you want to turn her from a friend to a lover, acting nice SIMPLY WON'T WORK. You have to do something MORE, and my Cocky & Funny strategies are a great place to start. Suggest grabbing a cup of tea... and then bust on her playfully. Lean back. Relax. When you do, she'll see you as the kind of confident, secure guy she's after... then SHE will come to YOU. Well, the problem in these types of situations is that most guys don't want to get a woman's number then be seen talking to other women or getting other numbers because they don't want to be seen as "players" or as insincere. My advice? Get over it. If you enjoy talking to a woman and you'd like to get her number AND go talk to other people (including other women), just say: "Here, write down your e-mail and number. I'm going to get back to my friends" and DO IT. She'll actually see you as an "in demand" kind of guy if she sees you talking to other women. Her competition mechanism will kick in, and that will actually AMPLIFY her attraction for you."

Given human variability, this may work with some women. But, to put it rather bluntly, if you aren't with her, someone else will be. And you're left behind at the starting gate.

Mar 15, 2007

It Seems that I shall have to move along. So a few more applications will be required. You will recall where in my previous post I said "if you're not with her..."? Precisely.

314

I shall drift along and see who is out there.
No one has signed up to accompany me to the races this weekend either. Oh well! And here you want people to believe you know how to party! Hah!
wandering off as felines will

Mar 16, 2007

You get what you give....so if you want ENTHUSIASM, PASSION, and total INVOLVEMENT...guess what? You have to GIVE them. Either meet me with fire in your eyes, heart, and loins (even if just for a tryst) - or go annoy some other woman.
Are you with me on this?

Very exciting, very fun, very fast, and very revealing!! LOL I was showing a LOT more than is pictured herein too! I'd like to publicly thank Phineas for 'preserving my dignity'! You ladies should try dancing with Wolf!!

Mar 17, 2007

My Specifications:
I prefer men who meet the following:
1. aged 45 to 55 although exceptional men as young as 40 may apply.
2. 6ft or taller as I am a tall, long-legged woman who requires a man my ardor cannot break
3. furry since I adore fur on men, it is a very masculine thing
4. nearby I require frequent attention
5. kneeling I am a domme after all and kneeling does put you where I want you to be, geographically speaking.
6. an alpha male if you have to ask...
7. more than half a brain so you can keep up
Finally - I am only interested in a discreet LT fwb R with a sincere and suitable man who is committed to "the lifestyle". Mildly evil, cute, witty teddybears without other encumbrances preferred.
Thank you! Wish me luck! Hope I find him!

Mar 18, 2007

I was reading The Economist, April 2007, in the bath, which is the only way to read it, because by doing so I could lightly cast water droplets over those articles I found inane, otherwise disagreeable or pompous. So there I am casting water droplets, shaving my legs, and reading articles on the private property rights legislation coming up for a vote in China this week - all at the same time. Then lunch was called so I dropped the magazine, not into the water, washed the green volcanic mud from my face, dried off, dressed, and went to get my tomato soup and grilled cheese sandwich and a glass of 2% milk.
How did you prepare to meet your Sunday?

Mar 19, 2007

Have I Mentioned how much I HATE getting 'stood-up'??
Of course I have. And I know you don't like it either so I
try very hard to NOT stand anyone else up. BUT it still
happens.
If you are meeting me for lunch, please inform me that you
CANNOT make it by 11am as this is when I leave my
computer and office to drive out to you.
For all other appt times, please give me, at least, a two hour
head's up if there are any changes in the schedule. You
know what traffic is like around here.
Can you do that for me, please?

I have created three "blings".
small square ones
1. tiger stripes
2. lightning bolt
3. skull and crossbones
Three little patches for you 'collectors' out there!
Enjoy!
Ok, ok it is now 4 bling patches. I added "burning sun" last
night.

Mar 20, 2007

Don't Review Your Blog!
I was so very happy. Ah me! But "the game is worth the
candle". So here I continue. Although so few of you are
willing to join me in happy polyamory.
The future remains obscured so love as many as you can as
frequently as you can!
May the devil take the hindmost!

Potato Soup Recipe

Proof that I can cook!

Sauté' the following in 1 Tablesp butter and olive oil:
2 slices of onion chopped
1/2 a pound of bacon chopped
1 teasp coarsely ground black pepper
5 large potatoes peeled and chopped
a scant handful of spring onion greens chopped
until the potatoes gain some color.
Add in 1/2 C of red wine and 1 teasp Worcestershire sauce.
Pour in chicken stock until covered and bring to a boil.
Then cover and simmer for 30 minutes.
Just before serving slide in 1 C of milk while stirring and
warm through.
Serve with red wine and bread. Yields 4 bowls.

Mar 21, 2007

I HAVE MISSED HIM
Off the injured list and back into my arms again, I had
almost forgotten what a wonderful lover he is. Almost. We
re-acquainted ourselves with kisses and body worship. I
love the feel of fur beneath my hands. His lips pressed
against the side of my neck - sheer bliss! Sliding down my
oiled body I received cunnilingus as done by a master of
the art. You had me clawing the pillows, my dear! You
moved up and caressed my labia with the head of your
penis before sliding in. Yes. So very good. This was a
quick beginning for what would be a long and sensuous
sexual interlude. More oil and an excellent back rub later,
and I went down on him. Nice to hear how well he enjoyed
it. Mmmm very expressive! I then rode and rode him. My
ejaculating all over him woke all of his cylinders; a wild
romp ensued as we slid from position to position. His
orgasms coming almost as fast as mine but he rejuvenates
without leaving me. His penis hardening again and again

inside of me. This is his most special skill. I like how he caresses my legs with the side of his face, kneeling, with my crossed ankles on his one shoulder. We ended up on our sides as a Y until I had finally exhausted him. WOW! I am the most fortunate of felines! Welcome back, baby! I have missed you!

and he gave a birthday gift too! Very nice and greatly appreciated.

I have never been impressed with mere 'appearances'. If there is no substance to support the appearance, then that appearance is worthless to me. This goes along with my dictum "you get what you give". If I once offered friendship and you showed no interest, then that offer will not be repeated. The public semblance of "friendship" is of no use to me. You are either there or you are not. I only deal with what is real. You understand?

Mar 23, 2007

Re: those clubs where single males are either excluded or charged more in order to subsidize the single females.
"My female date for the APG Mardi Gras party, which did allow single males, made a point in that the female half of couples are there for other females. The male halves of those couples are even lucky that they're getting any play. Why? It's simple...if they want dick, they have one at home, but when they go out, their female half wants pussy. Hence, these couples will shun all males (even their hubbies) and start searching for that unicorn. Unless of course you are that GQ/Playgirl centerfold, 10" hung-type, that kind of dick is NOT at home...LOL."
This is true ONLY for those women who are interested in women and not ALL of us are. (Now if only they'd toss

their husbands my way while they searched for those unicorns! Ah me!)
I say charge a set price for admission regardless of who the person is. If the club wants to encourage single females, then they should suck up the subsidy - not the single males. What do you think?

Over the last several years of my time here, I have run across those who have suffered abuse at the hands of those who should have protected them, nurtured them, and loved them - but did not. To you all I offer my deepest sympathy, warm hugs, and the words "it was not your fault". I was one of the fortunate ones; the one's whose mother was, and still is, a tigress dedicated to her children and willing to battle anyone at any time to secure their happiness and well-being. I wish that you all had had a mother like mine.
Thank you, Mom!

Mar 24, 2007

The Piedmont Fox Hounds Point-to-Point Races at Salem Course, in Upperville, VA.

W and I went out for a delightfully 'soft' day at the races and had a great time swigging wine (a shiraz) out of the bottle (someone forgot the wineglasses), watching the horses run past, and taking pictures in an "impressionist" style. W is of the partnership N&W one of our oldest play partnerships and a great guy! So we talked about everything - from the China scare a while ago to how pleased they were that we had found them.

but back to the races:

First Race: The George Robert Slater Memorial, a race for maidens 5 years and up, over timber, carrying 165 lbs. I selected Crypto Cousin and W selected Radio Flyer. Radio Flyer, a bay gelding aged 6 yrs from Ireland owned by Augustin Stables and ridden by Stewart Strawbridge, won. Field of 12 horses.

Second Race: The C. Reed Thomas, MFH Memorial, a race for owner/rider & foxhunter over timber for 5 yr olds and up ridden by gentlemen, carrying 180 lbs. I selected Bien Allure and W selected Where's the Wire. Bien Allure, a bay gelding aged 11 yrs, owned and ridden by James Whitner IV, pulled it out going up the last hill to the finish line to win. Field of 6 horses.

Third Race: The Thomas M. Beach Memeorial, the Lady Rider over Timber for 5 yr olds and up carrying 150 lbs. Enough shiraz having been imbibed by this time we just decided to take pix. This race became a hotly contested one over the final jump as Inca Colony, Edited, and Bulawayo fought it out for the win. Antonio Star was close but last. Not being able to hear clearly, W and I remain uncertain as to exactly which horse won. I rather thought Bulawayo had gotten it while W was certain the Inca Colony had proved triumphant. Rather than argue about it we went back to his place to continue the "conversation".

BTW these races are all 3 miles long - cross country.
Got home to receive the news that the shower had been leaking into the sub-floor. *SIGH*
Heigh ho for a quiet life in the country!

Mar 25, 2007

What was supposed to be a day of motorcycling has become a day of house projects (see previous post). Yes, we do all of our own work and we are very good at it. This can also be fun, of course, but it wasn't quite what I had planned for us. Ah well - it was a trifle cool outside anyway. So carefully removing tile, and linoleum in order to see how extensive the damage is will be our "fun" for today. As a break from that action, I can hunt up the papers the accountant wants.

I ask very little of men. I accept them for who they are. I enjoy them as both lovers and friends - yes, they have to be both. Since I am not going to change, I do not ask them to change either. Since I am not going to be exclusive - how could I possibly be exclusive? - I'm not going to ask them to be exclusive. I demand from men only what I am willing to give them. Sincerity, honesty, acceptance, strength, true friendship, and courage. This is in addition to wild, rampant, skin-on-skin, full-body contact sex, of course.

"When I have a quiet hour at work (I can rarely surf the web at home) I like to pop into AFF and scan its own little blogosphere…. Since I can so seldom reach out to anyone, reading the blogs is my principal point of AFF engagement…. There are some blogs I check regularly, of course. Almost all of them are women's…. Each of these women, in her own way, impresses me as exceptional. Each has overcome some recent sorrow. In no particular order:
One blogger is a woman I have met, and would be very sorry not to meet again. She lives life with an audacity that I find astonishing – and while we share many common interests (I mean besides sex!) she just plain baffles me! Which is a significant part of her appeal, I confess…. From time to time she recounts in her blog erotic adventures that leave me (and probably every other man who reads them) feeling envious/angry/hungry for her company… "I had almost forgotten what a wonderful lover he is. Almost. We re-acquainted ourselves with kisses and body worship…" The "he" there was most definitely not me! Drat!"

Thank you, Sweety! But I am not that difficult to understand.

"If a flying saucer landed in my back yard and a purple-people-eater emerged from it, stared at me with his three great, green eyes and announced: "Gracch threeble banzingo!", I could understand him better than I do you...."
SIGH

Mar 26, 2007

Cat Toy Appreciation Day:
May is coming up soon and I'd like to remind all of those delicious Cat Toys that their day is rapidly approaching. I do hope they are up for this! Last year's party was so much fun!

"But Your words posted yesterday and today, whether ya meant it as fact fiction or fantasy, may become the New Gospel According To You, Whole new religions, philosophies even cults and sects may arise to worship you as a mythological god or goddess... "
He writes a wonderful blog - but this idea is just - unsettling. THE GODS MUST BE CRAZY...OR MAYBE I AM.... S, my sweet - sometimes ya scare me!
What would my 'cult' look like, believe, and what rites would they practice?

Mar 27, 2007

If you are here, and if you are serious, then you would have completed your profile, posted a decent picture, and checked everything over twice to make sure that you are presenting yourself as attractively as possible - to your target audience, which you have chosen wisely. Go with your strengths. Specifically, point 1: what about you appeals the most; and point 2: to whom?

For example: I have always attracted a certain type of man. So my profile, my pix, etc., everything is written to appeal most strongly to my 'natural market'. My entire presentation 'package' is based upon my skill with words and with nuance, my love of seduction, my high sex drive, and my highly energetic zest for life - my 'audacity' *EG*.

You have a good idea of what I will bring to these 'negotiations' - what will you bring in exchange?

Does this help?

The Queen Bee Syndrome exists. Once an insecure female has what she wants, she deliberately prevents other women from achieving similar success. This can be seen, both professionally and socially and is usually dismissed as just 'her way'. It is deadly to other women. Only her boss/husband can stop this behavior but, oddly enough, often men do not see it or recognize it for what it is.

1. she comes in between you and others - possessive
2. she takes over tasks from others - is greedy
3. she subtly undermines and torpedoes other women while appearing to help/like them - "bless her heart, she tries"
4. usually operates one victim at a time then moves to the next - sneaky
5. uses/plays men to achieve her objective - esp her bosses - playing it 'safe'

What the Queen Bee wants is to be the only woman in an all-male shop. She wants to be the center of masculine attention - only socially, however. She doesn't want men - she wants drones. To men she always appears sweet, nice, and supportive. So if you look around and all of your women are gone except the one (speaking from experience here) or you have no real friends in your social circle other than those she doesn't feel threatened by - you now know what happened. **You were suckered.** Female rivalry is a fucking HUGE waste of time which is why I DON'T do it in spite of having been on the receiving end of it TWICE now in my adult life. Please see Mean Girls Grow Up by Cheryl Dellasega, PhD

The Book of The Dead
Funerary literature of ancient Egypt began with the Pyramid Texts. These evolved into the Coffin Texts which later became The Book of The Dead. While not "religious" in perhaps the strictest sense, there is an ideal moral value inherent in these writings. This can be most clearly seen in The Negative Confessions:

1. Have you done wrong?
2. Have you robbed with violence?
3. Have you stolen?
4. Have you slain another?
5. Have you defrauded the offering?
6. Have you reduced measures?
7. Have you plundered the Gods?

8. Have you spoken lies?
9. Have you spoken evil?
10. Have you caused pain to another?
11. Have you committed fornication?
12. Have you caused the shedding of tears?
13. Have you dealt with deceit?
14. Have you transgressed?

15. Have you dissembled?
16. Have you laid waste to the land?
17, Have you discussed secrets?
18. Have you brought false lawsuits?
19. Have you been angry but for just cause?
20. Have you defiled the wife of any man?
21. Have you caused terror?

22. Have you polluted yourself?
23. Have you been hot tempered?
24. Have you been neglectful of truthful words?
25. Have you cursed another?
26. Have you acted with insolence?
27. Have you stirred up strife?
28. Have you judged hastily?

29. Have you gossiped?
30. Have you sought for unearned honors?
31. Have you been garrulous in speech?
32. Have you done evil?
33. Have you disputed the King?
34. Have you fouled the waters?
35. Have you spoken scornfully?

36. Have you cursed a God?
37. Have you carried off goods by force?
38. Have you damaged the offerings to the Gods.
39. Have you plundered the offerings to the Blessed dead.
40. Have you stolen food from a babe?
41. Have you harmed the God of your place of birth?
42. Have you slain the cattle of the Gods?

Now, "confessions" as used here does not mean repentance and all is forgiven. There is no forgiveness available to anyone in this code. Your heart is weighed against the truth with a fine impartial objectivity in the Hall of Judgment. In The Book of The Dead you find 'spells' and 'prayers' to help you reach The Field of Reeds.

This all sounds very familiar, doesn't it?

Mar 28, 2007

FROM THE ANKLES UP

I walked in to find a naked man waiting for me. How very, very nice! I rapidly disrobed while he donned his collar. He gets this wickedly gleeful look in his eye when he straps that bit of leather around his neck. We begin kissing then its onto the bed for a bit of "hello how are ya?" sex. Some laughter, a few orgasms, lots of hugging and then I am on the sofa with a short scotch to sip and my hair's all messed up. On his knees at the end of the bed he begins licking from my ankles up. Very slowly, first one then the other, around, up, down, moving ever higher up my legs. A quick bit of cunnilingus and he keeps moving slowly upward, softly chuckling; he can feel the heat coming off my skin since my blood's roaring but he ignores my claws on his shoulders and my cries of delight. I can't take any more and grab hold of him, slide myself around him. I am totally, completely given over to passion. I am not holding anything back from him. OMG! He doesn't even have to move, just hold on. He's kneeling low on the bed with a wild kitten in his lap riding him, kissing him, clawing, biting and cumming all over him. I was wild and he didn't seem to mind. Wet orgasm after wet orgasm for me then he couldn't wait any longer and had his own orgasm. We collapsed onto the bed gasping for breath and cuddling. I walked sideways over to the sofa looking for my drink. Empty; so he brought me a soda and I looked him over for damages. He seemed quite proud of himself. Kept showing the marks off with a particularly complaisant air. He was cute. I had to agree that he certainly earned the marks. Wow! A short interlude this time but at lunch the next day he assured me that he was healing up very nicely. The sly devilish teddybear then snuck in more food when he ordered for us. Grrrrrrrr. Naughty teddybear!

Mar 29, 2007

-reposted by request
(refers to the roof of the vagina and how to induce squirting)

The Guided Tour
As you go in, you will find first a kind of squashed grape structure covered with goose bumps in the front and on the top. These goose bumps enlarge and become more prominent as her excitement mounts. Then there is a central raised area going further back with two grooves on either side. Further in, you come to a raised bar going from side to side followed by an area like a washboard. You may not reach the bar or washboard as she may be too excited to permit you to get back that far as she clamps down upon you or your hand. But if you stroke upwards gently while exploring these features, you just might get very, very wet. She has to be both relaxed and extremely aroused in order to ejaculate. Yes, a man can induce squirting using his penis as well. The female ejaculate is perfectly safe to drink; although it does not do very much for his contacts if he is wearing them at the time and you get it in his eyes. It does come out with some pressure and can be copious, so having towels nearby would be a good idea. The ejaculate evaporates quickly without a stain.

Spend some time with this.
It is well worth the effort!
Wheeeeeeeeee! LOL

Mar 30, 2007

Dominating Alpha Males:
Impossible, you say? Not at all. It may surprise you to know that the vast majority of sexual submissives are

328

dominants the rest of the time in all other areas of their lives. That is the standard profile. Consider this from his point of view. He has to do all of the work. Selecting, chasing, initiating and so on. How nice would it be if she selected you, chased you, and initiated sex with you for once? Most men would love it even if it did involve a few bits of leather.

1. He gets a vacation. 2. He receives intensely focused attention. 3. He learns more about himself.

Read the Playtime with Teddybears posts below. Now imagine how that would feel. Those few bits of leather only heighten the experience - making it more intense. The thought of claws lightly ghosting slowly over your skin and fur when you can neither see or escape doesn't excite you? (For the women reading this - if it excites you - it might excite him.) Also notice that while most people's idea of dominatrix means whips and harsh treatment - this is NOT necessarily the case. There are many levels to all encounters. Open your mind and forget those comic book notions.

Examples:

1. Receiving an erotic massage while being tied down onto her bed. Followed by fellatio and a male G-Spot orgasm.
2. Being blindfolded and told to take an active role when you cannot see but only feel her.
3. Being denied the use of your hands as she has you perform cunnilingus and then rides you vigorously until she's had 20 to 30 orgasms and had ejaculated all over you.
4. Any of the above with two dominant women simultaneously.

We are not talking about a 24/7/365 full power exchange here. There is no pain, abuse or humiliation involved. He is not asked to do what he does not want to do. There is no pushing of limits. There is an exploration of both mind and body. There is a total involvement of both partners, or more, in the process to the enjoyment of everyone involved. Does this help clear up the confusion?

"Ramble on Rose"
Just like Jack the Ripper
Just like Mojo Hand
Just like Billy Sunday
In a shotgun ragtime band
Just like New York City,
Just like Jericho
Pace the halls and climb the walls
Get out when they blow

(Chorus)
Did you say your name was
Ramblin' Rose?
Ramble on, baby
Settle down easy
Ramble on, Rose

Just like Jack and Jill
Mama told the sailor
One heat up and one cool down
Leave nothin' for the tailor
Just like Jack and Jill
My Papa told the jailer
One go up and one come down
Do yourself a favor

(Chorus)

(Bridge)

I'm gonna sing you a hundred verses in ragtime
I know this song it ain't never gonna end
I'm gonna march you up and down the local county line
Take you to the leader of the band

Just like Crazy Otto
Just like Wolfman Jack
Sittin' plush with a royal flush
Aces back to back
Just like Mary Shelley
Just like Frankenstein
Clank your chains and count your change
Try to walk the line

(Repeat chorus and bridge)

Goodbye, Mama and Papa
Goodbye, Jack and Jill
The grass ain't greener, the wine ain't sweeter
either side of the hill.

Did you say your name was
Ramblin' Rose?
Ramble on, baby
Settle down easy
Ramble on, Rose

Words by Robert Hunter; music by Jerry Garcia
("Ramble On Rose" composed and written by Robert
Hunter and Jerry Garcia. Reproduced by arrangement with
Ice Nine Publishing Company, Inc. (ASCAP)).

So cool!

Mar 31, 2007

Loot first; pillage second.
not vice versa.

"Your granddaughter is being very stubborn and cranky."
naturally - takes after her mother
who
takes after her mother
who
takes after her mother
so you see
- tis only to be expected
Just remember, daughter of mine, what you have so often counseled me - "serenity"
LOL & BIG BEAR HUGS

I went last night, with one dear friend, to celebrate our mutual friend's ascension to honors due her. I had nothing in common with everyone else there, other than my friend and my escort, and yet – the honest outpouring of affection for her, our friend, welded us all together. Nothing but the joy we shared mattered. We laughed, sang, and clapped our hands in exuberance and celebration!
I am so very proud of her!
I am so very happy for her!
She is magnificent!

April
2007

Apr 1, 2007

May's party is Cat Toy Appreciation Day - when the women come out and show the delicious Cat Toys how much we enjoy their 'participation'.
We will need as many women as we can get to come out!
So, ladies - NOW is the time to contact me!

Apr 2, 2007

Resistance is Futile I Say!!!
"Oh give me a home
where the naked men roam
and the kittens
and the teddybears play
where seldom is heard
that dreadful word
and the sex is rampant all day."
Just had to do it.

Apr 3, 2007

One and Only
This should develop over time with the aim being marriage.
The problem with demanding it up front is that one gets too tightly wrapped around the axle and then you end up clingy, needy, and willing to do anything or to put up with anything to keep him/her. Fear of loss rearing its ugly head. Date several and this does not occur.

No, I won't actually fuck anyone. Sorry, if this ruins your illusions but THAT part of the adventure is a long time over. Condoms are mandatory. If you do not have, then you do not get. Got that? Look, you may neither agree with me

334

nor even like me but stop thinking that I am stupid. One cannot mess around with men for 39 years now and escape entirely unscathed, which I have, without having intelligence. No one, not even me, is that lucky. For the record I have never been pregnant out of wedlock and I have never had, nor do I have now, any STDs; period. You may now stop emailing. Thank you.

Apr 4, 2007

CLAW MARKS
Forget foreplay. Forget collars. Wild rampant sex is what we shared yesterday. Him on top. We couldn't even make it through a smoke break without abandoning everything and racing back to the bed. Me riding him. I shredded his back because he felt so good! Having sex at the end of the bed. We rolled around on the bed stopping periodically to take a few more pictures and then it was back to the sex! Where did the bottom sheet go? He kept trying not to orgasm but with little success. Try to not have an orgasm with me, will you? Hah! Take this! A bit of snuggling then we went out for a bit. When we returned, he barely had enough time to remove his clothes before I pounced upon him and had my way with him again. Yes, just socks is not a good look for a man. Fortunately, I wasn't looking. He was a tired teddybear and I was grinning while I tried to not walk sideways. Wow, Baby! That was great!
I might even post the pictures.

Apr 5, 2007

Calculating Cost Basis:
There are four methods to figuring out cost basis. Just remember choosing one method over another could result in tax savings.

1. First In, First Out - (FIFO) The first shares you bought are those that you're selling now. This is the default method so unless you choose otherwise, the IRS will assume this is the method you used. While this is also the easiest, it is the one method that usually results in the biggest tax bite.

2. Single-Category Averaging - This is where you take all shares, regardless of when you bought them, total cost of shares divided by the number of shares and there you are - your average cost basis. Be aware that if you choose this method, the IRS will have to approve if you change to another method later before you change.

3. Specific Shares - For meticulous investors only! If you've kept careful records of what you bought when and for how much, you can specify precisely which shares you want to sell thereby controlling your cost basis and the taxes paid on any gains. Keep in mind your holding period when making this decision.

4. Double-Category Averaging - Short term shares owned and then long term shares owned - compute each category's cost basis as in #2 above.

Note that you have to tell your broker/mutual fund company in writing which shares and how you are computing your cost basis.

I recommend Method 3 myself.

Apr 6, 2007

Happy Birthday, Pookie!
The most courageous and loving man in the world!!

Guys, When All Else Fails.... Try these female attracting tactics:
1. Show off your handsome feet, then pick up your chin and say "ooooo" very loudly and repeat. Then ask her if she's hot yet?
2. Fling yourself up into the air, fluttering your arms and shout "Look at me! Look at me!" and repeat. Then ask her if she's hot yet?
3. Catch yourself a fish then circle around the ladies saying "Hey baby, baby! See, fish! Fiiiish!" and repeat. Then ask if she's hot yet?
You know you want me. LOL
Hey, if it works *shrug* it works! Right?

The Seven Deadly Sins
Seven sins whose seriousness was based on the degree from which they offended against love with this escalating severity representing increasing fixation with the self; vanity being the most egregious of the sins. So here they are in order from least to worst.

GLUTTONY
LUST
SLOTH
WRATH
ENVY
AVARICE
VANITY

The common everyday sorts of things people do, is not what is meant here. The true target are those persons who give their entire lives over to the sin as a drug addict gives everything over to the drug. The sin consumes him/her and becomes their only reality. They have no moral 'brakes' to stop them. Thus the envious person will never be satisfied. The wrathful person will always reach for deadly force first. The avarice person always will covet more, will want more, will need more. The vain will believe themselves even better than the divine let alone you and the rest of humanity.

None of you, I hope, are truly guilty of any of them.

Apr 7, 2007

She asked:
1. If you've met me in-person what was the first thing you felt/thought when you saw me?
2. If you've only "met" me online what was your first thought/feeling upon reading my blog/profile, seeing my photo (and which one ... *lol*), or a combination?
I said to her: Strength & Joy: meaning strength of character and a joyous heart.
She replied: Felt: Such a full-on passion for life. I love learning from her!! Thought: Beneath the steel there is a tender, giving, kind heart. I am blessed she is my friend ... always, always. *much love*
Now it is your turn to answer the two questions above!

Apr 8, 2007

Happy Easter!
The rebirth of the world has long been celebrated by those whose existence was challenged each winter. There is a reality behind the symbolism. Starvation, lack of shelter, poor clothing were very real threats, and remain so for some. The hierarchy of needs is eternal. The prolific rabbit and bird eggs were often the only food available at this time of year.
Easter egg hunts are wonderful - a test of tenacity and ingenuity as well as a race against others. We have a set of painted wooden eggs that we hide (more or less) in plain

338

sight outside of the house each year. She/he who finds the gold egg gets the larger chocolate rabbit.

The parallels are unmistakable.

When one has enough, the necessary live rabbit becomes the unnecessary chocolate rabbit and life becomes a party! Rejoice and be Generous

Party Report

Three women and four men with scented body oils, two beds, and 6 hours at our disposal. A little something for everyone! Even two men at once! Very nice! All of those hands, penises, and mouths. I had a wonderful time. At one point all three women were 'singing' at once! Then S had two fellows on the sofa, N was with M in the other bedroom and J and I were on the main bed. YES!! A little networking, a few cookies, and then back at it for the second half! Thank you, M - you're a wonderful host! As for J, I may have created a monster here! LOL!

Apr 9, 2007

The Best?

Men might say it but I do not do anything in particular that is "the best". What I do have are a zest for living, an unparalleled love of sex, and a deep acceptance and understanding of human frailty. I hope that is enough because no one's going to stick with me for my exquisite hand-jobs. "I bet you say that to all the women." LOL

I am the same person day to day, month to month, year to year. A man knows who I am and who I am going to be when he wakes up each morning. That has to count for something because he's not going to like my driving. "Oh, is THAT what you call it?"

What do you value in a partner, people?

An internet friend of mine, a very charming woman, wanted me to join in a sex symposium in Las Vegas teaching my seductive subjugation techniques, as depicted in my book beguile, to paying attendees. Decidedly a great opportunity but, alas!, I cannot go. It would have been fun. It may have been profitable. But I cannot take the time away from my business here. I may even have taken a friend with me. Ah well! Perhaps next year?
What do you think? Would people pay to go to such a symposium?

Apr 10, 2007
I don't treat men as "commodities" or as "interchangeable parts". Each one is a unique human being and most are well worth the time it takes to know them. I object to the idea that one "uses" another person for anything. This should be a mutually beneficial and supportive cooperation with joy as its goal. Perhaps I am letting my deep appreciation for men get the better of me but I do not think so.
Are you with me on this? Or are you not?

A Cat Toy, and they know who they are, is a highly skilled and delicious man of proven worth. All Cat Toys have been specifically selected by my WWG partner and I. There is an inauguration involved.
If you have to ask...you AREN'T one.

PURRRRRRRR
A man with a vibe is a wonderful thing esp when he licks along with it. Dancing the vibe around the clitoris and around the lips of my vagina - teasing, tantalizing. Caressing my G-Spot with it while he licked, nibbled, and sucked. He drove me into a frenzy then I grabbed him, drug him on top and in me. Oh yes! Tore the poor man's flesh! Complete and unbridled passion! A few pix were taken. I put a blindfold on him, laid him out onto the bed and dared

him not to move - to just feel and accept what I would do to him. I began from the top down. Kissing with a bit of tongue the corners of his eyes and lips, nibbling on his ears, breathing on the side of his neck slowly, ever slowly, ghosting over him just touching his fur as I slowly slid gently down the length of his body; sensuously caressing his body with my own. Skipping over his groin for the moment and slowly licking up his legs. I turn on the vibe and hold it up against him just behind his testicles and then begin sucking his cock, up and down with a twisting motion. Up on top and a bit of riding - sshhh don't move now! Slowly moving the vibe to his prostate and gently rotating it as I reach over and sprinkle a few drops of scented body oil onto his penis and have him masturbate for me. Love seeing how a man does himself! "May I cum?" he asked. "Yes you may." I answered. Caught the semen on my tongue and gently removed the vibe. I left him there to recover as I tidied up. Very purry by this time, I laid face down onto the bed. I heard him remove his collar and felt him begin moving lips and hands up my legs. Mmmmmm very nice! Aah! He kissed me right there! I sooo love that! Up over my rump and onto my back and shoulders. He put his hands in my hair moving it up to reveal the nape of my neck and kissed there. I rolled over and we began a slow sensuous and fully involved bit of coitus that left us both breathless and the bed entirely soaked. He tried but didn't make it back to the sofa and sat on the floor instead. When I began caressing his thighs he asked me not to start what he doubted he could finish but "damn, it feels good"! then it was time to put the Kitten out for the night.

Apr 11, 2007
Next vetting is this coming Friday, Apr 13th, at The Firehouse (upstairs) on University Road in Fairfax, after 9pm. $5 cover charge. Dress casual.

There is a website and you can Mapquest for specific directions. Beware that parking is a bear. Will we see you there?

Apr 12, 2007
TEDDYBEAR PICNIC
A halfnaked teddybear greeted me at the door. There was a bit of scotch and Oatmeal Raisin cookies on the table. But nevermind that, there's a now completely naked teddybear on the bed. How I could I resist such a delicacy? A slow shedding of my black garments and then pounce! Rolling about kissing and laughing and then sliding him inside of me. Bears. Oh my! Several orgasms for me and one for him. Next he dragged me to the side of the bed for some cunnilingus and then more 'blast me past Jupiter' coitus. More orgasms for me and another for him. Then, as he sat there collasped on the floor, I was a very, very bad Kitten and teased him just so. He got all muscular. So I waved my tail at him at the end of the bed - with the inevitable results. Then, in a first for him, I "machined" him. Just for a few minutes because the torque would have made him orgasm before he wished to. He had to slip out, gasping for oxygen, to regain his composure. Quick as a wink the sly Kitten had hopped up further onto the bed rump down this time. He then dragged me back to the end and more wild sex ensued with him becoming all covered in my ejaculate and his lower left side covered with my claw marks. Wow! What a man! We were both walking sideways after that one! I did manage to sip the scotch and nibble two cookies however - so I did get my picnic.

Apr 13, 2007
OMG, did I write that? What a mess! Typo, typo, and then the formatting isn't what it should be. The actual content is good, however, so all is not lost. Checkmark the errors on the page then dog-ear that page and move along, move

along - have 214 pages to get through. Damn! There's even a typo on the dust jacket! Help!

Apr 14, 2007
"The consequence of that release is stress-free mice. Dr. Lowry was able to measure their stress by dropping them into a tiny swimming pool. Previous research has shown that unstressed mice enjoy swimming, while stressed ones do not. His mice swam around enthusiastically." –*The Economist*
Mice swim???

Apr 15, 2007

May's party is Cat Toy Appreciation Day - when the women come out and show the delicious Cat Toys how much we enjoy their 'participation'. We will need as many women as we can get to come out! Let's see how much they can take! **So, ladies - NOW is the time to contact me! Yes, this group is run by a woman, thank you. As if a dominatrix would let anyone else have control - tsk tsk!*EG***

No, there's nothing you can do about the chemistry check. This is one of those "its there or it isn't" things. It is also impossible to predict. She/he could be the most attractive person on the planet and yet...ICK! The idea of actual sexual congress with her/him leaves you cold and unmoved except for wanting to put as much space between you two as possible. Even more mystifying is the person who doesn't appear to be "all that" who hits you like lightning! The one who you simply must have as soon as possbile please lay down naked right here. Do not ask me - I know it happens, having felt it, but I cannot explain why. He was sitting on the barstool across a crowded bar. Pheronomes don't work at that distance but something said "yes". Ah

343

well.Perhaps you can explain it? Do you have a similar story to tell?

Apr 16, 2007

Look, guys, much as I adore you - generally speaking - do you ever READ? Please, pay attention to the words and do NOT just fixate upon the picture. FOCUS!! **If you are not yet 40 years of age, do NOT contact me for sex. If I can physically pick you up, or fear breaking you in two, do NOT contact me for sex.** You have to meet ALL of the criteria before you can even consider contacting me for sex. **Ahem... now then - all suitably aged big furry teddybears out there - PLEASE contact me for sex. *EG* I have sufficient at this moment but you never know when a date might be cancelled.**

Heartfelt condolences to all involved with VATech shooting. This is a truly horrific thing to have happen to anyone. My sympathies to you all. **Treat each other gently.**

Apr 17, 2007

Tired of the old, cheesy-creepy tunes normally used as background "mood" music? (Sorry Marvin Gaye!) Try these!

for slow erotic sex: Moonlight Sonata, the Adagio by Beethoven
for dark beguiling power sex: Love You to Death by Type O Negative
for energetic sex with a pause: Clubbed to Death (Kurayamino Mix) by Rob D
for long relaxed sex: Nara by E. S. Posthumus
for gentle sex: Watermark by Enya

but to tell the truth, almost any music turned down low will do for sex once the blood's roaring.

For those wishing to sensitize a man to the point where picking lint off of his cuff will cause him a *frisson* of sexual excitement, even when in public; do this:
With him lying prone and face down, do slow erotic body worship with hands, mouth, hair, claws, nipples, while murmuring indistinctly - leaving nothing unexplored. Alternating between 'ghosting' the barely felt touch and heavy pressure. Do not be afraid to add a small touch of pain to the pleasure. Incorporate both straight lines and graceful arabesques as you roam all over him. Firmly and moistly kiss the nape of his neck after bowing down his head. Have him roll over and then do the same on this side, leaving his genitals for last. Be sure to kiss the corners of his eyes and the base of his throat beneath his adam's apple. Do not neglect his hands and feet either. Repeat as you will. This is especially effective if he's blindfolded. Add a vibe if you'd like to blast him past Jupiter.
Men spend so much of their time and energy being outwardly focused on their partners or focused upon penetration, that they have no idea how utterly amazing they themselves can feel just by receiving.
This works!

Apr 18, 2007

Playtime with Teddybears
CHANGE
Far too many clothes, baby. Hmmmm those cuffs aren't fitting correctly so I will modify the scenario. Such a naughty teddybear trailing the metal D-rings of his cuffs gently down my spine - their chill contrasting nicely with my warmth. You're just one big tease, aren't you, baby? We

345

began with both of his wrists tethered and blindfolded with me on top. I slipped both feet beneath his rump for a different angle. Oh my! The differences one can get from such small changes! We'll have to work on this again - only 5 orgasms for me. Blindfolded with one wrist tethered he was asked to take an active role. This is something else - having to lie there and take it while blindfolded is one thing - this is quite different although it seems such a small change going from receiving to giving. Operating entirely by touch he caressed, manually stimulated, and body worshiped me into a white heat before sliding inside. I came all over him, much to his delight. Listening, having to judge my excitement and work out his movements when he could not see me requires careful attention to my responses. I leave very little doubt. After having another 10 orgasms, it was his turn. I love that second gear he finds just before he orgasms! I released him then wandered back to the sofa for cookies and scotch. But I have always found it difficult to not attack naked men so the rest period was a bit short. I laid face down onto the bed and was massaged, my right shoulder was giving me trouble, and cuddled; then my very sly teddybear turned on the vibe. I rolled over "you devil, you" grinning at him. He slowly vibed all over my body which feels amazing! I was quite pink! This proved too much and he dragged me to the edge of the bed for a wild fuck wherein I collected more orgasms and he collected a few clawmarks before having another orgasm of his own. I wonder, does he have more in him? Lets find out. I took advantage of an almost entirely drained teddybear by giving him a vibed g-spot orgasm via fellatio. Then I watched as his limp body slid off the sofa onto the floor and became a quivering puddle of protoplasm. He even tried to say 'plotoprasm' but quickly gave it up. Once he regained the power of speech, he remarked, somewhat amazed, "you look as energetic as when you walked in". Teee heeeee! I do sooo love sex!

Apr 19, 2007

For those new to the concept of polyamory, the usual pattern is a 'triad' (FMF or MFM) or a 'quad' (MFFM), (FMMM) or (MFFF). Yes, there are strong emotional bonds involved even if there is or isn't marriage. They don't all have to live together either.

One person is 'primary' the other is a 'secondary'. If there's a marriage then the spouse is the 'primary'. One can have as many 'secondaries' as one desires since these terms describe the relationship not the person.

I myself have 1 primary and 3 secondaries - a FMMMM quint. I am a secondary to each of my three secondaries. Some of them have or are seeking primaries of their own. As you can imagine scheduling requires advanced mathematical skills especially since we all work and there are kids and families involved.

And here you thought YOUR relationships were 'difficult'! *W*

Apr 20, 2007

An extremely wonderful friend is teasing me in his post Fact-Based, Too, I Do Not Doubt!
"Ah, that wicked woman! I sometimes think that she does it just to torment the remote and encumbered...."
Now would I do that..? *VEG*

new pix for you to view!

Apr 21, 2007

The CPA has spoken! So we sign the forms and now, we wait - for my SRM to come out of his funk. Hey, we got some back - no, not a lot back; some. One would think he'd be happy. I had told him she'd make us as 'poor' as possible,

347

but he still went into a funk. At least we avoided the AMT. **There's just no pleasing some people!**

Can we talk?
I know you've been to exposed to women who talk a good game and everyone knows how thick you guys can spread it on - but, seriously, it isn't how long you can go for - it is how WELL.
Some women take FOREVER to orgasm and then they only want the one. They require lots of work for very slender rewards. The request for a man who can "go all night" is something of a red flag to the more experienced men.
Similarly, women do not want a man who cannot have an orgasm unless he's been pounding away seemingly for eons. Just as much as men enjoy a woman's orgasm so to do women enjoy a man's. Please, be 'generous'.
Given the differing capcities a nice exchange would be 10 to 20 orgasms for her to every one of his. Then repeat the cycle for a total time, including breaks, cuddling, and foreplay of about 4 hours.
Now that I've been the heretic, it is YOUR turn. What do you propose as a fair exchange?

Wisteria:
Oh yes, it looks all nice and pretty but anyone who has ever planted one and then has had to deal with it knows precisely how much of a monster it is!
Last winter it ripped its support to shreds (we're talking 4x4 posts here), grabbed three of the neighboring trees, and tangled itself into a mare's nest!
So there I am, clippers in hand, untangling (Let go! Stay over there! Stop it!), detaching it from tree limbs well over my head (Get out of my hair!), and generally (Let go of my ankle!) sorting the damn thing out. Yes, I was talking to it,

(Will you behave?) as well as snipping it (That will teach you!) here and there.
Snip! Snip! Snip!
It will not do any good, of course. This thing grows 30 feet per year. This time we're going to weld together an iron wisteria tree to support it. One grows wisteria for the same reason one play's golf - for the **exasperation!**

Apr 22, 2007

Going motorcycling with my Pookie!

Apr 23, 2007

Here it is the nicest day forecasted for this week and I have spent the entire day inside awaiting a computer tech and beating myself up for having been stupid and destructive last night.
Damn! Damn! Damn!
Now that I've painted a bull's-eye on my back, I am going out onto the library deck to let the paint dry. I dropped the phone into the hottub as well.
Я очень огорченн. Пожалуйста простиньте мне.
Know what I mean?

Apr 24, 2007

Spring has arrived when the season pass form for polo at Great Meadows arrives! $150.oo for general admission and $900.oo for reserved second row tailgating spots. But it is Saturday evenings. If you just want to go once, for your truck (and 6 persons) it is $20 general admission. Directions: take Interstate 66 to Exit 31, heading toward Warrenton, several miles and it is on the left, use the last entrances.
You may or may not see me. My polo night is usually

Friday. But if a bunch of you would like to go we could caravan and make a party out of it.

Whadda ya mean "No Snitchin'? Hell, I'd give your ass up in a heartbeat, Baby! I'd sing like a canary with a hundred-foot wingspan! I'd even be happy to supply the police with video and stills! Because here, we don't put up with that nonsense! No, no, no - that's not happening in my neighborhood. **NIMBY big time baby!**
You want 'street cred' - the kind that counts?
JOIN THE MILITARY.

Apr 25, 2007

Playtime with Teddybears
NIRVANA
The door will be open, he had said. It was, and there he was, a naked man napping on his bed. Very attractive these naked teddybears! After nuzzling behind his knees and caressing his rump - he woke up too soon, I, wearing my undies (black satin with black lace), relaxed on the sofa while he collected himself. Snuggling up close to me, he began kissing my shoulders and unhooking my bra, slipping the straps down, and caressing my skin. Leaning over toward him, I nipped his shoulder a little bit and smiled at him. Between the sofa and the bed I lost my undies. We laid there until the inevitable occured as it so often does when a man slowly kisses down your body while the lady has her hands all over him. Mmmmm, nice! Today was going to be a one orgasm day for him. I didn't let this keep me from enjoying him and his torment as I orgasmed again and again while ejacualting all over him. An orgasming kitten beneath, around, and on you and you cannot orgasm yourself. Exquisite torture. Slide on out, wrap me in your arms, and think of the steps involved in rebuilding transmissions. I laugh my way back to the sofa

350

as you follow muttering - you got hung up somewhere during your rebuild. Who ate up all of the cookies? At least he had the grace to look guilty. Kittens cannot survive on 1 and 1/2 cookies. Bad teddybear! I had to torture him some more after that transgression. So I leaned over the end of the bed with my rump toward him and waved my tail at him. He slid inside and I machined him while he held on, and held out. He slid out to maintain control but I wasn't done with him just yet. I then rode him, keep your hands to yourself, until he cried out for mercy. Back to the sofa! He has this large comfy leather chair over there and I am highly flexible. He's so very good at cunnilingus! That led, as it does, to coitus. Not the best situation however so we kept it short. Still no orgasm for him. Not that I'm trying to make him orgasm, of course. Back onto the bed, he dragged me down to the edge and slid in. Then it happened. That perfect concordance between both minds and bodies where the orgasm takes over and lasts. One eternal simultaneous orgasm for both of us. Total annihilation of space and time. All one can say is: **yes**.

The article on Princess Culture in BeE, April 2007, extolling the Victorian virtues, and modes of dress and behavior, blithely ignored the realities of the past. The reason why society required women to adopt those attitudes and behaviors was not a good one. Since her virtue was her most prized societal value, any woman who lost hers, however she lost hers and whatever her social rank, was both doomed and damned. All the good works in the world would neither save nor redeem her. The perception of licentiousness and materialism in our current culture is a superficial one. The truth is these latest less elegant modes are the wingbeats of fledglings exercising the powers they cannot yet effectively employ. With the more robust rule of law to protect her, today's young women can explore and develop their own value according to their talents and

351

abilities. If that means a bit of reveling in "pink" for a period of time, then so be it.

We all come to character and elegance in our own time.

www.ingramcontent.com/pod-product-compliance
Lightning Source LLC
Chambersburg PA
CBHW030413100426
42812CB00028B/2938/J